D1245206

1. Does Catholicism Still Exist

DOES CATHOLICISM STILL EXIST?

Does Catholicism Still Exist?

JAMES V. SCHALL

ALBA·HOUSE house NEW·YORK

SOCIETY OF ST. PAUL, 2187 VICTORY BLVD., STATEN ISLAND, NEW YORK 10314

Library of Congress Cataloging-in-Publication Data

Schall, James V.
    Does Catholicism still exist? / James V. Schall.
        p.   cm.
    Includes bibliographical references and Index.
    ISBN 0-8189-0694-4
    1. Catholic Church — Apologetic works.   I. Title.
BX1752.S29   1994
282 — dc20   94-2855
                                                                CIP

Produced and designed in the United States of America by the
Fathers and Brothers of the Society of St. Paul,
2187 Victory Boulevard, Staten Island, New York 10314,
as part of their communications apostolate.

ISBN: 0-8189-0694-4

Printing Information:

Current Printing - first digit	1	2	3	4	5	6	7	8	9	10

Year of Current Printing - first year shown

1994	1995	1996	1997	1998	1999

Table of Contents

Acknowledgments

The following chapters have appeared in different forms in various journals. I would like to thank the individual publishers for permission to use this material here: Chapter 3 in *Social Justice Review*; Chapter 4 from *L'Osservatore Romano*, English Edition; Chapter 5 from *Faith & Reason*; parts of Chapter 6 in *The Month* and in *Crisis*; Chapter 7, *Proceedings* of Fellowship of Catholic Scholars; Chapter 9, *Homiletic and Pastoral Review*; Chapter 10, *Seminarium* and *Social Justice Review*; Chapter 11, *The Living Light*; Chapter 12, *Spiritual Life*; Chapter 13, *Homiletic and Pastoral Review*, and Chapter 14, *Modern Age*.

"People were waiting for the Church to affirm something. . . . Some people no longer practice (the faith) because they no longer know what to believe or what not to believe. Now (with the publication of the *General Catechism of the Catholic Church*) these people are told the articles of the faith. This strengthens them, this comforts the people; they are delighted. Finally, they have a Church that affirms instead of cultivating doubt. They are rediscovering the 'assertive' Church, if one can use this word that has gone out of fashion, a Church that affirms, which says 'I believe,' because one is beginning to ask oneself the question: 'Does the Church still believe in something or is she beginning to doubt everything?'"

— André Frossard, Interviewed by Etienne de Montety, *Catholic World Report*, 3 (February, 1993), 61.

"In your apostolic work do not let yourselves be dazzled by the idea that everything can be solved by denouncing the evils which block or burden social development, nor by the noble desire to share the lot of the disadvantaged. . . ."

— John Paul II, Homily to Priests and Religious at the Cathedral in Santo Domingo, October 11, 1992.

Are We Beginning to Doubt Everything?

At Lyons, in France, on the Feast of St. Ignatius, July 31, 1937, Henri de Lubac completed his monumental work, *Catholicism*.[1] A major reason why he wrote this book, as he explained, was due to neglect of a clear and proper understanding of dogma, of doctrine, of what is actually taught and held in Catholicism. This neglect "increases the extent of moral failures," de Lubac thought, so it is not a merely indifferent topic or concern.

Even more fundamentally, however, after reading and observing what was said about Catholicism in the learned circles of his time, de Lubac concluded that there seemed to be little accurate or adequate understanding of this Catholicism.

> If so many observers, who are not all lacking in acumen or in religious spirit, are so grievously mistaken about the essence of Catholicism, is it not an indication that Catholics should make an effort to understand it better themselves?[2]

de Lubac's monumental study was directed at the question of the social nature of Catholicism, at its essentially communal aspects in

---

[1] Henri de Lubac, *Catholicism: Christ and the Common Destiny of Man*, Translated by L.C. Shepphard and E. Englund (San Francisco: Ignatius Press, 1988). The original edition was *Catholicisme: les aspects sociaux du dogme* (Paris: Cerf, 1947).

[2] *Ibid.*, p. 16.

all its teachings over against an overly individualistic understanding of God and man.

This book, *Does Catholicism Still Exist?*, however, does not arise directly from de Lubac's book. Nor does it come from Karl Adam's earlier (1924) book, *The Spirit of Catholicism*.[3] And yet, de Lubac's worry about a general lack of understanding Catholicism remains unsettling even into the twenty-first century. Karl Adam's question is, likewise, still pressing on us some seventy years later: "We ask what is the single basic thought, what is the essential form that gives life to the great structure we call Catholicism?"[4]

The concern that I have in mind in this book is not the "essential form," "social aspect," or "spirit" of Catholicism, though these aspects remain fundamental. In fact, I would stress that we do have, or perhaps, can have a better understanding of Catholicism today than at almost any time in history, granted that either Catholicism is a constant throughout history or it is not Catholicism. What needs to be addressed is Catholicism's effective and intelligible existence.

In these considerations, I have also in mind something of Chesterton's perceptive remark that Christianity has not been tried and found wanting, but tried and found difficult. That is to say, any obstacle that Catholicism may have need not be rooted in its own intrinsic intelligibility but in the spiritual wills of its own members and those who would consider it. Truth still has to be chosen.

What I would add to this observation of Chesterton is that when Christianity and Catholicism are found difficult, other ways are tried, with whatever justification. These "other ways," even if pronounced in the name of religion, are not intellectually or morally superior to Catholicism. The explanation by Catholicism of itself is, ironically, not challenged, as it has been in the modern

---

[3] Karl Adam, *The Spirit of Catholicism*, Translated by Justin McCann (Garden City, N.Y.: Doubleday Image, 1957).

[4] *Ibid.*, p. 1.

era, by say evolutionism, now itself under grave suspicion, nor by science, nor by Marxism, itself spiritually crippled. We have the curious and unprecedented phenomenon of an entire culture finally faced with the suspicion that what it has consistently rejected may in fact be the truth.

If Catholicism's existence seems problematic, then, it arises from sources more mysterious, more willful. Harold O.J. Brown has written:

> What is the most significant intellectual movement in the United States in the 1990's? The answer is now becoming clearly evident: the anti-Christian *Kulturkampf*. . . . The frenzy of many of the major media is directed against Christianity in general, notably against Roman Catholicism.[5]

Catholicism has spent the past century arguing that it could accommodate itself to the culture, to the modern state. Suddenly, the culture is rejecting what is most distinctive about Catholicism. The state is making theological decisions about what it will tolerate. The relation between "moral failures" and erroneous doctrine, de Lubac's warning, seems to be evident here.

What I am suggesting in this book, then, about the very existence of Catholicism, is that something quite different is going on. No sudden or credible intellectual or spiritual alternative to Catholicism has appeared. Catholicism has not ceased itself carefully to consider what other religions, philosophies, or ideologies say about themselves. In fact, it has devoted unprecedented effort to this task. It is increasingly becoming more dangerous, however, both in terms of citizenship and even of life itself to be an orthodox believer. Direct and indirect supports of the culture for Catholicism's being itself are disappearing.

Jean Danielou, in his still moving book, *The Salvation of the*

---

[5] Harold O.J. Brown, "The Continuing *Kulturkampf*," *Social Justice Review*, 84 (March-April, 1993), 1-2.

Nations, wrote a brief passage at the end of his reflections on the "sin against the Holy Spirit." In the context of the relation of Catholicism to all other cultures, the subject matter of his book, Danielou sought to state the essence of this famous "sin" that could not be forgiven.

> Many men see only the human side of the Church and reject it because of that: their sin is not the sin against the Spirit, and we can believe that they will be forgiven. The sin against the Spirit. . . would be the sin of those who are cognizant of the divine nature of the Church and yet refuse through pride to acknowledge it.[6]

The issue of the existence of Catholicism, even at times for Catholics themselves, is increasingly at this level.

No credible alternative to Catholicism exists, none that so comprehensively deals with every aspect of life, world, and God. Catholicism is of its very nature, moreover, a critique of the culture in many of its accepted practices and beliefs. Catholicism is rejected out of a pure act of the will rooted in no real philosophic basis that can be dialectically sustained. In this sense, the evangelization of the world is more complete than we might suspect. That is, the issue is not what Catholicism believes, but whether one will accept it.

The twentieth century has been a century of "isms" — communism, socialism, fascism, deconstructionism, secular humanism, capitalism, racism, sexism, scientism, multiculturalism, not forgetting Hinduism, Buddhism, and Mohammedanism. I do not, of course, wish to treat Catholicism as another "ism," as something abstract and made up by a human thinker, even though this is often how it is considered from outside its own fold.

This book is not a polemic with other rival claims about

---

[6] Jean Danielou, *The Salvation of the Nations*, Translated by A. Bouchard (New York: Sheed & Ward, 1950), p. 109.

understanding the world, though it does recognize that there are in fact rival claims that can be accounted for. This book is rather an effort to consider the existence of Catholicism as a coherent and intelligent understanding of man, world, and God. It maintains that this Catholicism is a complete and harmonious explanation, one that leaves out nothing and one that considers the alternatives in their intelligibility.

We do not live in a time, moreover, in which Catholics themselves are triumphalistic about their understanding of the world. Quite the opposite. If anything characterizes Catholics about their own intellectual reasons and doctrines, in short, about their Catholicism, it is a lack of confidence in them, a kind of corporate demoralization. This lack of conviction would be understandable if the reasons for this lack were objectively verifiable. The embarrassment of Catholicism is not over the strength of its rivals, but over their weakness.

Most writers throughout the twentieth century have argued as if Marxism was either the wave of the future or the principal alternative to Catholicism. In the end, largely as far as we can tell because of something that began in the country in Eastern Europe with the most Catholic population, in Poland, that is, Marxism collapsed. This rather precipitous decline of Marxism has resulted in a kind of retrospective analysis that now wants to maintain that communism as an intelligible threat was overblown and not the menace that most people had thought during much of the century.

But there is a strand of Catholicism that thinks that this decline of Marxism was due much more to supernatural forces than we are generally willing to admit. Neither economics, nor sociology, nor political science anticipated or predicted the fall of Marxism. The social sciences were as surprised as anyone else. Yet, Marxism was in fact the threat that most sane people thought it was, something that makes its crisis even more mysterious.

The third millennium is upon us. We expect Catholicism to belong also to this new era. But the question is whether it will belong as something that has conformed itself to ideological or religious systems at variance with its own inner logic? Or will it belong as that abiding and coherent system of beliefs, doctrines, and sacraments that has characterized it throughout the first two millennia?

Catholicism is a claim to be true.[7] Were it not for this claim, we would need to pay little attention to it. This claim is not to be confused with the question of whether individual Catholics, oneself always included before all others, practice what they believe in all cases. Obviously, they do not. The fact that the purpose of the Good News was to call not the just but sinners by very definition means that failure to practice Catholicism is itself a part of the self-understanding of Catholicism.

When we ask about the existence of Catholicism, therefore, we do not ask about whether there are so-called "bad" Catholics. There are and always have been. They are never very far from our own souls, from our own hearts. This awareness is one of the reasons Catholicism itself exists — to deal with bad Catholics, to deal indeed with disordered souls wherever they might appear. Generally speaking, however, bad Catholics hold the tenets of Catholicism. Sinners are also believers.

Moreover, the capacity of Catholicism to explain itself has never been greater. There are really no intellectual or moral views of the world or man that present a serious rival to Catholicism. By that I mean, that there are within the tradition and resources of Catholicism long standing and coherent studies and reflections that are able to grasp and evaluate any other understanding of God, man, and world, whether arising from science, philosophy, or other religions. Again, the focus of this book, though it does not exclude this aspect, is not about Catholicism insofar as it specifically responds to any alternate system.

The focus of this book is Catholicism as it understands itself. If this book is "against" anything, it is against those priests, bishops, theologians, professors, laymen, and yes, non-Catholics

---

[7] See John Paul II, *Veritatis Splendor*, 1993.

and non-believers, who explain what Catholicism says about itself falsely or wrongly or incompletely. It is one thing, then, to be a Muslim or a skeptic and to suggest Catholicism is different from such a position. It is quite another thing to suggest that basically Mohammedanism and skepticism say the same things that Catholicism does. Catholicism may or may not be inherently credible. But it should rise and fall on what it says of itself alone, not on an explanation of itself that is not what it really holds about itself.

The French journalist, André Frossard, as I noted in the brief citations at the very beginning of this book, was grateful to see that Catholicism is again "asserting" itself. People have in fact been asking whether the "Church still believes in something or is she beginning to doubt everything?" It is sometimes remarked that Protestantism and atheism can safely go their ways so long as they themselves believe that the historic stability of Catholicism remains to return to. This book is written in the awareness that Frossard's question about Catholicism's doubting everything is a real concern.

Likewise, in the second citation from John Paul II, I would suggest that it is not enough to identify oneself with the poor nor to denounce evils. We must really know why the poor are poor and what causes them not to be poor. We need really to know the truth lest our denunciations sound hollow. Catholicism has been too often marked by the very "dazzled" spirit that the Pope rightly saw to be a weakness.

Secular culture itself, moreover, has taken over the cause of the poor as its own non-transcendent justification of its own deeds. Everything from abortion to heavy taxation is justified in terms of the poor even by the modern state. Most modern tyrannies in truth have been promoted in the name of the poor and the underprivileged. Something has been missing and this something, to recall de Lubac's remark, is right thinking about Catholicism itself.

This book is divided into two parts. The first part is called "On the Lack of Catholic Apologists," while the second is called

"The Revolution That is Catholicism." In the first part, I discuss the reasons why Catholicism is increasingly becoming an object of hatred and contempt. To understand this ominous turn of civil life, it is necessary to talk about intelligence and its place within Catholicism, where it has a unique and special standing. We must be clear that Catholicism does claim intelligence, does claim that its most essential doctrines and even those that do not seem so, do in fact intellectually make sense, however much they might be ridiculed or rejected.

In the second part of this book, I want to say something about what Frossard called "assertive" Catholicism, that Catholicism that is conscious of itself and of the force of its own teachings. From the new *General Catechism* to the new Encyclical on social order (*Centesimus Annus*), from the new Code of Canon Law, to the Encyclical on the missions (*Redemptoris Missio*), to those on the family (*Familiaris Consortio*) and on morality (*Veritatis Splendor*), we have an extraordinary re-presentation of the coherence and grounding of Catholicism.

Moreover, it is not enough to address the things of this world, be they poverty, family, war, or social order. The ultimate things must themselves remain central — joy, evil, death, sadness, life everlasting. Catholicism is not itself, not loyal to its own vocation, if it neglects to inform both believers and non-believers of what is given to it to know about these ultimate things.

We do not have one Catholicism that speaks about this world and another that speaks about the next. We have one whole in which the life we lead on earth and the life to come belong together. "Seek ye first the Kingdom of God and all these things will be added unto you." "Man does not live by bread alone." Man does need bread. He needs many other things. This too is essential to Catholicism.

But we need not lower our standards as if somehow this neglect of higher things is the proper way to solve our human needs or problems. Quite the opposite. We live in a time of lowered standards and they are not working. What we need, in short, is a revolution. The irony is that the revolution remains so new, so extraordinary that we no longer see it because we think we know what it is. We think we need to reject it in the name of what we are, when we do not even know what we are.

The question then needs to be posed: "Does Catholicism still exist?" "Does the Church still believe in something or is she beginning to doubt everything?" Is Catholicism "dazzled by the idea that everything can be solved by denouncing the evils?" Do we really not think that "the noble desire to share the lot of the disadvantaged" will solve our spiritual and temporal problems?

The existence of Catholicism depends on our awareness that Catholicism does believe something, that this belief is intelligible and intellectually coherent. But we need also to be aware that precisely this essential belief is becoming an object of hatred in a culture that begins to live in ways that are contrary to the order of right living, to the order of being that Catholicism maintains about the nature and meaning of God, world, and man.

Part One

On the Lack of Catholic Apologists

CHAPTER I

Does Catholicism Still Exist?

I

Catholicism, of course, still exists. A Pope can still be heard in Rome, and John Paul II has been almost everywhere; he was once even at Laguna Seca in Monterey in California as well as in Denver. Bishops are in Sees around the world. There remains a widespread organization of dioceses, of religious orders, of universities, schools, hospitals, and other works of mercy under the auspices of the Catholic Church. Millions of people, perhaps a fifth of the human race, call themselves Catholic. We can find Catholic Churches in most of the cities of the world, even in countries that are not Catholic in population, even in places where the Church is under persecution or political pressure. We can find a Catholic press and a Catholic presence in the secular media, though it is not a particularly influential one. In short, Catholicism, which maintains that the Lord will be with it all days even unto the end of the world, has not disappeared, nor is it likely to do so in the near future.

So why, then, should I pose the deliberately provocative question, "*Does Catholicism still exist?*" The immediate cause of this question came from a letter I received from a friend of mine living in Rome. In early 1993, he wrote the following rather caustic lines after the American Election:

3

> I have been told Clinton has not appointed one Catholic to
> any major or minor office. If true, where is the mul-
> ticulturalism that reflects America? The U. S. bishops do
> not present a consensus on doctrinal matters; ergo, no
> Catholic identity; ergo, no point in Clinton's selecting a
> "nothing" — "Catholic" means nothing in theological or
> moral matters.

Clinton did have two Catholics in his initial staff, one a pro-
abortion congressman from California, the other a Latino; he did
receive some 45% of the Catholic vote, one margin of his victory.

Russell Shaw wrote: "With the advent of a new administration and a new Congress, the Catholic Church's capacity to
influence national policy is at its lowest ebb since the 1920's."[1] In
short, a distinct mood exists, and not merely in the United States,
that (1) whatever its numbers, an acute feeling of disunity exists
among Catholics about whatever it is they might hold and (2)
there is a down-right cultural hostility shown to Catholicism itself
when it does adhere to its own defined doctrines. Thus, Catholicism, whatever the statistics, appears to be in considerable trouble,
with no effective national leadership, episcopal or lay, on the
scene.

Not merely is there talk of lack of Catholic influence, but
there are reasons to worry about actual persecution. The Archbishop of San Francisco told a group of students:

> If you want to be a Catholic today, you have to be prepared
> to be ridiculed, to see the Pope ridiculed, to see the Mass
> and the Sacraments profaned as KQED did during the past
> year. There is no longer room for ambiguity. We have to
> know where we stand and with God's help we have to
> stand firm in the midst of these increasing attacks. The
> Catholic Church... is the one thing in American society

---

[1] Russell Shaw, *Catholic Insight*, February 3, 1993, p. 1.

today which is exempt from the rules of fair play and which can be openly ridiculed and held up to contempt.[2]

James McFadden is, if anything, more forthright:

> However "compassionate" he (Cardinal John O'Connor) is to sinners (he is), he cannot stomach the blasphemous *sins* perpetrated against the Church he loves: the infamous desecration of St. Patrick's three years ago remains an open wound. Last month he wrote (in his *Catholic New York* column) that an "AIDS activist" had done it again: a woman "took the consecrated host — the Holy Eucharist — from the deacon, crushed it and threw it on the ground" — O'Connor called it "so inexplicable as to border on the demonic."[3]

Ironically, the apparent political ineptitude of a disorganized Catholicism is matched by an increasing and organized threat of hatred and persecution especially against those who remain faithful to the basic teachings of the Church as it understands itself, not as it is too often confusingly understood in the universities or media.

The paradox of this sense of impotence and disarray over against a growing contempt for the faith that is undoubtedly felt throughout much of the Catholic world is that the intellectual case for Catholicism has never been stronger. Not only have we had the most intelligent and articulate Pope in modern times, if not in any time, but also we have had a series of formal statements of the Church, even following those of Vatican II, that have clearly and forcefully identified and clarified the precise meaning of Catholicism in its doctrines, rites, practices, and spiritual life. The *General Catechism of the Catholic Church*, the Encyclicals on the economy

---

[2] John R. Quinn, Archbishop of San Francisco, *Lay Witness*, 14 (January/February, 1993), 9.

[3] James McFadden, *The Catholic Eye*, January 24, 1993, p. 4.

(*Centesimus Annus*), on moral theology (*Veritatis Splendor*), on the missions (*Redemptoris Missio*), on the family (*Familiaris Consortio*), the new *Code of Canon Law*, and a host of other teachings and reflections have made it possible to know the unity of and arguments for Catholicism in a way never before available in the history of the Church.

One could almost argue — indeed, I do so argue — that Catholicism, properly articulated, has no major intellectual opponent in the modern world. When it comes to the truth of things, the relation between a true and valid science of whatever discipline and the basic teachings and practices of the faith, there is no essential conflict. The growing modern opposition to Catholicism does not come from science, but from what must be called politics or will, even personal disorder of soul.

Moreover, the empirical results of examining the lived out values and positions that have replaced the classical Catholic views of morality and right living are proving not merely unlivable but even degrading. We are more and more confronted not merely with the theme of "alternate" life-styles and uncertain truths, but with the almost everyday themes of decline and human depravity.

The general thesis that I will argue in this book is that the case for Catholicism has never been stronger, that the Church's political and moral life among its faithful is in considerable disarray, and that the general society is reaching a level of moral degeneracy that is undermining the civilization itself. The civilization we live in, furthermore, is not an isolated or solely inwardly-directed one.[4] Rather, it is a civilization that is itself the universal civilization, "dedicated to a universal purpose," and therefore our disorder directly contributes to the undermining of civilization on a world scale.

---

[4] Leo Strauss, *The City and Man* (Chicago: University of Chicago Press, 1964), p. 3.

II

Does Catholicism still exist? Let me begin to approach this perplexing question by recalling an Address given at the 1987 Meeting of the Catholic Commission on Intellectual and Cultural Affairs. Thomas Langan, from St. Michael's College in Toronto, asked, with not a little irony, "Do we still have any Catholic universities?" Such a question must be asked, I am sure, with considerable circumspection and in obscure places. In spite of the great obeisance to academic freedom in Catholic universities by which they have reduced more and more their "Catholicism" and increased, so they presume, their "university rank," the one question that is not brought up, except in a most oblique way, is precisely Langan's question: Are these universities in any meaningful sense Catholic?

This concern about the content of the Catholicism actually taught — and it is not an inquisitorial question but one of fact — is one query that will not be tolerated lightly, either administratively or academically, even though in Catholic teaching this is the one thing about which a local bishop should be most concerned. Neither parents, benefactors, alumni, nor students, it is said, ought to be much disturbed by controversies about the school's relation to the faith in terms of what, if anything, is actually taught *as* Catholic. It hurts morale and giving if any bad publicity arises, while it hurts reputation if it appears that the Church has anything at all to say in a university context about what it stands for as Catholic. Academic freedom, and with it Catholicism itself, comes to mean whatever the academic freely says.

The definition of Catholicism, in academic practice, thus turns out to be what is taught in these academic halls, *whatever it be*. Despite considerable public wonderings on this topic, the question of the truth and content of Catholicism's understanding of itself is never frankly and openly addressed. This silence means in effect that it is not permitted to question academic self-identification of what Catholicism is. "Catholicism" means what selected Catholics — but not the ones appointed in the Church itself — say it is. To hint otherwise is to violate an assumed good faith or good feelings arrangement. Pluralism now comes within religious bodies, not just between them. It means that there will be no discussion of fundamentals or real issues that might indicate something higher is at stake. If Rome continues to worry about the rumors it hears, well, that is due to a foreign pope and a closed Vatican bureaucracy, not to anything really wrong with what is taught.

In non-Catholic universities, the equivalent question concerning academic freedom and intellectual honesty, I assume, would be: "Can in any honest sense the clear, authentic statement of what the Catholic Church holds about itself, with the reasoning to support it, whether one agrees with it or not, be anywhere presented or objectively heard within their confines?" And if not, can the institutions claiming to be really intellectual, open to all that is known among men, be anything other than sophisticated closed societies? This question is not one of freedom of worship, but of intellectual integrity, or rather, of what intellectual integrity and freedom presuppose, namely, honesty of statement and completeness of presentation of all claims for truth. Catholicism, if it is anything, is a claim of truth, both a theoretic claim that truth is possible and a practical claim that some things are true and these truths, granting the finite nature of the human intellect as such, can be spelled out with careful attention.

Invariably, it seems, whenever in academic or media circles the "case" for Catholicism is to be presented, it turns out to be, most often, that the presenter of "what Catholicism holds" is someone alienated, in one or other basic point of doctrine or practice, from Catholicism itself. Thus, the audience will assume that what it has heard is the Catholic position, whereas what it has heard in fact is a deviation from it. No wonder so few are persuaded or even challenged by the radical newness of Catholicism, no wonder the increasing attacks on Catholicism.

In Catholic universities, on the other hand — there are

exceptions — even if there can be found in their curricula courses on Catholicism, little thorough or adequate presentation of any or all the classical Catholic doctrines as the Church maintains them will be heard. Even when prominent faculty and administration members support or tolerate abortion, homosexuality, feminism, versions of Marxism, paganism, or whatever, it remains dangerous to say in public that the school itself is not "Catholic." Only bishops can say this and they are almost completely quiet in these areas. Because no attempt to challenge or correct such academic situations is made, even when it is clear what is happening, the impression is left in the minds of many that the Catholic Church really does, with a few appropriate distinctions, quietly approve birth control, abortion, divorce, relativism, population control, homosexuality, feminism, environmentalism, and, even after its death, Marxism.

Yet if we admit that the Church does indeed oppose these controverted teachings and actions in very specific and clear ways, the Church's view, usually in some interview with a prominent Catholic intellectual, is then boldly described as anti-modern and distinctly benighted. My own impression is that a young student in a Catholic university can usually get in his courses a more objective account of Buddhism or liberation theology than of Catholicism. Further he can get equal credit for these and other such religious courses and many other similar topics to fill his religious credit requirement, if there be any.

What is to be emphasized here is that the criterion of truth has become "what a modern man can hold," not what was taught and argued in the Catholic tradition. However, "what a modern man" can hold is itself a philosophic problem based on the reduction of philosophy to a kind of truncated scientific method now taken to be an absolute. These sanitized and pious versions of "modernity" are everywhere in evidence.

A young friend of mine, for example, a professor in a local college, once decided to teach seventh graders in her local parish CCD program. To her amazement, she discovered that the required text book (*Growing with the Catholic Faith*) was filled, as she quaintly put it, "entirely with leftist crap" about oppressed minorities, who were always called "the poor," as if there were no unoppressed poor or oppressed well-offs. Further, she added, "fully two-thirds of a weekly lesson was how the students feel about Scripture. There was constant encouragement to 'decide what feels right for you'."

Likewise, one of my very best students one year came in to see me. This young man was up for several prestigious scholarships. He was, as I recall, a wise and reflective sort. I asked him what he had been doing. He replied that he spent some time with a branch of a university-sponsored religious volunteers' program, a kind of service organization. "How did you like it?" I asked him. "Well, I quit after a month," he told me.

> I got the picture on the first Mass that was celebrated, when God was called a "He/She/It" sort of being. The United States, in the group where I was working, was pictured consistently as the epitome of evil and corporations apparently were the cause of it all. During my time at the Center, there was not a sign of any reflection on the truth of this analysis. Moreover, there was a terrific pressure to conform to this sort of persuasion.

One might hope that such experiences were rare, but they seem rather common.

III

In any case, the day of worrying about the specific "Catholicity" of historically Catholic universities, if judged by the Church's own understanding of itself, is probably over. This battle is already lost, however quietly this must be whispered to our neighbors and benefactors as well as to the heathen. The only thing missing is the honesty on the part of the universities and the hierarchy itself formally to admit the fact. Indeed, as Josef Pieper perceptively remarked, the only real courage in today's world is for some intellectual actually to agree with the Church.

"Could not the intellectual manifest his non-conformity," Pieper mused,

> by expressing his disagreement with those criticisms of the Church which are now being shouted from every rooftop (and which thus have come to represent the 'Establishment'?)... Or, what about the pleasure the intellectual might derive from the risk of himself "going it alone," i.e., taking a truly unpopular stand. It does not take a grain of courage to attack the Pope.[5]

That we have had, no doubt, in John Paul II the most interesting and intelligent Pope of any time, only leaves Pieper's remarks more poignant.

If the cause of opposition to basic Catholicism, however, is because of Catholicism's stand in regard to certain propositions of "modernity," those essentially having to do with man's self-creation of himself and of his world, as I think it does, then the hostile reception of John Paul II becomes more explicable. For he cannot be written off as someone who does not also know in his own right the order of being. John Paul II is himself a man of the greatest intellectual stature. No one certainly in the American hierarchy or in our universities surpasses him.

Truth, we must not forget, is a great risk because it must be received by those who can choose not to accept it. Not only will the "truth make us free" but we are "free to make our own truth," even though the truth we make ourselves will not be itself "true," that is, in conformity with *what is*. Some of the most interesting passages in Scripture, in St. Paul in particular, have to do with the

---

[5] Josef Pieper, "The Problematical Metier of the Intellectual in Relation to the Church," *Problems of Modern Faith* (Chicago: Franciscan Herald Press, 1985), p. 263.

refusal of philosophers to see the wisdom of revelation, a refusal that seems, evidently, to result in an inability to acknowledge any truth if revelation is consistent with it. We have lost our profoundly spiritual sense of the contradictions that can arise when we contest the truth of faith. The validity of any truth, in this case, not just the truth of faith, eventually comes into question for all truth has the same source.

The courage to think clearly about what Catholicism means does not flourish in many mainline religious schools where the central ethos is rather that of redefining the faith so that it conforms with contemporary ideologies. The great problem with the faith arose when modern intellectuals decided that their problem was first to reduce the truths of the faith to what modern science would "allow" religion to hold. The classical view of this faith was quite the opposite, namely, that faith teaches intellect wherein intellect has its own grounding and dignity. The methods of the sciences are not the measure of reality, but only of that aspect of reality that these methods allow to be presented to the mind.

Nothing perhaps is more ironic in today's academic world than the figure, among others, of Stanley Jaki, who has argued brilliantly and clearly — in *The Road of Science and the Ways to God*, in his biography of Pierre Duhem, in his discussion of Chesterton and science, and in *Chance or Reality* — that the case against the faith from modern science simply does not exist.[6] Rather Jaki argues that modern science is possible only because it followed the direction of questions originally posed by faith. Indeed, as I would argue, modern Catholic intellectuals lost their faith at precisely the time when the same faith was becoming most

---

[6] Stanley L. Jaki, *The Road of Science and the Ways to God* (The Gifford Lectures) (Chicago: University of Chicago Press, 1978); *Chesterton, A Seer of Science* (Carbondale: University of Southern Illinois Press, 1986); *Chance or Reality and Other Essays* (Lanham, MD: University Press of America, 1986); *The Absolute Beneath the Relative and Other Essays* (Lanham, MD: University Press of America, 1988); *Uneasy Genius: The Life and Work of Pierre Duhem* (Boston: Martinus Nijhoff, 1987). See Peter Hodgson, "Science and the Church," *Clergy Review*, LXII (February, 1987), 71-4.

credible, most intellectually plausible. But this position had to be argued carefully in the schools.

Here, in any case, I wish to broaden the scope of the discussion. By now not merely the universities and media are caught up in this evaporation of the essence of Catholicism but more and more the seminaries, diocesan bureaucracies, some bishops, not a few parishes, even the prayer life given to the people are involved. I want to ask rather, at least so it will at least once be asked, "Do we still have a Catholic Church in any meaningful sense, and if so what does it hold and do?"

I am aware, to be sure, that the Church can decline in some parts of the world or in some nations and not in others. I consider myself an orthodox Christian so I do not expect the Church ever to disappear, but I do expect it will be bitterly opposed in some times and places more than others, especially when it teaches what it should. What is characteristic of the present time is a clear isolation of Catholic teachings and practices from the general culture in which civil law, as reflective of this opposition, is making the practice of specifically Catholic principles increasingly difficult if not illegal.

But I am also a realist. I am tired of having to say that not just anyone claiming to be a Catholic is a Catholic. I rebel to hear that any position "sincerely" held must therefore, on account of some subjective feeling, be a part of the corpus of the faith. Nor do I think that any action done with "compassion" is *ipso facto* able to be fit into the general confines of this faith as doctrine. If in fact everybody is Catholic, then no one is and we need not worry about it. Indeed, it can rightly be argued that this very "compassion," designed as it is to prevent us from challenging the truth or content of anyone's claim to authentic faith on his own testimony, is responsible for undermining the intellectual structure of the faith itself. Compassion as such prescinds from truth. It can be a kind of pride, a refusal to admit that there is an order even to our emotions.

I am reminded of this problem of compassion and sincerity

when I recall a Session on "Catholicism and Politics" that I once attended at an American Political Science Association Convention. The proposition was presented that we could not, in practice, even for the sake of argument, exclude anyone from being a Catholic if that is what he claimed to be, no matter what he held. Granted that there is an official way to declare who or what is or is not Catholic, still one ought not to carry this form of doubt about the main outlines of faith to an extreme. In the light of the clear propositions that it claims about itself, we can indeed say something about what the faith maintains. For many versions of Church, however, membership, even an "official" definition of the Church, does not deprive someone of his "right" to be a Catholic if he chooses to be such. Catholicism becomes simply self-proclamation, with no ecclesial limitation of thought or practice.

Consequently, up until the publication of the *General Catechism of the Catholic Church*, it has been practically impossible to say in public what Catholicism is or is not (see Chapter IX). Even the secular media has been as confused on this issue as has everyone else, though this same media seems infallibly to know what view it wants to be declared "Catholic," usually its own. Most local bishops or clergy do not dispute in any meaningful sense what is claimed to be Catholic, especially if a dubious interpretation agrees with prevailing or apparently popular cultural positions. The Pope is left to do all the work himself. The result is that what is traditionally thought to be Catholic and in fact is properly considered to be so considered is held to be simply another "minority opinion" even within the Church. And this minority opinion, which is what the Church does teach, is the one that is most circumscribed and restricted. The horrendous stories of the liberals criticized openly by the Roman offices are well-known. Hardly a word, however, is spoken in defence of those considerable numbers of priests, nuns, professors, and laity who are effectively marginalized or silenced because they are orthodox.

IV

Josef Ratzinger made the same point in another way. Speaking of the confusions caused by many examples of modern biblical scholarship, he took up the happy case of the Devil. Ratzinger examined what is really behind this sort of evaporation of traditional Christian doctrine on this subject:

> "In this special case, they (scholars) admit —they have no choice — that Jesus, the apostles, and the evangelists were convinced of the existence of demonic powers. Then they (scholars) go on to take it for granted that to this conviction of theirs they (Jesus and the Apostles) were "victims" of current Jewish thinking. But since they (scholars) have already taken it to be absolutely certain that 'this idea can no longer be reconciled with our view of the world,' they have simply removed, by slight of hand, whatever is regarded as unintelligible to today's average man."

> Consequently, he (Ratzinger) goes on, "in 'saying farewell to the Devil' they (such scholars) are not basing themselves on Holy Scripture (which supports just the opposite view) but on our world view. Thus they are saying farewell to every other aspect of faith which does not fit with the current conformism; and they do so, not as exegetes, as interpreters of Holy Scripture, but as contemporary men."[7]

This observation, of course, goes to the heart of the problems that Catholics have in identifying exactly who they are. Doctrine is not, to be sure, all that Catholicism is, but it is distinctly at the center of debate because this faith does direct itself specifically to reason.

Catholicism has been and is a religion of doctrine. Some writers, even an Eric Voegelin, seem to want to understand that position about the centrality of doctrine to be a sort of idolatry that would substitute "ideas" or "definitions" for realities. However,

---

[7] *The Ratzinger Report* (San Francisco: Ignatius Press, 1985), pp. 143.

even though Voegelin points to a real danger, Catholicism has always been clear that its doctrines are about persons, about real beings, about the being of God, of the Persons of the Trinity, of definite human beings with particular names. It is doctrine—that is, mind formulating conclusions on the basis of evidence—that formulates what is believed. Christianity insists, whatever the limits of finite intellect, that the mind remains itself and craves for true knowledge. And for Christians, the "what" of faith is ultimately a "Who."

The long tradition within the Church of analyzing heresy, a word that has a perfectly objective meaning, is instructive here. Catholicism, indeed, is the one religion that can and must take ideas, even erroneous or deviant ones, seriously. They all have something to teach. This is the abiding brilliance of Chesterton's *Heretics,* that he saw the modern propositions within the broader scope of the intelligence of faith. That is, Chesterton argued the validity of revelation on the grounds that it was more "reasonable" in practice than any of its proposed alternatives or refutations. The cliché, that "ideas have consequences," is quite literally true. This is especially the case with the basic doctrines of Trinity, Incarnation, grace, redemption, eternal life, the Fall, Sacraments, and Church. Heretical positions, moreover, properly and accurately stated, do not arise primarily from religion.

What does it mean that orthodox doctrines do not "arise" from religion? Certainly, these doctrines are typically and uniquely Judaeo-Christian in their original formulations. That is, whatever it might have in common with other religions, whether they are said to be revealed or natural, this faith has its own unique and unalterable positions, ones which indeed it may have taken centuries to have hammered out clearly. Without the truth and the exact statement of each of these positions, the faith has no inner unity or cohesiveness.

But what I am getting at here is something more fundamental. A Catholicism explained in such a way that the intelligibility of these revealed truths comes to be modified or subsumed into a notion of what men "can" believe changes the religion's inner coherence and meaning. It also alters the doctrines' attractiveness to human intelligence as such. It obscures why men might want to believe in them in the first place. What is at stake, in other words, is the fact of Catholicism itself. In that inner core of what it is, Catholicism wants us, as intelligent beings, to be attracted to it, to the realities its doctrines point to and stand for.

This brings me back to the notion that the essential doctrines of Christianity do not "arise" first from religion. What the faith teaches us is meant to be an answer to questions and problems rooted in human life as *already* lived and formulated by us. In other words, unless we have certain problems deeply and poignantly presented to our minds because we ourselves have experienced them, we will not know why doctrine or dogma, as set forth by Catholicism in its essential form, is important and important to keep as it is. This theoretical position confuses us because today we think the most important aspect of religion is what it can "do" for the social or political order, as if somehow religion were not also itself valid on some other grounds. Most of our deepest feelings and problems have become so politicized that we no longer understand the limited value of political issues, even if we were able to solve them by political or religious processes.

No doubt Catholicism rightly conceives of itself as having a contribution to make, perhaps the fundamental contribution, to the civil order, because faith insists on the intrinsically limited scope of politics. Catholicism arrives at this view of itself, both from the experience of history in which other principles of worldly order are operative and from the view that the created world is one, only a part of which, a valid part to be sure, politics can account for. Whatever is said to have its origins in God by whatever source, whether reason or revelation, will help and strengthen the relation of all aspects of human life to one another. However, Catholicism is primarily a thesis about the hierarchy of being. Some things are more important than others, even though all things have their respective importance. Human beings ought to find out what this importance is. For, as Aquinas intimated, the most practical thing we can do is to keep our attention correctly directed to the highest things. Otherwise, we will begin to insist that the highest things are in fact political.

V

The central teachings of the faith — the revelation of the inner nature of God, the Incarnation of the Son of God, the establishment of the Church, the inner life of each person, his life and death, his promise of resurrection, the Last Things — these are not themselves somehow impositions, inconveniences of an arbitrary God. Rather they are intended to be and are answers to questions that we human beings have always asked about ourselves, about our internal disorder, about our origin and destiny, about our friendships, about our uniqueness, about our permanence. We simply have these questions, and we have many and varied answers to them given in the history of philosophy and religion.

Catholicism, in its turn, has a body of doctrine, based on the sending of the Son of God into this actual world, that addresses itself to each of the essential questions that a man can have about himself and about his being human. The real cause of Catholicism's self-crisis — it is not today somehow an attack totally from the outside, either physically or intellectually — is that, aside from the Pope who does it constantly, it no longer asks clearly enough how its doctrines relate to these lived human questions. Rather too many modern Catholic intellectuals ask, "How can modern man believe these odd truths presented by the faith?" What governs the reflective enterprise is not faith seeking reason, but rather modern reductionist methods of knowledge excluding the parameters of faith in the name of the absolute truth of these very methods. The critique of this particular method, then, is the initial intellectual endeavor in behalf of revelation.

Take, for example, the doctrine of the resurrection of the

body, which St. Paul remarked was the one doctrine, that, if it were not true, would make all other religious doctrines vain. Many modern explanations of the resurrection so attenuate it, mollify it, that no one in his right mind would find it attractive or credible. When Hans Küng, for example, gets done with the resurrection, who could possibly think it worth the effort? Classical thought, of course, had already elaborated the notion of the immortality of the soul, quite a perceptive insight in fact as far as it went. And probably it could not have gone any farther than it did in the name of man's own reason.

But if we examine carefully, say, Aristotle's teachings about friendship, among the most beautiful of the heritages we have from the ancient world (*Ethics*, Bks. 8 and 9), a heritage that still reads exactly true on its own basis, we can see that the most perplexing aspects of this deepest of human experiences are challenges, almost, to some power to supply what is so obviously lacking. Aristotle noted that no one would want to be a god or a king, if this meant in the process that he must become some other person. He observed too, that when we love someone, we want to remain ourselves and we want the other to remain the other. We do not want some suffusion of one being into another essentially third being. Aristotle grasped that the "whole" of us included our history, our bodies, our spirit, and the events of a lifetime. He also inquired about friendship with God. And he argued that friends exchange the highest things, if they be good.

These are clearly legitimate observations. Aristotle was quite right; these are the things that we are brought to when we reflectively analyze the best in us. No one, of course, would hold that the best answers to these questions must exist because they are the best theoretical responses that the human mind might conceive. As a matter of fact, the human mind did not by itself conceive the best answers to these perplexing questions that the human mind, in the reflections of Aristotle, was able properly to formulate. The two doctrines of the Incarnation of Christ and the resurrection of the body are, in some uncanny way, "possible" answers to the questions as posed. That is to say, there is a strange sort of "reasonable" correlation between the questions as posed by the greatest philosopher of our kind and the answers posed by revelation.

We must remember, however, that it is strictly against the faith itself to conclude that *therefore* the classical Christian positions are true as philosophy. The fact that they are not unreasonable still does not prove that they happened. On the other hand, this coherence of reason and revelation makes very uncertain any absolute exclusion of the possibility of revelation as a source of answers to authentic questions, particularly when the answers arose through an actual history with sufficient testimony to make us hesitate to reject them outright.

VI

To conclude this approach to considering whether Catholicism still exists, I wish to refer to a comment Henri Cardinal de Lubac once made in an Interview with Angelo Scola in the Italian journal, *Trenta Giorni*. The question de Lubac was asked was precisely about whether Catholicism still exists. Doubt about this continued existence is the motivating force behind all those movements within the Church that would confine it to the ideologies of this world. Does the human mind, by itself, penetrate to the full truth of things to such an extent that it can afford to exclude, by virtue of its own authority, any source in revelation?

What generally takes the place of the validity of the orthodox answers, then, is a projected world view, devised by a few, usually intellectual politicians, who seek to impose or inspire their total view on mankind as a, perhaps reluctant, substitute for the transcendent destiny of each individual that the faith presupposes to each existing human life. The alternative to orthodox Catholicism seems to be one that is "reasonable" once we are satisfied that the Christian answers are not possible. The philosopher Eric Voegelin, in his *Science, Politics, and Gnosticism,* observed that modern ideology in fact arose from the weakness of faith in Christian intellectuals who, doubting the truth of the revealed answers, insisted that the Kingdom of God must be visible in this world as a product of their own work.[8]

Thus no exclusion of the answers provided by Catholicism to man's experienced problems and questions is possible except by deliberately excluding the direct confrontation of Christian truths with the questions as asked from reason reflecting on individual human reality. Normally, in modern times, at least, the alternative to Catholicism will take on collective or political overtones. The destiny of the "race" or nation or civilization will substitute for the destiny of each individual (resurrection in the orthodox Catholic view). Each person's meaning will only be that of a part of a collectivity and therefore as such expendable. This is why the obscuring of Catholic and Christian theology is so devastating for those who really seek answers for their own ultimate questions and for their own transcendent meaning as a particular human being (see Chapter XII).

For de Lubac, "modernity" is the "refusal to see in man any sort of transcendent aspiration.... Modernity would be therefore the triumph... of finitude, the certain acquisition of the knowledge that man knows in the end how to destroy himself." But this destruction would not be by the nuclear bomb, that had for a while in recent years come to have a sort of apocalyptic inner worldly meaning as if the continuance of life on earth were in fact the only mission of man. Rather, "modernity is the refusal of any sort of faith. It follows on the rejection of mystery. Modernity will always 'know' more, will always 'explain' more, but in reality it will not 'comprehend' more, because it has refused mystery."

Here, de Lubac is in agreement with von Balthasar and

---

[8] Eric Voegelin, *Science, Politics, and Gnosticism* (Chicago: Regnery/Gateway, 1968), p. 109-10.

Voegelin that this situation can be seen as a form of gnosticism, something very old in Christian history.[9] And what is going on in gnostic spirituality that seeks to substitute itself for the truths of Catholicism? "It is the attempt to reduce the profound sense of Christian revelation to a sublime consciousness, integral, reserved to an elite, the only depository of the capacity and the right to interpret the hidden significance of the Gospel or some other original revelation." For those who have followed the twistings of the politicized religion and ideological theologies of recent decades, surely this is the spirit we have seen at work.

Do I think Catholicism still exists? It does not exist in the growing dominance of secular ideology or its religious imitations that increasingly show almost violent hostility to the classic truths of the faith as presented in the tradition and represented by the Church. On the other hand, if we examine the alternatives presented by these ideologies, secular and religious, we again see that they are not adequate answers to the vibrant questions presented by human life as such in each human being. Aristotle was most perceptive in seeing that we could not have many friends in the course of one life-time, because he saw that it took the whole of life to do justice even to one good friend. And this very observation is sufficient to make us realize that precisely in the historical and present multiplicity of individual human lives and their friends, there remains room for the ultimate questions presented by each of these lives, particularly room for the answer that is known as resurrection.

John Paul II has never hesitated to urge us to live well in the world. But he constantly reminds us that salvation is not a political or economic liberation in any ideological sense. Rather it is the intense relationship that each created human person has with God. This is the meaning of each individual life actually begun in this world in whatever time or place. The friendships that may or

---

[9] James V. Schall, "The Abiding Significance of Gnosticism," *The American Ecclesiastical Review*, CXLVII (September, 1962), 164-73; "Gnosticism Reconsidered," *Crisis*, 10 (May, 1992), 41-43.

may not happen in a lifetime can only reach their completion if the doctrines of the faith are true. Catholicism still exists where we are allowed and taught to ask the ultimate questions. If we will not experience them, ask them, we will never know whether revelation exists to answer them. That these places of inquiry remain perhaps only a few, only isolated, does not mean that there, in the hidden intellectual or familial Nazareths of this world, places no one ever heard of, the great truths are not still being kept for us.

When John Paul II was in Monterey in California, at Mass at the Laguna Seca Race Track, not far from my brother's home, the following remarks of a young mother and a young soldier from nearby Fort Ord were recorded in *The Washington Post* (September 19, 1987):

> As the Pope paused for a long moment of silent prayer, a deep silence pervaded the crowds on the hillside. No coughing, no child crying, not even a bird could be heard, as 50,000 people focused their attention on the distant figure in white whom they had come to see and hear—and be blessed by.
>
> After the Mass, Edith Lenz explained what the Pope's visit meant to her. Balancing Christopher, the youngest of her brood of five on her hip, she said, "I'm so thankful that he has come here to see us, to teach us what is right.... I really see him as the Christ figure and I admire him so for traveling all over the world and trying to teach people.... I admire him for standing for what is right."
>
> Not everybody at Laguna Seca was Catholic. Army Pvt. John Whitefleet, 20, in civilian clothes and wearing a white nylon jacket stenciled "Papal Volunteer," had volunteered to help out "because I wanted to." "I volunteered," he said, "even though I'm not Catholic because I think he has the power to bring out the spiritual in people."

Does Catholicism still exist? Somehow, a young mother and a G.I. vividly remind us that it does, and where. *Ubi Petrus, ibi Ecclesia.*

CHAPTER II

The Problem of Intellectual Infidelity

I

I f Catholicism's existence can be considered to be at all problematic in a given time or place, this difficulty can be traced back to a number of reasons, some of which are simply moral in the sense that men chose not to live well or properly. While this moral stance is a problem in its own right, it becomes much more pressing and dangerous when writers and thinkers go on to evolve a theory of why what is being done, what is said to be wrong or evil by classical standards, might be justified or explained.

Catholicism has always held that the most dangerous sin or disorder was pride. Pride was, in its most pejorative sense, the worst of the vices. Usually it was irremediable. It was the sin of Lucifer. It was really the sin of Adam and Eve in wanting themselves to be the cause of the distinction of things. Their eating of the fruit of the Tree of the Knowledge of Good and Evil meant that they wanted to obey only their own commandments, not those of Yahweh. No profound understanding of the human soul can neglect this most serious of all disorders, the problem of "intellectual infidelity" before the *things that are*.

On March 20, 1776, James Boswell and Samuel Johnson visited Oxford where the two proceeded to look up sundry friends at University College, then to Pembroke College, Christchurch, Magdalen, and finally Trinity. At this latter college, lively conversation centered on a rather "mellifluous" book, then much in vogue, that was, however, by common opinion merely "artful infidelity." The author of the book, it seems, was an Oxford man who once, of all things, as it was quaintly put in the language of the times, had "turned Papist."

However, this otherwise inexplicable deed was rendered more intelligible, Boswell pointed out, if it be recalled that this same smooth-talking author had already changed his religion "several times" before "from the Church of England to the Church of Rome — from the Church of Rome to infidelity." Boswell added, rather wittily of this vacillating record, "I did not despair yet of seeing him a Methodist preacher." To this, Samuel Johnson responded, laughingly, "It is said that his range has been more extensive, and that he has once been a Mohammedan. However now that he has published his infidelity, he will probably persist in it." To which Boswell retorted, "I am not quite sure of that, Sir."[1] Infidelity in its very nature, it seems, can be so artful that it can go beyond even the definitiveness of one's own printed word, can be unfaithful even to itself.

We live in a world, of course, in which the Church of England, the Church of Rome, infidels, Mohammedans, and Methodist preachers by the law of the land exist side by side in the same polities. Or at least, we live in certain polities in which these sorts of people are allowed and encouraged, though to be sure sometimes also forced, to dwell together. Many existing states, however, have established religions or ideologies that, to varying degrees, only barely tolerate or actively suppress divergent opinions.

Some writers think, moreover, that liberal democracy is ultimately to be based on the Hobbesian theory that we must reduce all philosophic and religious truths to civic indifference

---

[1] *Boswell's Life of Johnson* (London: Oxford, 1931), I, p. 659.

and threaten force if any religious or philosophic controversy makes any splash in the public order. Other writers maintain that there is no truth anyhow so that the best we can do is wait until these outmoded beliefs finally disappear. Still others insist that everyone should be mixed together and redistributed on some quota basis no matter what the race, creed, nation, sexual or personal differences might be, since the only "truth" is that no distinctions hold.

On the other hand, we can recall the Head of State in Iran threatened to kill a novelist who, in the religious politician's view, blasphemed his religion. We are perplexed by such passions that seem to run contrary to the laws of civility in a society that is not allowed by the laws of propriety to see any blasphemy in anything, not even when organized homosexuals desecrate the Eucharist in St. Patrick's Cathedral. We are frightened by ideas that mean what they say, by ideas that demand public acknowledgment. We tend to think that the many erroneous claims to truth must mean that there is no claim to truth at all. Whatever we think of the importance of ideas, it seems to be impolite if they are taken too seriously.

The crisis in communism was at bottom an intellectual crisis, a loss of faith in the validity of its own workings. In a reflective piece just at time of Marxism's predicament, *The Economist* of London wrote:

> (Communism) was an idea that threatened to take the twentieth century by storm.... Yet communists the world over now peer fearfully into the next century, out of puff, out of converts and increasingly out of ideas for recovering their lost glory.... Communists have always been loath to recognize failure. By any measure of people's well-being, from health and welfare to the quality of the sausage on the dinner table, market-led economies have outperformed communist ones. Yet communists in power have blundered on regardless.[2]

---

[2] "Communism at Bay," *The Economist*, January 14, 1989, p. 15.

The failure of communism, moreover, makes particularly poignant those branches of Christianity, both Protestant and Catholic, that have thrown in their lot with the Marxist cause as if it were
the philosophic form in which the public life of the Church ought
to be expressed. Not only was the theory of Marxism contrary to
the Catholic faith on essential points, its practice had no stamp of
success to argue in its favor.

Yet, the failure of Marxism as an economic agent or a
political regime does not necessarily spell the end of the utopian
ideology from which it arose. Nor does it prevent us from suspect-
ing, as Paul Johnson has written, that other similar and related
systems will not take its place.[3] The modern mind is itself in some
sense ideological. The failure of one ideology does not ruin the
chances of ideology itself, rooted as it is in a certain view of the
relation of the human mind and will to the world, to its origins and
destiny. Indeed, if there is anything characteristic of the years
since the 1989 crisis of Marxism, it is the replacement in the public
forum of other varieties of statism and other attempts to put into
existence the theoretical principles out of which Marxism originally flowed. Any anticipated return to religion and classic morality has not occurred.

This century, the twentieth, and not some previous one, is in
fact the century in which full totalitarianism was actually perfected and employed as a political system. The possibilities for an
even more dire form of civil and moral totalitarian disorder are
much greater at the end of this century than they were at the
beginning. Richard Pipes pointed out that the great political
scourges of the twentieth century were caused not by brutal
tyrants seeking their own ends, but by intellectuals who have
seized political power in the name of doing good. Pipes has
stressed the difference between rebellion and revolution. Rebellions, he maintained, are usually against some specific problem
that needs remedying; revolutions, however, are intended to

---

[3] Paul Johnson, "Is Totalitarianism Dead?" *Crisis*, 7 (February, 1989), 9-17.

change the whole system if not man himself. The difference between the two is based on the relation of intellectuals to each.

"Why?" Pipes inquired.

> Because it (revolution) brings intellectuals to power, at least initially, to roles they think they deserve. And they become dangerous because they have utopian longings to remake the world. It is one thing if you're just a day-dreaming intellectual but something else when you're an intellectual equipped with an army, secret police and firing squads.[4]

The key question, about which Aristotle also hinted (*Politics*, 1267 a12), is "what is it about intellectuals that causes them to think that they can reform the world?" From a Catholic point of view — remembering that Catholic intellectuals are subject to the same temptations as other men — the cause of this temptation is itself spiritual, rooted in someone's choice of accepting or rejecting a world which in its essentials is not made by man.

But there is a fine line here. Catholicism is itself an intellectual religion that holds that the highest act of the human spirit, including the final vision of God, is, while including the whole of man's being, itself an intellectual act. On the other hand, this very fact of the centrality of intelligence in Catholicism is also the reason why the intellectual is much the more dangerous presence when he chooses not the world that God created but the one he would himself have created were he given a chance. The content of several strands of modern thought, including democratic thought, make it clear that, for many intellectuals and politicians, there are no longer any philosophic or theological reasons for not trying to put their own imagined world into existence to replace the one *that is* and for which they see no order or purpose, particularly no divine order or purpose.

---

[4] Arnold Beichman, Interview with Richard Pipes, *The Washington Times*, February 13, 1989.

II

The Catholic alternative to this position is that there is in principle such a thing as truth. This position necessarily maintains that there is also a difference between one way of acting and another. That is, not all ways of acting or thinking are right in what they hold. Action follows being, that is, truth. Aristotle's affirmation that every action of ours is either to be praised or blamed finds strong reaffirmation in the doctrine of sin and reward that are found in Catholic teaching.

One of Ogden Nash's poems, with a title itself from the Jesuits via James Joyce, namely, "Portrait of the Artist as a Prematurely Old Man," began:

> It is common knowledge to every schoolboy and even
> every bachelor of Arts,
> That all sin is divided into two parts.
>
> One kind of sin is called a sin of commission, and that
> is very important,
> And it is what you are doing when you are doing
> something you ortant,
>
> And the other kind of sin is just the opposite and is
> called a sin of omission and that is equally bad
> in the eyes of all right-thinking people, from
> Billy Sunday to Buddha,
> And it consists of not having done something you
> shuddha.[5]

This splash of Nash, as it were, contains our tradition.

St. Augustine, moreover, was said to have practically invented the concept of the will, that faculty by which we can opt for one or another of these acts of commission or omission. The freedom of the will was not meant to deny the distinction between

---

[5] *The Pocket Book of Ogden Nash* (New York: Pocket Books, 1956), p. 66.

praiseworthy and blamable actions but to suggest how the distinction was possible in the first place. The problem did not arise because men created this distinction by themselves. Rather it arose because, whatever it was that caused them to be men in the first place, they recognized such distinctions already implicit in the structure of the sort of being they were, whether by doing things they "ortant" or things they "shuddha."

The freedom of the will meant, ultimately, that it was not possible to locate evil in any other source but in the human will itself. Nothing created was in itself evil. Evil thus had to reside in something that itself existed, something that was good. Evil was explained as the real power of a rational being to choose the good. But in choosing, the free human being was also able to direct his action to a purpose less than the best, to a purpose contrary to the right order of man's actions. All evil comes into the world in the pursuit of what is itself lovely.

Since evil is not a "thing," however, but a lack in something in itself good, evil had to be located in the sort of being for whom the risk of serious choice existed in his very being. Ultimately, evil had to be found in a being that could reject what it ought to do. This very capacity in a negative way illustrated the terrible power that was in the soul of every human being, the power to choose between good and evil in an action that could be carried into the very world itself, indeed into eternity itself (See Chapter XII).

Dante, in the Fifth Canto of the *Paradiso* recounted Beatrice telling him:

> The greatest gift that our bounteous Lord
>   bestowed as the Creator, in creating,
>   the gift He cherishes the most, the one
> most like Himself, was freedom of the will.
>   All creatures with intelligence, and they
>   alone, were so endowed both then and now.[6]

---

[6] Musa translation, Penguin, 1986, p. 56.

What this doctrine means is that no political regime can directly interpose itself between the creature and God when it comes to the ultimate decisions that count. In what really matters, that is, in the condition of soul, there is ever a possibility either of rejecting or choosing good. This position means that evil can come about in even the best regimes and good in even the worst ones. It will also mean that our condition is ever precarious, that drama and risk and, yes, excitement or terror are possible in our every act, in every life.

The freedom of the will, no doubt, is a fundamental fact that Catholicism defines and defends. We do not, I think, take seriously enough the depths at which we operate in our moral lives. Without the radical freedom of the will, there is no other way to make human life in its particular existence in each person significant.

III

In the account of the Fall in Genesis, the fruit of the Tree of the Knowledge of Good and Evil that was forbidden to the first parents is no merely neutral symbol. If we think of it, this famous "Tree" stands rather close to the deep disorder noted in Greek philosophy. "The wickedness of human beings is insatiable," Aristotle remarked in the *Politics* (1267 b1). Plato also recognized that the corrupt philosopher-king could attempt to arrange everything to himself, to his own vision of right order independently of any relation to order itself. The power to define the very distinction between good and evil and to order every action to one's own definitions and to one's own life is the location of the ultimate power to act against God.

The greatest crimes, Aristotle also observed, are caused not by hunger or even by greed but in the service of some philosophic theory (*Politics*, 1267 a13). Adam and Eve, it is to be stressed, are enticed by no small aberration. They are tempted to claim a god-like power, namely, the power to decide by themselves the very distinction between good and evil. What they said was good was to become good, what they said was evil to become evil.

Herbert Deane, summing up Augustine's thought on this point, put it this way: "This lust for power also has its root in the primal vice of pride, in revolt against God and the insane desire to 'be like God'."[7] This desire is what the "temptation" was really about. Yahweh had already indicated that this distinction between good and evil was His to make. That is, His distinctions, His commandments, are the reflection of His order in the created beings that were made in His image. This discovered order reflected a good that is in fact better for human beings than anything they could figure out or choose for themselves.

What each human being, in the end, is asked to choose — and this choice defines his being — is the truth that God's order for him is what he really wants. He wants it because it is in fact a more wonderful and beauteous thing than any alternative he could conceive for himself. In a sense, human history is the working out of this thesis, of the alternatives to God's order, none of which ever proves to be comparable in glory to what is found already in being.

Free will, that power that made anything outside of God to be really worthwhile, invited man to understand and affirm this superior reality that God had put forth out of His own freedom as a gift to man. But it was possible for man to claim to establish his own order in his own soul subject to no order but himself. Unless we understand this possibility, we will never understand the problems of any existing human life nor of any existing political system composed of such choosing human lives. The myth of Prometheus or the account of the Fall was designed to show both the power and the autonomy of man in the sense that man could impose his own order in his soul and in a world given over to his "dominion." God and his law could be rejected by the free

---

[7] Herbert Deane, *The Political and Social Ideas of St. Augustine* (New York: Columbia, 1956), p. 49.

creature. And this rejection would have an intelligible form compared to the natural and divine law also existing in reality.

If we would understand modern politics, we must begin, I think, with the clear realization that there is something recognizably wrong, something disordered in man at the deepest level of his being and in all phases of his voluntary life. Man is not by nature evil, nor are his faculties evil, but there is a disorder that potentially surrounds his every act and choice. Thus all reflection must begin not outside of ourselves but in our own souls. We will never understand the problems and temptations of man in the state until we understand and acknowledge our own sins and temptations, something remarkably difficult to do, as any honest person knows from experience (see Chapter X).[8] The spiritual notion that man can choose an absolute self-sufficiency dependent only on man himself underlies the political and social turmoil of our era, at least where these conflicts are not caused rather by the wars of the gods, that is, by divergent conceptions of the Deity itself.

Even when we understand the principles and ideas at work here, we can choose the wrong way to do something about it. In the light of the myriads of wrong deeds and disordered institutions that we know to exist, we can seek to find some force or power outside of our inner-selves that will "make" us good in spite of ourselves, that will relieve us of the responsibility of doing something about our lives. Such a position, be it noted clearly, is exactly contrary to classical and Catholic notions of virtue and its coming to be in our souls. This process of finding an external cause to make us to be good, however, would relieve us of any internal effort or any spiritual reliance on such means as grace, discipline, sacraments, or prayer, that presuppose that the ultimate drama is within, inside our wills.

---

[8] See Vatican II, "The Church in the Modern World," #10, *The Documents of Vatican II* (New York: Angelus, 1966); "Le péché originel," *Le Catéchisme de l'Église Catholique* (Paris: Mame/Plon, 1992), #396-409.

Nevertheless, we have to recognize that what is wrong, even though it begins in our inner-selves, is not an illusion, as some philosophies would have it. The realism of Catholicism is such that it cannot deny the sins that we do "do" to ourselves and others. Machiavelli claimed that he was going to found a politics based on what men in fact do. The difference between Catholicism and the sort of Machiavellianism at the root of so much of modern theory and practice is not that they differ about what terrible things men might do to one another. The difference was that the Catholic denied that such evils could ever be anything but evils, even if men frequently performed them, even if they were backed by positive law and coercion.

This recognition, moreover, did not make Catholicism utopian and Machiavelli realistic. Rather it enabled Catholicism still to call evil evil, wherever it occurred, while it did not allow it to "use" evil to control evil or good. This latter "freedom" was the freedom that Machiavelli proposed to himself. The one way we cannot forgive the sins of others or be forgiven of our own is to deny that sins are sins. Catholicism maintains a doctrine of the forgiveness of sins; it does not believe that what is sinful can be redefined to make it good. Nothing distinguishes the true Catholic position in public life today more than this principle that remains at the heart of all modern opposition to Catholicism. Catholicism claims that evil is already defined by our nature and nature's God, that it is not something for us ourselves to determine on the basis of nothing other than ourselves, than our own wills.

IV

In Robert Short's *The Parables of Peanuts*, to return to the disorder of our nature and the willfulness of our acts, there is a sequence that goes as follows: Lucy, with her hands behind her back, rather coquettishly approaches a thoroughly innocent Charlie Brown. "Charlie Brown, I want to ask you something." With a growing frown on his face as if he knows the worst is about to happen, Charlie listens to Lucy's question: "Do you think I'm a crabby person?" Charlie, the epitome of frankness and openness, responds to a non-plussed Lucy, "Yes, I think you're a very crabby person." At which point Lucy yells back with a force that turns Charlie upside down, "WELL, WHO CARES WHAT YOU THINK?"[9] The order of truth can be rejected by the order of will.

And what secures our capacity to recognize truth and to guide our wills to embrace it is nothing less than the discipline of virtue and the presence of grace. Again Aristotle put the problem well: "Without virtue (man) is the most unholy and the most savage of the animals, and the worst with regard to sex and food" (*Politics*, 1253 a36). Aristotle made this observation not on the basis of any religious theory but on the basis of simple observation. Without virtue, it seems, men will have to be coerced to do some minimal things for the protection of society if not of themselves. Indeed, as St. Thomas said, such minimal purpose is what coercion should be used for (*Summa Theologiae*, I-II, 96, 2). We will always find citizens in any polity who will not act virtuously so that some force likely will be needed to prevent others from being harmed. This too is no doubt what St. Paul meant when he wrote to the Romans that magistrates "do not bear the sword without cause" (13:4).

The word "liberation" has been in much use in Catholic circles to describe what seem to be mainly political and economic problems and purposes, though it can have a much broader religious meaning. The Catholic religion is sometimes proposed as a direct solution to these problems not as they exist in some transcendent plane but as they exist in actual civil societies. To be sure, it is not the Catholic position that man is a passive being, nor that it is impossible for him to discover and address problems that

---

[9] Robert L. Short, *The Parables of Peanuts* (New York: Harper, 1968), p. 54.

beset men in economic or political orders. His capacity to act in these areas is what, in part, his free will means.

But it is also the fundamental Catholic position that each human being does have an ultimate problem concerning his relation with God no matter in what sort of political regime he might live in during his one lifetime. This relation to God will manifest itself in all man's relations to himself and to others. When all is said and done, Catholicism does not deal primarily with one's citizenship or economic well-being, but with one's final status before God as such. That status may indeed have something to with how men deal with their neighbors. The City of God, however, is not of this world even though those who belong to it will have been born, will have lived and died here.

John Paul II with his characteristic accuracy addressed this tendency that does not separate the distinct Catholic doctrine from many current theories that hold that "the concept of salvation is confined to the temporal reality." These theories mean that man can "find in himself and in his earthly progress all that is necessary to achieve it."[10] Behind the Holy Father's concern is the old Pelagian doctrine, now dressed up in contemporary form, that man can save himself by his economic, political, or social activities. The Catholic position does not deny that men can act. Nor does it deny that the world is markedly better because of the presence of grace within it. Nevertheless, in back of so many modern social and political philosophies, many of which individual Catholics have adopted, lies the idea that men can, in all essentials, save themselves primarily by their own socio-economic forces. In this position, neither Church nor redemption are necessary for the true good of mankind to be achieved.

The root political problem of modern life, in the Catholic view, then, is the diagnosis of human structures by ideological

---

[10] John Paul II, Address to Missiology Congress, October 7, 1988, *L'Osservatore Romano*, English, November 28, 1988, p. 2. See also his Encyclical *Redemptoris Missio*, of 1991.

means rather than by metaphysical or religious ones. These humanly formulated forms or structures are then imposed on man (or sometimes positively chosen by him) and his society by the state power as the solution to man's deepest spiritual difficulties. This position is essentially a claim for self-redemption. This claim is what I have here called "intellectual infidelity." It is not merely a question of evil-doing but of redefining evil and its cause so that the unique instrument of man, the state, can be used to replace the man of nature and revelation. This replacement will manifest itself by denying the sources of virtue and grace that have always been considered by Catholicism to be the primary causes of human worth and betterment insofar as this is possible in this world.

John Paul II is, therefore, correct to address himself to the claim for "self-redemption" as the central spiritual issue that manifests itself in any public order.

> Because salvation is a total and integral reality, it concerns the individual person and all people, and touches also historical and social reality, culture and community structures in which they live. However, salvation cannot be confined to the framework of merely the earthly necessities of man or of society; neither can it be reached by playing with historical dialectics. Man is not his own saviour in a definitive manner; salvation transcends that which is human and earthly, it is a gift from above. *There is no self-redemption*; God alone saves man in Christ.[11]

The "intellectual infidelity" that is most dangerous in the modern world is precisely the one that denies the affirmation that "there is no self-redemption" for man. The claim that such self-redemption is possible, however it be formulated, is the identical claim from the Garden to be "like Gods" determining good and evil by the powers of man and his institutions.

---

[11] John Paul II, Missiology, *ibid*. Italics added.

V

What is further to be emphasized is that the most likely, indeed the most logical location for the spiritual claim of self-redemption by man to surface will in fact be in the state. The very nature of man incites him to put his inner life into external being in a definitive way. And this self-redemptive claim will be made in the name of those who are most likely to have addressed themselves to the human condition, namely, intellectuals with their allies and followers in the general culture.

Aristotle had remarked that politics was the highest of the practical sciences, that is, of those sciences that were indeed proper to man as man in his life in this world. Aristotle, however, did not think that man was the highest being as such. This conclusion meant that politics was not the highest science. It was understood that man was subject to some higher or transcendent power that was the origin of his being man in the first place. So long as no metaphysical or transcendent order is recognized, wherein the goodness of human being as such is acknowledged as not originating from man himself, there will be an abiding temptation to rebel against the very human condition itself, as Aristotle also understood (*Metaphysics*, 982 b29).

The terms of this rebellion, of which certain modern political movements have proved to be their most dangerous and subtle manifestations, consist essentially in the political claim to possess the power and authority to decide *what man is*. Whether it be a Supreme Court deciding what a human being is or is not in an abortion case, or an ecology theory that holds that nature is more important than man so that man becomes a function of the ecosystem, or a hegemony that so wants to educate and care for children that the family is effectively undermined in the name of compassion and good will, behind these claims lurk the signs of self-redemption. Such claims do not appear as some abstract theoretical opposition but as active interventions in the public order that would deny the distinction of good and evil to be anything more than what the state claims and enforces. The only law becomes the positive law.

When it is not countered by virtue or a theoretically limited polity, "the wickedness of human beings is insatiable" — to recall again Aristotle's memorable phrase (*Politics*, 1267 b1). Even when human nature is so countered, human experience has found that something more is required, something from outside the human experience itself, something called traditionally grace, something that might both explain and guide men to the true causes of their disorders. Philosophy, even to be philosophy, may not have all the resources it needs for its own achievement.

If Catholicism still exists, I might say in concluding this Chapter, it must exist as fully aware of the problem of what I have called "intellectual infidelity," something that can harass the souls of even the most spiritual, even of theologians and bishops. In his *Autobiography*, G.K. Chesterton reacted to George Bernard Shaw's idea of a better "superman" than the kind of beings that we are. "I have defended what I regard as the sacred limitations of Man against what he (Shaw) regards as the soaring illimitability of Superman.... For in fact all these differences come back to a religious difference; indeed I think all differences do."[12]

The "sacred limitations of man" in this world are the condition for the protection of his own being. It is to these limitations that we must be faithful in our very choices. The claims to be able to reconstruct man by our own efforts are not unknown. Indeed, they appear every day in our political, economic, and intellectual proposals if we but recognize them. These proposals arise from differences about what man is. They are indeed ultimately religious differences.

The main intellectual contribution of religion and faith to any civilization, however, remains the explanation of what is

---

[12] G. K. Chesterton, *The Autobiography*, in *The Collected Works of G. K. Chesterton* (San Francisco: Ignatius Press, [1936] 1988), Vol. XVI, p. 215.

man's ultimate destiny. Without this active explanation and the spiritual resources to understand and live it, men will actively seek alternate worlds, alternate definitions of what they are. And the makers of these alternate definitions, since they have no theoretical reason to recognize limits, will seek to reorganize the world with its natural configurations, configurations not caused by man nor by the world itself. The fact that these efforts will arise primarily from disaffected intellectuals who seek political power should not surprise us. This is what we should expect on the grounds of our understanding of pride and the human heart.

I arrive at this conclusion, however, as a hopeful thing. Understanding evil with its ramifications in family, social life, and state is itself a good, something that should be part of our deepest meditation and, yes, education. The Church of England, the Church of Rome, infidels, Mohammedans, intellectuals, ecologists, feminists, Marxists, and Methodist preachers are all actively present in our midst seeking to explain to us what it is we are. The one conclusion that we should continually draw from the politics of our time or any time is that there is no self-redemption for our kind. Without understanding why this is so, we will continue to experience in any existing public order metaphysical rebellions. These metaphysical rebellions will seek to refashion man into some other sort of being but the one God created. He was instructed not to seek by himself to define, in his habits and in his politics, the distinctions between good and evil as if this were his and not a divine power.

In the end, to recall Boswell and Johnson, intellectual infidelity remains a "fine art." Whether or not with Ogden Nash, Billy Sunday, Chesterton, Shaw, or the Buddha, we think this ultimately also a religious question, we "shuddha," for that is what it is. Intellectual infidelity engages the human mind when that mind has rejected *what is* and the revealed answers addressed to the basic questions man poses to himself.

CHAPTER III

Thought and the Difference It Makes

I

Thus far, I have asked in several ways whether Catholicism still exists? I have suggested that this issue arises most often in the hearts and minds of the most intelligent and those in authority, either in academia, the culture, or even in the Church. I reflected on the nature of this "intellectual infidelity," as I have called it, but only to emphasize that faith itself is always a substitute for vision and for full intelligence.[1] Faith always has the characteristic of a second best or a substitute knowledge. Perhaps it is a necessary substitute, perhaps an unsatisfactory one, but to do faith "justice," as it were, is to understand it exactly for what it is. In a number of different ways, I want to present the case for intelligence and for a spirituality based on it, even when that intelligence and that spirituality may begin or continue because of revelation.

Henri de Lubac, I think, provided a necessary caution. Superior intelligence does not necessarily mean superior holiness.

---

[1] See Yves Simon, "The Search for Truth," *A General Theory of Authority* (Notre Dame: University of Notre Dame Press, 1980), pp. 81-132; Josef Pieper, *Problems of Modern Faith* (Chicago: Franciscan Herald Press, 1985); *The Truth of All Things* (San Francisco: Ignatius Press, 1989); John Paul II, *Veritatis Splendor*, 1993.

> We know all too well — unfortunately — that the profes-
> sion of Catholicism, even militant Catholicism, does not
> automatically confer sanctity, and we must admit that
> among us . . . much human narrowness often places
> obstacles in the way of the action of the Spirit. Yet we also
> know that the humblest of our saints is freer, interiorly,
> than the greatest of our masters of wisdom.[2]

The "masters of wisdom" here are not being denigrated in the
name of revelation. The very real knowledge of the philosophers,
a knowledge that, as I shall constantly emphasize, is both necessary for the faith and glorious in itself, is only a slim inkling of
knowledge itself, as Aristotle already reminded us in the last book
of the *Ethics*.

Living rightly, moreover, is a function of thinking rightly.
No doubt we all know those who think incorrectly but who live
decent, even heroic lives. Likewise, we know those who think
correctly enough but who do not live well. Most of us are, in fact
and at the same time, in both of these latter categories in many
things. So, what is the point of maintaining that living rightly is a
function of thinking rightly?

We need to be reminded, I think, of the unity of human
nature in thought and action. Aristotle's observation that "a little
error in the beginning will lead to a large error in the end" (*On the
Heavens*, 271b 9-10) is not only memorable but extremely accurate.
The real battles in the world are won and lost in thought before
they ever appear in deed and speech. Conversely, the restoration
of moral order initially lies in the restoration of intellectual order,
even in the heart of the person, even in the most obscure of places.

In the minds of many observant people today, as I have
suggested (Chapter I), what characterizes Christianity in general
and Catholicism in particular is the practical loss of its intellectual

---

[2] Henri de Lubac, *The Splendor of the Church* (San Francisco: Ignatius Press, 1986),
p. 309.

institutions, even of its intellectual center. I do not mean that intellectual institutions inaugurated by Catholics do not exist, nor even, in a kind of worldly way, that they do not flourish. But I do mean that in them, some exceptions granted, there is found little distinctly Catholic intelligence operative.

"Philosophy is not the reading of books; philosophy is not the contemplation of nature; philosophy is not the phenomenology of personal experience; philosophy is not its history," Frederick Wilhelmsen has written.

> These are indispensable tools aiding a man to come to know the things that are. But that knowing is precisely knowing and nothing else. We once were given this, not too long ago, in the American Catholic Academy. With a few honorable exceptions, we are given it no longer. This is why philosophy is no longer talked into existence. It is no longer talked into existence because it is no longer taught into existence.[3]

What has replaced philosophy in Catholic academic institutions is either ideology or a social activism that is aimed at presumably reforming the world without the prior effort to know *what is* (see Chapter IX). Social activism by itself cannot justify its own tenets, which is why it too often appears as but an aspect of Marxism, liberalism, or ecology, themselves aspects of modern autonomous philosophy.

Curiously, we also live in a time when the distinctive mark of Catholic intelligence persists and even blossoms in the papacy and within the spheres of its immediate influence. But this vibrant source is largely unknown and unattended to within many of the intellectual institutions claiming Catholic origins. Briefly I might suggest that the Holy Father knows what modernity is and how

---

[3] Frederick D. Wilhelmsen, "The Great Books: Enemies of Wisdom," *Modern Age*, 31 (Fall, 1987), 329.

Christian thought might be directed to it, whereas so many Catholic intellectuals accept prevailing thought and seek to reinterpret Catholicism in its light.

At first blush, then, this position might seem merely rash or subjective. I have no doubt that it is, in a way, at least brash if not wholly rash. I would not have perhaps decided to spell my concern out, even for myself, had I not chanced on several quite similar and equally blunt observations. It struck me that the crisis of intelligence in the Church and its nature is in fact quite visible to many acute observers when it is not so visible to Catholics themselves.

II

The first critique that grabbed my attention was an editorial in *The Wall Street Journal* on the occasion of a rally convoked by Billy Graham in Central Park in New York City. Some 250,000 people gathered there to hear this now venerable and powerful preacher. The editors of the *Journal* instinctively recognized that something important went on in New York's most famous park when even Cardinal O'Connor "encouraged his flock to attend" Billy Graham's Crusade.

The Wall Street Journal editors wondered what explained this amazingly large turnout for "a religious message"? They thought that essentially it was due to a loss of authority in the mainline churches, including the Catholic Church. This loss resulted in a consistent failure in recent years to teach basic religious truths, something the Church itself has come to recognize with the publication of its new *General Catechism* (see Chapter IX).

Thus, it can be observed that bishops in their pastorals and conferences talk mostly of public policy issues, not, like the Holy Father, of basic doctrinal and spiritual teachings and practices of the faith. At most Catholic colleges today, moreover, what can fulfill theology or religious studies requirements is a vague course in God-talk and a second course in some other faith or ideology. The schools have obviously lost confidence in the truth of their faith as itself a worthy object of systematic study.

What caused this extraordinary flight from mainline churches and a desire to find places where the Gospel is preached in a purer form? "Somewhere along the way those churches began to de-value and even dispense with their traditions and their identities as primarily spiritual institutions," the *Journal* editors percep-tively observed.

> Spiritual life was now to be fully integrated with more secular political goals flying under the rubric of "social justice." At its most extreme, the main-stream Protestant churches and the Catholic Church in America fell victim to the radical-left ideology of the times on foreign affairs and whatever domestic agenda the most liberal wing of the Democratic Party was promoting. In the Christian churches throughout the country, social concern and activism have for some time now been the main mode of religious expression. One of the ironic effects of this turn was that administrative talent, especially of the Catholic Church, was decimated (September 24, 1991).

At first sight, such remarks might seem to be mere "liberal bashing" or "capitalist complacency." Yet, there is no doubt that much of "social justice" preaching is, on the basis of any objective content analysis, a kind of pious version of ideology. The flight from the mainline churches is not unrelated to the laity's recogni-tion that what they are getting is not the Catholicism they have a right to know, but some version of political pleading for aberrant social practices and institutions.

Understanding justice, of course, is not alien to religion. However, the New Testament is not a handbook in political philosophy or economics. It leaves our basic analysis of political and economic life to our good sense, experience, and reason. But of late religious leaders and teachers, in an extraordinary lack of perception, have followed a fashionable social or psychological ideology and have confused such ideology, in the minds of the faithful and many other sympathetic observers at least, with good policy and even with good sense or with faith itself.

Thus, to give a second random comment on how intellectual life in Catholicism is seen, in a review of a book written by a Jesuit on St. Ignatius of Loyola, Anthony Burgess wrote in *The Times* (January 17, 1993) that

> It's dangerous to generalize but one finds in American Jesuits a distressing lack of concern with theology. Good and evil seem to be embarrassing terms, and I read a recent Jesuit symposium on communication techniques which did not even list Jesus Christ in the index.

One hesitates to take such remarks lightly.

John Paul II, in his social Encyclical, *Centesimus Annus*, moreover, frankly stated that "there can be no genuine solution to the social question apart from the Gospel" (#5). He then, as if to prove his point, went right ahead and embraced most of the ideas and institutions opposed by the socialists and the radical left for the last hundred and fifty years (see Chapter X). Unsurprisingly, his words have been met with a stony silence by the same "faith and justice" movements in the churches that have so alienated the congregations, the very folks now found showing up to hear Billy Graham in Central Park.

The current problem of religion, I suspect, is not that its leaders are too authoritative or too dogmatic. Rather it is that they have practically yielded any proper intellectual and decision-making authority to academic, media, and special-interest movements. These movements in their intellectual roots stem from the modern liberal and socialist notion that man can "make himself." Christianity, in many ways, has been made to sound exactly like that "autonomous man" whose intellectual world contains no norms but those which "human rights" people "give" to themselves. Sympathy with the deeds of others, whatever they might be, becomes itself an intellectual criterion deciding the validity of these same deeds.

The leaders of these latter movements called generically "social justice," when themselves ensconced in posts of religious authority, as many have been, are most assiduous in rooting out adherents of classical Judaeo-Christian understandings of man, God, and society. By not using authority, we suddenly discover, we do not escape it. We just transfer it to antagonists and they use it.

Speaking of a kind of popular sovereignty based not on norms of a stable human nature but on the will of the majority as the only norm of rightness, Josef Ratzinger remarked, as if to recognize the seriousness and nature of this problem:

> Sovereignty must always be linked to the laws of human nature. To preserve human dignity, some fundamental aspects cannot be overlooked, aspects which concern more than majority rule. Respect for basic human rights — and the right to life, the right to live as a human being, is fundamental — is a necessary condition for any legitimate sovereignty. A sovereign who feels free to decide that certain human rights are less valuable becomes inhuman.[4]

Nothing is more obvious today than that the problem of inhuman rule or totalitarianism has shifted from concern about Marxist states to concern about the intellectual principles of democratic states themselves.

We do not, in this context, have a surfeit of religious authority in our society, but a surfeit of its *lack*. If there is a "decimation" within the Catholic Church in particular, it is primarily because religious authority has allowed "more secular political goals

---

[4] Interview with Josef Cardinal Ratzinger, *The Catholic World Report*, 1 (November, 1989), 9-16.

flying under the rubric of 'social justice'" to determine the religious content and agenda of what it is to be a clergyman and a Catholic.

The third reflection along these lines that caused me to wonder about the intellectual condition of the Church was an observation of Irving Kristol. "It is secular humanism that is the orthodox metaphysical-theological basis of the two modern political philosophies, socialism and liberalism," Kristol wrote in his essay on "The Future of American Jewry."

> Christianity and Judaism have been infiltrated and profoundly influenced by the spirit of secular humanism. There are moments when, listening to the sermons of bishops, priests, and rabbis, one has the distinct impression that Christianity and Judaism today are, for the most part, different traditional vehicles for conveying, in varying accents, the same (or at least very similar) sentiments and world views. Of other-worldly views there is very little expression, except among the minority who are discredited (and dismissed) as "fundamentalists" or "ultra-Orthodox."[5]

Again there is this theme, that what acute observers hear in the churches is nothing similar to what the churches are known for and are obliged to teach. What such critics actually hear, and are sure the people also hear, is merely a kind of baptized secular humanism. Since authorities in the mainline churches apparently cannot bring themselves to admit the seriousness of their condition, the people more and more seek other religious centers or often no doubt simply join the ranks of a dying secular humanism because they seldom encounter anything else.

---

[5] Irving Kristol, "The Future of American Jewry," *Commentary*, 92 (August, 1991), 23.

III

Something else that has occasioned these reflections in my mind is the Encyclical of John Paul II on the missions (*Redemptoris Missio*) together with the Document known as "Dialogue and Proclamation" from the Congregation for the Evangelization of Peoples and the Pontifical Council for Inter-religious Dialogue (May 19, 1991). Two things strike me as particularly important about both of these documents.

The first is the recognition on the part of the Holy Father that the Church must state or proclaim *what it is* to the nations. The Church is not what other philosophies or religions are, even though it can respect them and encourage them in some of their aspects. The Church says what no one else says. It cannot not seek effective means to state what it is. This truth must be made known even to those Islamic or absolutist states, including democracies, that recognize no norms but their own wills, that use every political and police method to prevent any presence of Catholicism.

The Holy Father is particularly annoyed with those states that officially interfere by civil or extra-legal sanctions with the freedom of the people to hear what specifically the Church maintains about itself, God, and man. To a gathering of Oriental Patriarchs from the Middle East, John Paul II emphasized that he recognizes that their faithful

> are exposed to a thousand difficulties, the greatest of which is that of being unable to express themselves as Christians while they are minorities in Islamic societies which, depending on national or regional policies, tolerate, esteem, or reject them. In this regard, I cannot pass over in silence the fact that today there are still communities which do not allow Christian communities to be implanted there, to celebrate their faith and to live according to the demands proper to their confession. I am thinking particularly of Saudi Arabia.[6]

---

[6] John Paul II, "Building a Future?" (March 4, 1991), *The Pope Speaks*, 36 (#6, 1991), 326.

Sometimes it takes a brave, frank man to state what is obvious. It is especially fortunate when the man also happens to be the Pope, with his own peculiar authority.

The second thing that is remarkable about these documents on missions and proclamation is the pains that the Church has been taking in recent years to engage every organized religion, scientific discipline, and philosophy in direct, systematic discussions about what each stands for and how it relates to human knowledge and revelation. Some time ago it struck me that the Holy Father not merely took his, shall we say, religious obligations seriously, but also his philosophical ones. If the Church is essentially "mission" oriented, this will include efforts directed specifically at the thought of other religions and philosophies in their most sophisticated positions.

That is to say, many human things can be pursued or attempted in order to bring faith forward before the nations and the various kinds of peoples within them. Conferences, audiences, commissions, writings, addresses, colloquies, and study groups are to be employed. The Church understands that civil and religious freedom in all polities also applies to itself, to its freedom to present its considered case without political interference. All these human endeavors could and should be used to clarify and to state the nature of disagreements and of agreements. The problems are between religions and between religion and science, literature, politics, economics, and the thousand other things that can be touched by a right understanding of what man's destiny really is. Dialogue is not just for the sake of talk but it is to find out how much agreement and disagreement really exists intellectually. Proclamation exists to state specifically what the faith holds.

The Holy Father has a particularly magnetic quality and I suppose this charism is peculiar to him. He has a capacity to go over the head of the media to speak directly to people, particularly to the young. On the other hand, John Paul II is demanding. It is not enough to say that Lutherans, for example, have a different position than Catholics. The Holy Father, and the general spirit of

Catholicism, wants to know what this difference precisely is and what can be done to state it clearly. In this sense, the Holy Father has long insisted that the climate be created in which serious discussions about differences can be held.

This approach will be valid for Marxists, Buddhists, Mormons, astrophysicists, abortionists, and a myriad of other groups that claim some aspect or some whole understanding of God, man, and the world. When this human work of dialogue and intellectual understanding is done, the Pope thinks it is still necessary to proclaim and to teach what clearly it is that Christ has taught and Who He is. The Pope takes life and faith seriously because he takes intelligence seriously, an intelligence that is addressed to mankind under the reality of "the Word made flesh."[7]

IV

Not just any philosophy, however, can bear this discussion of intelligence, which is why philosophy itself is a basic interest to Catholicism in particular, as Leo Strauss once recognized.

> For the Christian, the sacred doctrine is revealed theology; for the Jew or the Muslim, the sacred doctrine is, at least primarily, the legal interpretation of the Divine Law. The sacred doctrine in the latter sense has, to say the least, much less in common with philosophy than the sacred doctrine in the former sense. It is ultimately for this reason that the status of philosophy was, as a matter of principle, much more precarious in Judaism and Islam than in Christianity: in Christianity philosophy became an integral part of the officially recognized and even required training of the student of sacred doctrine. This difference explains partly the eventual collapse of philosophic inquiry in the

---

[7] See also Josef Pieper, "Philosophy Out of a Christian Existence," *Josef Pieper — an Anthology* (San Francisco: Ignatius Press, 1989), pp. 164-70.

Islamic and in the Jewish world, a collapse which has no
parallel in the Western Christian world.[8]

The status of philosophy today in seminaries and in Catholic
universities seems to suggest that the collapse has finally found a
"parallel" in the Western Catholic world, a collapse that more
than anything explains the ideological susceptibility of Catholic
and Christian thinkers and students in recent times.

Catholicism is a proud faith. It is a faith, indeed, that also
maintains that pride is the greatest of sins and human disorders.
It even locates this disorder not in external social and political
things but in the human heart, from whence it can always appear,
even in the holiest of places. But when I say that Catholicism is a
proud faith, I mean here rather that its historical mark is the
pursuit of intelligence. It makes no concessions to error except to
understand it. Catholicism first had to know if its faith was
"credible."

But is this not dangerous, to "understand" error as error, to
inquire whether faith is credible? Again, the proud tradition of
Catholicism is the claim to seek out error, to first understand it. We
are taught this in the very structure of St. Thomas' *Summa Theologiae.*
In this sense, Catholicism is not first a faith of "sympathy" or
"compassion." Compassion is misplaced if it is located in the
intellect. The intellect is to know, to know *what is*. Without this
latter knowledge, compassion and sympathy can lead, as they are
leading, to transforming the distinction between good and evil
into an approval of evil.

In 1937, Etienne Gilson published a short essay entitled
"Medieval Universalism and Its Present Value." In it, he wrote:

> For it is a last and all-important feature of medieval
> philosophy that its rationalism was not only a realism, but

---

[8] Leo Strauss, *Persecution and the Art of Writing* (Westport, CT: Greenwood, 1972),
p. 19.

a personalism as well. Just like trees and any kind of living things, men are individualized and distinct from each other by their bodies. Such is the metaphysical reason why, grounded as it is on matter, individualism is always a source of divisions and oppositions. When men consider themselves as mere individuals, the so-called Liberalism is bound to prevail, until political disorders and social injustice make it unavoidable for the State to become totalitarian.[9]

The state becomes totalitarian when persons, each with a direct transcendent origin and destiny, are held to be merely living individuals, replaceable divisions of matter. Gilson's social metaphysics was remarkably perceptive.

In an Interview in 1989, to illustrate this point further, Josef Pieper recalled the problems under which his students at the University of Münster in Germany labored because they had no opportunity to learn in their theology courses the intellectual side of the faith.

One of my students wrote me that he had been studying theology for ten years and never heard one lecture on what a priest is. The priesthood, the nature of the sacraments, what happens in the Mass: these are the things that must be taught. I asked one of my female students if she knew what a sacrament is. She said no. I asked her what kind of theology book she had in the Catholic school run by nuns that she attended. It turned out that in that book there was no definition of sacrament. I went to my bishop and pointed this out, and he told me to look at the curriculum of the theological faculty in the University of Münster. There are not any lectures on the sacraments.

---

[9] Etienne Gilson, *Medieval Universalism and Its Present Value* (New York: Sheed & Ward, 1937), p. 21.

We can suspect that this situation is not confined to the University of Münster.

Catholicism is not a faith that maintains that thought makes no difference. Rather it is a faith that forces the curious to describe what it maintains; it seeks to be clear and, yes, dogmatic about this content. Many schools of thought, both philosophical and theological, have fumed against what they call doctrinairism or dogmatism. No doubt these "isms" are also dangerous when they mean, as they cannot mean in classical Catholicism, confusing the articulated statement of doctrine with the reality it seeks to clarify. On the other hand, the human mind is not the human mind if it does not seek accurately to state *what is*, even of God. Catholicism has always maintained that the effort of the mind to state what it can about God is not an aberration, but the very purpose of the mind itself. This very effort includes the awareness of the limits of human knowledge. But it also includes the nature of intellect as such, which is precisely to know the reality cast before it.

V

A.N. Wilson, the biographer of Belloc and C.S. Lewis, has recently startled the world by what his publisher calls a "counter-blast" against religion. He begins, "It is said in the Bible that the love of money is the root of all evil. It might be truer to say that the love of God is the root of all evil. Religion is the tragedy of mankind."[10] This rather classic type of book is the not untypical account of a man who began as an agnostic, became a Catholic, then an Anglican, wrote books on religious subjects and finally turned "against religion."

What struck me about Wilson's heavy-handed attack on religion was my recollection that I had earlier reviewed Wilson's

---

[10] A.N. Wilson, *Against Religion* (London: Chatto & Windus, 1991), p. 1.

book *How Can We Know? An Essay on the Christian Religion.*[11] I recalled, on seeing this book of Wilson, how unsurprised, in a way, I was about this recent rejection of religion in the name of his newly rediscovered secular intelligence. I went back to read the review that I wrote of his theology book. I had many uneasy feelings about "an essay on the Christian Religion."

Wilson was not a prey to modern ideology in the form of Marxism or secular liberalism, yet he seemed skeptical and willing to indulge in obvious misunderstandings of what Catholicism held. It strikes me now in retrospect that Wilson's understanding of Catholicism was never well-grounded, that he becomes a contemporary reincarnation of the professional agnostic who has tried religion and found it wanting, a kind of English Voltaire, if that can be imagined.

"Wilson seems to be himself a kind of 'will' theorist," I wrote in my review,

> when it comes to the reason why one Christian 'sect' might be true and another in error on a given point. "Is it the kind of God who cannot be found and cannot reveal himself in many different ways?" The implication of Wilson at times seemed to me to be that God did not do as He did because Wilson cannot imagine Him so acting.... I still suspect that more may be said for identifying errors than Wilson seems prepared to acknowledge. "I do not believe that human beings can be protected from error, any more than they can be protected from sin." This can be merely a statement of Christian prudence or the theoretic grounding of a yet more subtle skepticism.

That in fact it turned out to be the grounding for "a more subtle skepticism" should surprise no one. The point is that our thought does make a difference.

---

[11] James V. Schall, Review of A.N. Wilson's *How Can We Know?*, in *Homiletic and Pastoral Review*, LXXXVI (June, 1986), 76-78.

Wilson's attack on religion in general, and on Catholicism in particular, seems grounded, as he himself said about his study of Belloc, in an inability to connect revelation and reason. Strauss was right here. The strength of Catholicism is in its insistence that philosophy is itself necessary for the faith of intellectuals. The difference between Wilson and the political intellectuals whose faith was so weak that they passed into ideological political movements, the more common turn of those who lose the faith in the Twentieth Century, is that Wilson reverts to almost a pre-modern atheism. He does not sound like the Marxist atheists of whom John Paul II spoke in *Centesimus Annus*, but more like Epicurus or Lucretius in the ancient world, though it should be noted that Marx did his doctoral thesis on Epicurus.

This non-Marxist atheism is aware of the ravages of twentieth century ideology so that it has no place to go except to a kind of suave skepticism. This skepticism is content to abuse religion for the very failures that Christian dogma, with the affirmation of original sin, maintained would always be present among men in this vale of tears. In this sense, Wilson does not, in spite of himself, wholly escape the utopianism he has castigated in Christians. He has, in fact, blamed religion for the failures of believers, as if the effect of religion were to change mankind so that it would no longer be free enough frequently to commit the same old errors and sins.

The purpose of religion rather is to explain man to himself. Wilson's impatience with religion, as I said, has itself a touch of utopianism to it. John Paul II warned that "by presuming to anticipate judgment here and now, people put themselves in the place of God and set themselves against the patience of God" (#25). The impatience of the newly found atheism of an A. N. Wilson needs to be seen in the light of the "patience of God" whose purpose is precisely the salvation of fallen men.

VI

Orthodox Catholicism, in other words, remains not to declare that the world can be wholly reformed by ourselves but to preach salvation to those in the world who err and who can be forgiven. The proclamation of the truths of original sin, of the understanding of God's inner life, of the Incarnation, and the ways to salvation within the Church, the sacraments and doctrines, is what faith owes to thought. The truth of revelation leads to the truth of philosophy by forcing philosophy to understand why revelation is at least believable, at least non-contradictory.

John Paul II, moreover, in an attitude that is wholly Catholic has insisted in recent years that Catholicism confront and be confronted by the other religions and philosophies that claim to know the truth. John Paul's is a confident faith. In this sense, the Holy Father in *Centesimus Annus* maintains that grace does make a difference. "We need to repeat that there can be no genuine solution to the 'social question' apart from the Gospel" (#5). But grace is a gift and need not be accepted. Grace and truth even can be hated, not perhaps in themselves, if they are seen and known, but in those who imperfectly embody them.

With the death of socialism and the religious enthusiasms based on it, notably liberation theology, we can expect, I think, more and more A.N. Wilsons to appear among us. These individuals would be intellectuals who have lost their faith but who have not lost their dreams of a perfect world once, supposedly, the confusions of religion be abolished. They will again examine the Christian reality and find it wanting because it does not teach what they want to hear.

Josef Pieper put this issue very well, perhaps prophetically well:

> It might well be that at the end of history the only people who will examine and ponder the root of all things and the ultimate meaning of existence — i.e., the specific object of

philosophical speculation — will be those who see with
the eyes of *faith*.[12]

In many ways, this situation is already the case. Henri de Lubac
suggested that the humblest of our saints is freer interiorly than
the greatest masters of wisdom. By this, he did not mean that the
masters of wisdom should not be masters. He meant that they
should also be humble so that they too might see the true objects
of even our intellects, the true doctrines of the faith that complete
the reality we in fact experience.

---

[12] Pieper, "The Possible Future of Philosophy," *ibid.*, p. 181.

CHAPTER IV

Division Not Peace

I

C atholicism claims to know what it believes and the arguments that sustain that belief. It is a claim to truth, to a living truth. On the other hand, widely varied controversies on fundamental issues seem to be typical of intellectual life of classical, medieval, and modern times, controversies that exist also in Catholicism. What are we to make of the fact and nature of this phenomenon? Are these merely signs of vitality for a finite creature who cannot be expected to know everything? Or do they indicate something even more fundamentally at odds in the human condition in its relation to God?

We cannot be familiar with Scripture without recalling certain passages that seem to indicate that we should expect deep disputes and radical disagreements to accompany the truth. However much we might think that the world ought to live in peace and harmony, we are aware that Scripture does not expect this happy situation. "I have come to bring fire to the earth, and how do I wish it were blazing already!" we read in the Gospel of Luke.

> Do you suppose that I am here to bring peace on earth? No, I tell you, but rather division. For from now on a household of five will be divided: three against two and two against

three; the father divided against the son, son against
father, mother against daughter, daughter against mother,
mother-in-law against daughter-in-law, daughter-in-law
against mother-in-law (12:49-53).

Such a passage goes against a version of Catholicism that would
make it very sanguine about improving the human condition.
Peace at any cost is not, evidently, the teaching of the Gospels. And
the history of mankind seems to bear out the fact that this division
exists wherever men exist, including those who stand within
Catholicism.

Fire is a striking image. Christ said that He came to bring
"fire" on earth. He wanted it to be "blazing already." Of course, He
did not mean that He wanted to start forest fires or abolish
volunteer fire fighting companies. Nor, by this desire to bring
"fire" on the earth, did He intend directly to promote the invention of matches or of coal-burning stoves. Nor was He some kind
of divine arsonist. The "fire" that He spoke of was a vivid symbol.
He did not want lukewarmness (Revelation 3:16), nor coldness,
but precisely that "fire" which incites us, brings us out of our
spiritual laziness and unconcern with important things.

The symbol of fire suggests not that we are too satisfied with
ourselves and our existing world, but that we are too dull to
imagine anything better, anything beyond ourselves. A "fire"
needs to be "lit under us," as the saying goes. The abiding
"newness" of the "good news" (Mark 1:1) has too often left us
unresponsive, not because it is not the most exciting thing that
ever was told to our kind, but because we have dampened, not
inflamed, hearts. We are, as C.S. Lewis remarked in his essay, "The
Weight of Glory," "far too easily pleased" with what we already
have ever to realize the wonder of what is promised to us.[1] Thus,
in this context, it is not overly surprising that we are asked at the

---

[1] C.S. Lewis, *The Weight of Glory and Other Addresses* (New York: Macmillan,
   1965), pp. 3-19.

very beginning of this "good news" precisely to "repent," as if something within us, within our choices, prevents us from seeing this good, this "good news" for what it is (Matthew 3:2).

John the Baptist at the Jordan said that he baptized with water but someone is coming after him "who will baptize you with the Holy Spirit and fire" (Luke 3:16). Fire contains both the idea of enthusiasm, of becoming alive and active, of spreading like "wildfire," and the notion of purifying, of destroying what is wrong. To be baptized with "fire" is no flaccid thing. The Holy Spirit is precisely the gift, the completion, as it were, of the inner life of God. What Catholicism means is that we believers, each of us, if we will accept it, are offered the inner life of God, this living "fire," as our purpose and destiny.

In Isaiah, consequently, we read, that we should be fired by nothing less than the best, the word.

> Woe to those who for a bribe acquit the guilty and cheat the good man of his due. For this, as stubble (Exodus 15:7) is prey for the flames and as straw vanishes in the fire, so their root will rot, their blossom be carried off like dust, for rejecting the Law of Yahweh Sabaoth, and despising the word of the Holy One of Israel (5:23-24).

Here, fire is associated with punishment for rejecting the Law of Yahweh (see Amos 7:4). Not merely is there punishment for the guilty, for those who cheat good men, but there is a description of the souls of those who would so cheat. They are seen not merely to cheat others, but to "despise" in this very act the word of the Holy One of Israel. We do not deal merely with ourselves in our relations to others. We necessarily formulate justifications for ourselves. We articulate a reason why we hate. We can "explain," often on profound theoretic grounds why we despise what is against our wills when we choose against Yahweh. Clearly, if Yahweh has commanded something of us, if there is an inner law of our being that we did not ourselves constitute, then in seeking our own wills alone we necessarily oppose God.

In the very context of Isaiah, then, we are reminded of the
classic definition of justice — "to render to each what is due." We
are also told that fire punishes. We are warned of the gravity of our
actions. The guilty do not escape the Holy One of Israel, just as in
the last book of the *Republic* of Plato, the unjust do not escape the
punishments that civil society is unable to inflict. In one of his
sermons, St. Augustine wrote to this point:

> Whenever we suffer some affliction, we should regard it
> both as a punishment and as a correction. Our holy Scrip-
> tures themselves do not promise us peace, security and
> rest. On the contrary, the Gospel makes no secret of the
> troubles and temptations that await us, but it also says that
> *he who perseveres to the end shall be saved.*[2]

A peaceful world is not promised, while suffering has a purpose,
to punish and to correct, to sacrifice.

And yet, we are aware that the innocent suffer so that some
higher law exists into which this innocent suffering can be subsumed. The innocent suffer from the sins of others precisely that
others may see and repent their actions. If we are to be free beings,
however, we must have the unsettling capacity to choose ourselves as our final law, to choose against God's laws. Our spiritual
depth depends on our seeing these dire consequences of our
choices in the innocent, in others and seeking to reestablish the
Law we have broken in our "despising."

The 84th Psalm also associates the notion of fire with the
enthusiasm of seeking God.

> My God, bowl them along like tumbleweed, like chaff at
> the mercy of the wind; as fire devours the forest, as the
> flame licks up the mountains, drive them on with your

---

[2] St. Augustine, "Sermo," Caillu-Saint Yves 2, PLS 2, 441-552, in Breviary,
Twentieth Week of Ordinary Time, Second Reading, Wednesday.

whirlwind, rout them with your tornado; cover their faces
with shame, until they seek your name, Yahweh (84:13-
18).

Here fire is a purifying scourge designed not for itself but that we
might see by its light. Fire is associated with tornados and whirl-
winds. It aims to prod us into doing what we are for, what we
ought to do.

Lethargy and lukewarmness seem to incite the Lord to anger
almost more than sinfulness, almost as if to say that it is wrong not
to be excited and moved by what is beautiful or good or true.
Psalm 119 remarks, in a memorable passage, "I have no love for
half-hearted men" (113). This "half-heartedness" emphasizes the
need of this fire that ought to inflame our hearts. It is no accident
that love, its "flame," is associated with fire and spirit, while its
violation leads to alienation and punishment, with their symbols
of pain and darkness.

When Jesus appeared to the disciples after Emmaus, He said
to them "Peace be with you" (John 20:24). This appearance evidently frightened the disciples. "In a state of alarm and fright, they
thought they were seeing a ghost. But he said, 'Why are you so
agitated, and why are these doubts rising in your hearts?'" (Luke
24:37-39). Jesus does offer peace, yet on His terms. This peace must
be chosen as it is.

II

At the Last Supper on the eve of His crucifixion, after
reminding the disciples that the Advocate who was sent by the
Father in Christ's name would "remind you of all I have said to
you," Christ invoked peace. "Peace, I bequeath to you, my own
peace I give you, a peace the world cannot give, this is my gift to
you" (John 14:26-27). Christ's resurrection caused doubts but only
because this resurrection was true, too shockingly true to be easily

believed. The way to prevent such "alarm and fright" is not to deny the newness, the extraordinarily exciting fact of the resurrection, but to grasp what it is, in the truth — "see my hands and side."

The peace of Christ causes divisions when human life is not based on "all I have said to you." There is a peace that lies in the mystery of what "the world cannot give." What does not belong to God's order and peace has itself a certain unity. "Now if Satan casts out Satan, he is divided against himself; so how can his kingdom stand?" (Matthew 12:26). Radical divisions on what is true and how to live do exist. The teaching of the New Testament is that such divisions when they are based on false ideas of man and God cannot be reconciled. The only thing that can be done is to recognize what is true, as true, and what is false, as false.

In the Acts of the Apostles, the Pentecost account likewise associates fire with astonishment and the Holy Spirit.

> When Pentecost day came round, they had all met in one room, when suddenly they heard what sounded like a powerful wind from heaven, the noise of which filled the entire house in which they were sitting, and something appeared to them that seemed like tongues of fire; these separated and came to rest on the heads of each of them. They were all filled with the Holy Spirit . . . (2:1-4).

It was this "fire" of the Holy Spirit that enabled the apostles to go forth, to incite that "blaze," that "fire" that Christ spoke of. Peace, as it were, lies beyond the "fire."

If we were to ask, at random, any fair-minded person about the purpose of Catholicism, whether it is designed to bring peace to men of good-will (Luke 2:14), no doubt, he would acknowledge that peace was its stated purpose. We hear so much about the "Gospel of Peace and Justice," that we are downright appalled to find Jesus Himself telling us that He has come not to bring "peace" on earth but "division." This affirmation about division certainly serves to temper a good deal of misplaced rhetoric about "peace."

Did Luke perhaps misquote Christ? Or is there some necessary connection between right thought and right deed, so that following Jesus will in fact bring not peace but persecution and division? The situation gets pretty basic when we find that even in families, the very soul of faith and culture, the most radical of divisions take place (see Micah 7:6; Luke 12:52-53). These divisions are at bottom over what is to be believed about God, love, and life, about how we are to live. Christ says that these familial divisions will be over His teaching. No society, including families, can hold together without common grounds that are accepted and lived by all.

Peace is a rather enigmatic thing in any case. We are familiar with the notion of "peace at any cost." The Roman historian, Tacitus, writing of the first century of our era, explained: "I am entering on the history of a period rich in disasters, frightful in its wars, torn by civil strife, and even in peace full of horrors" (*History*, I, 2). This sort of peace at any cost, I suspect, is not a virtue. We can have peace very easily at a price, the price of principle and duty.

Both the notions of "ecumenism" and "inculturation" are premised to some degree on the primacy of peace. They presuppose a civil dialogue in which real differences can be frankly acknowledged. When they are based, however, on a kind of theoretic relativism, as they often are, they cannot work for peace, but division. No unity exists that is not in some sense also a unity of spirit and understanding.

Tolerance has paradoxically become almost our central and only universal virtue. Tolerance for differing beliefs and respect for differing cultures are valid ideas as far as they go. But the fact is that different religions, differing sects within the differing religions, and differing philosophies and ideologies do not believe or maintain the same things. We are too hesitant to admit this fact, even though we should be able to recognize common principles when they exist.

Yet truth requires us to recognize differences in ideas and

practices. Peace in this context means disagreement; it means something provisional and temporary. Tolerance often means also that no agreement about a possible resolution is possible in theory. Yet the fundamental nature of differences needs to be accounted for. Peace means acknowledging that divisions exist and that these divisions may well be unresolvable if the truth is to be clearly maintained. Clearly, Christ's teaching about division and peace means that peace is not to be gained at the cost of truth and order.

Likewise, within the cultural practices of most civilizations, themselves often based on religious or philosophic traditions, there are operative norms or principles that are at variance with the stated positions of Catholicism. Again, "respect" for the culture of another may well imply acquiescence in a principle that is most dangerous and evil. The notion that other cultures demand absolute respect for what they hold or do represents an abdication of intellectual honesty and good sense. Respect for another religion or philosophy or culture involves the capacity to state what it is that other religion, philosophy, or culture holds, together with a precise statement of why it cannot in logic or principle be held. Agreements to disagree, then, are much more principled than agreements that cover over fundamental points of difference in belief or practice as if they were not important.

Many know St. Augustine's famous definition that "peace is the tranquillity of order." This definition would suggest that where there is no order, there is not likely to be peace. This conclusion forces us to wonder about order, order of soul, of polity, of truth. If Christ came not for peace but for division, it must have something to do with this notion of order. That is to say, some correspondence must exist between what we believe and how we live. Our speech should correspond to and explain our deeds; our deeds should reveal what we hold. Both should acknowledge an order of soul and truth found in our being, in the law God gave to us in creating us to be human beings.

Moreover, there ought to be some relation between what

Christ taught and the peace on earth that we heard tell of at His coming. One way of putting this is to argue that there will be no peace on earth as long as Christ's teaching and example are not followed. Another way to state it would be to say that any life or society that embodies principles or deeds at variance with Christ's teachings will not be at peace, even if there is no overt fighting allowed within it. The legacy of Hobbes, in some sense, is that wars and strife are caused by ideas and beliefs. Everyone fears death and violence, so the way to control ideas is to use force, it does not matter for what purpose. The price of peace in this sense is theoretic skepticism in which no ideas make any ultimate difference.

III

No doubt, one of the most fundamental controversies at work in Catholicism today concerns the relation between living rightly in one's personal life and living in a well-ordered society. It is the mood of our era that we cannot live well unless society is well-ordered. This position at first sight seems logical enough and can be defended at some level. On the other hand, the notion can be a dangerous one because it seems to remove from each person responsibility for his own life and place it in the hands of some civil formula.

If we cannot be good until our society is good, then, since all societies are not good, we can hardly be held responsible for what we do. Our conforming to what the society does becomes our virtue. We are either irresponsible in a bad society since what is wrong is not within us but within society or we are working for a new society so our morality is, at best, tentative. Even in a good society, in this view, we are not good by our freedom and choice but by the structure of society.

Examining why there is so much effort to make homosexuals with AIDS to be "victims" and therefore guiltless and to be taken

care of by society rather than making them men responsible for
their own actions, Irving Kristol wrote:

> For a century now, the liberal-progressive point of view
> has had, as one of its basic premises, a belief in the original
> innocence of human nature and a profound resentment
> against the "distortions" that society and its traditional
> values have imposed upon it. One such distortion is "sexual
> repression," which leads to all sorts of neuroses, all sorts of
> aberrant behavior, all sorts of social problems. Since it is
> society that causes this state of affairs, it is pointless to
> expect individuals to be capable of responsible behavior.
> We would then be "blaming the victim."[3]

Kristol has identified this Rousseauist background to so much of
our public confusion, the notion that men are by nature good, that
original sin does not exist, and that all errors or wrongs are caused
by faulty institutions, that our personal choices have no moral
consequences.

Eric Voegelin, in a reflection on the far-reaching profundity
of Plato, has explained in more detail the intellectual background
to this confusion that makes society not ourselves responsible for
the disorders in the world:

> The symbols of the myth (or right order) become perverted
> into intra-mundane, illusionary objects, "given," as if they
> were empirical data, to the cognitive and active functions
> of man; at the same time the separate, individual existence
> suffers an illusionary inflation because it absorbs into its
> form the more-than-human dimension. Man becomes
> anthropomorphic — to use a phrase of Goethe's. The
> symbols of the myth are translated into realities and aims
> of anthropomorphic man: the nature of man is basically
> good; the source of evils is to be found in the institutions;
> organization and revolution can abolish such evils as still

---

[3] Irving Kristol, "AIDS and False Innocence," *The Wall Street Journal*, August 6,
    1992.

exist; the powers of man can create a society free from want
and fear; the ideas of infinite perfectibility, of the superman, and of self-salvation make their appearance.[4]

It is precisely this erroneous explanation of man's life and purpose
that cannot be accepted.

The divisions among us are divisions that are often rooted in
theories that are designed to justify an understanding of life at
variance with what Christ taught. The disappearance of personal
moral responsibility, in other words, finds its theoretic roots here,
in the necessary construction of an alternate world view once the
basis of Christian order is denied in thought or practice. Voegelin,
in fact, found the beginnings of modern ideology here, in the
efforts of believers to secure, instead of the Kingdom that Christ
promised, an inner-worldly order made by man alone.

John Paul II, acutely aware of this effort to assign moral
responsibility to institutions rather than to human will, told a
group of workers in Italy:

> Ethical recovery at the personal and social levels are
> closely interrelated. Social injustice and evil, authentic
> structures of sin or social sins . . . are due to the accumula-
> tion and concentration of many personal sins. There is,
> therefore, a responsibility, which no one can evade, claim-
> ing that the structures of sin are stronger than the power of
> individuals. Just as the "structures of sin" exist, there can
> and must be the "structures of good," of justice, solidarity,
> mutual respect, and peace, the result and concentration of
> personal actions.[5]

Here the Holy Father acknowledges that the sort of society we live
in, with its laws and customs, can and does affect us for better or

---

[4] Eric Voegelin, *Plato and Aristotle* (Baton Rouge: Louisiana State University Press,
1957), p. 188.

[5] John Paul II, "Church Is on Side of Human Person," Address at Castellammare,
March 19, 1992, *L'Osservatore Romano*, English, March 25, 1992, p. 1.

worse, though this external structure of sin or virtue is not the most fundamental root of good personal or civil order.

IV

The discourse about our laws and customs is a necessary one. But whether our constitutions and laws are good or bad, there remains a personal responsibility, both in concentration camps and in the best of actual political systems, for what each person does. The center of the social order remains at the level of the will of each person. Social disorders, as the Holy Father understood, are themselves the accumulation of serious personal disorders. The effort to understand man apart from this relationship is at the heart of the "cultural wars" that are in fact prevalent in our society.

Such misunderstandings of the essence of Christianity affect us at all levels. In his recent Instruction *Pastores Dabo Vobis*, on the formation of the clergy, John Paul II added:

> There are also worrying and negative factors within the Church herself which have a direct influence on the lives and ministry of priests. For example: the lack of due knowledge of the faith among many believers; a catechesis which has little practical effect . . . , an incorrectly understood pluralism in theology, culture and pastoral teaching which . . . ends up by hindering ecumenical dialogue and threatening the necessary unity of faith; a persistent diffidence towards and almost unacceptance of the Magisterium of the hierarchy; the one-sided tendencies which reduce the riches of the Gospel's message and transform the proclamation and witness to the faith into an element of exclusively human and social liberation or into an alienating flight into superstition and religiosity without God (#7).[6]

---

[6] John Paul II, *Pastores Dabo Vobis: On the Formation of Priests in the Circumstances of the Present Day*, March 25, 1992, *L'Osservatore Romano*, English, April 8, 1992.

Again, the divisions within the Church have to do with this same modern spirit and philosophical understanding underscored by Kristol and Voegelin as an alternate to any properly Catholic concept of the world.

The Gospel message, even in certain sections of the Church, then, is not seen as a question of personal reform out of which social disorders are re-oriented but as exclusively human and social liberation efforts. This reality of division even in the Church comes from theories and thoughts that prevent the sort of peace that Christ was sent to bring. If we look at divisions among men, then, behind them is something of basic importance. It is, in this sense, better to have the divisions than to achieve a sort of external peace not based in the principles and practices that Christ taught. Divisions at least are an honest sign that ideas are important and have their consequences in lack of unity.

From all we can tell of Christ's teaching, He was willing to accept these divisions rather than to change His teachings to arrive at some apparent peace. The tares were to be allowed for His judgment.

> The sower of the good seed is the Son of Man. The field is the world; the good seed is the subjects of the kingdom; the darnel, the subjects of the evil one; the enemy who sowed them, the devil; the harvest is the end of the world; the reapers are the angels. Well then, just as the darnel is gathered up and burnt in the fire, so it will be at the end of time. The Son of Man will send his angels and they will gather out of his kingdom all things that provoke offenses and all who do evil, and throw them into the blazing furnace, where there will be weeping and grinding of teeth. Then the virtuous will shine like the sun in the kingdom of their Father. Listen, anyone who has ears! (Matthew 13:38-43).

The divisions are radical and fundamental. Christ's purpose is that His teaching and the life based on it remain. The divisions are not to be praised, but they are to be allowed on their own terms. They are not to be destroyed except through the spiritual processes found within Catholicism, those of truth, repentance, forgiveness, and penance.

V

There are two possible responses to the disorder caused by false doctrine and, through it, to the doing of evil on its basis. The first is the doctrine and practice of punishment; the second is the doctrine and practice of forgiveness. Since Plato's *Gorgias* and *Apology*, it has been clear that it is wrong to do evil, even in the face of death. It is better to suffer evil than to do it. Death may or may not be evil, but doing wrong certainly is. Evil cannot harm the good man who does not fear death. Even if the state promote evil by its policies or acts, they do not become right. The death of the philosopher itself upholds the order of what is right and good. His witness lives on and prevents the truth from disappearing.

If wrong is done, what should we want to do about it? Again, in a surprising statement, Socrates said that we should want to be punished. The worst evil is to do wrong and to be praised for it because that locks us into our wrong. If we do wrong, however, we can restore the good by acknowledging our wrongs by accepting the appropriate punishment. This punishment upholds the good and the truth both in the eyes of the world and in the eyes of the doer of evil.

Moreover, there are ways to restore the good even in evil by admitting what it is. As finite creatures, we will likely do wrong. But we need not be locked into our wrongs. This is the marvelous aspect of God's creation of the free creature. We need not especially be locked into the notion that what is wrong is right, or what is right is merely what the state or culture upholds. Christ came also as a judgment, a fire, even for the nations to whom He sent His disciples to teach what He had told them in word and deed (Matthew 28:19).

Thus, what we need to do is precisely "catch fire" about what Christ has given to us. "I remind you to rekindle the gift of God that is within you," Paul told Timothy (2 Timothy 1:6). In *Pastores Dabo Vobis*, John Paul II elaborated on this theme of "rekindling" our lives in the light of the "fire" of the Spirit.

> Paul asks Timothy to "rekindle," or stir into flame, the divine gift he has received, much as you do with the embers of a fire, in the sense of welcoming it and living it out without ever losing or forgetting that "permanent novelty" which is characteristic of every gift from God, who makes all things new (see Revelation 21:5), and thus living it out in its unfading freshness and original beauty. But this "rekindling" is not only the outcome of a task entrusted to the personal responsibilities of Timothy, nor only the result of his efforts to use his mind and will. It is also the effect of a dynamism of grace intrinsic to God's gift. God himself, in other words, kindles his own gift, so as better to release all the extraordinary riches of grace and responsibility contained in it (#70).[7]

Again the enkindled fire is designed to alert us to the novelty and newness of God. The "extraordinary riches" need to be seen again, to be seen anew in order that we might have a proper reaction to their wonder.

The teaching of Plato about punishment, the theory of which is addressed to all reasonable men, has its resonance within the Catholic teaching of forgiveness. Punishment refers to the doer of the deed. It is designed to indicate the gravity of the wrong and thereby uphold the right or good. Forgiveness refers to the one injured, the one who is not returned his due. The divisions that prevent peace relate to actions and thoughts that we insist on doing or holding, things that have their own consequences. Christ's example and teaching lead us to expect that upholding His

---

[7] John Paul II, *Pastores Dabo Vobis, ibid.*

example will lead to strife and divisions over against those who insist on another doctrine and practice, those with power and force. The innocent will suffer, as a result. But this suffering is not lost. The suffering of the innocent too appeals precisely to those who, by their theories or actions, cause the suffering. The accepting of punishment indicates a sorrow and a recognition of the validity of the law.

Both on the side of punishment and of suffering, then, there is a spiritual appeal back to the holders and doers of false doctrine or wrong actions. At first sight, it is startling to think of suffering and punishment as intellectual appeals directed at precisely those doers of evil or thinkers of false ideas. Physical punishment, however, is by itself merely a deterrent designed to teach the one acting against the good of others the meaning and seriousness of his actions. It is designed to show the rational order in the very context of disorder.

VI

The fact is, however, that at the depths of forgiveness and punishment, this spiritual appeal contained within them is precisely why God could create a world in which evil could happen. He could not create a free creature who was not free to accept Him on any other terms but truth and freedom. Logically and actually, this creation of a fallible but rational being would mean God not only takes a risk in creating us, but takes us seriously. The great meaning of Christ's death by suffering is found here.

The argument with God is the ground or essence of each human life, the argument about what it is we are, what it is that constitutes our meaning and happiness. When we are fired by grace and insight to see the wonder of God, we are called to, attracted by God as He exists in creation, in His works, and in Himself as the only thing that will ultimately satisfy us. However, when we feel the fire of God's wrath and punishment, we are to recreate ourselves, to rewrite our own histories, but in His image. We can do this redeeming and refashioning our lives and histories through Christ's surprising teaching about forgiveness and punishment.

The person who suffers, either innocently or justly, and the person who suffers precisely punishment in order to acknowledge his violation of order, both maintain the same teaching about what is good and about what is true. We do, in a sense, rewrite our lives when we acknowledge that our deeds, which at the time of their doing were signs of a theoretic disorder in our minds and souls, now mean their opposite, now mean that they ought not to have happened, even as they did happen.

In explaining his vocation, with its relation of fire and choice and punishment, the prophet Isaiah wrote:

> Then one of the seraphs flew to me, holding in his hand a live coal which he had taken from the altar with a pair of tongs. With this he touched my mouth and said: "See now, this has touched your lips, your sin is taken away, your iniquity is purged." Then I heard the voice of the Lord saying: "Whom shall I send? Who will be our messenger?" I answered, "Here I am, send me" (Isaiah 6:6-8).

The prophet is punished, is purged. His iniquity is admitted, acknowledged. His history is rewritten.

But the prophet does not simply re-establish order according to God's law. He is presented with a choice. The choice is his to follow. It is no longer a repentance, an acknowledgment of an order not one's own. Rather, it is a call to carry the burning message. The prophet will be sent, not to do his own will, but the Lord's. Thus his status is that of a "messenger"; he is to stand for God's words that will, though this is not their purpose, cause division, not peace, because they must be chosen. They must be recognized as our good. Words that cause division are, nevertheless, words of order and peace.

Repentance, punishment, and forgiveness are signs that we

do not always choose the order that gives us the peace that Christ leaves to us. But they uphold God's word among men, among the rational creatures who can rewrite their history and refashion their lives. God does not spare us because of our actions, but He does redeem us in our freedom. This is the only choice God has that allows us to remain the finite creatures we are created to be and allows Him to remain the God *that is*.

"Do you suppose that I am here to bring peace on earth? No, I tell you, but rather division."

"And if anyone does not welcome you or listen to what you have to say, as you walk out of the house or town shake the dust from your feet. . . . You will be hated by all men on account of my name; but the man who stands firm to the end will be saved" (Matthew 10:14, 22).

The realistic understanding of how Christ's message will be received is an intrinsic element in the Gospels. It is a doctrine of peace, but it is also a doctrine, a statement of truth about man, the world, and God. The Gospels are addressed to human freedom with a message of human and divine order. This means that they will explain man to himself even when he rejects the order of God.

It seems quite clear, in conclusion, that Christ did not want His teaching compromised on the grounds of a kind of cultural or civic peace. He knew that good would allow us to choose its opposite. This was the lesson of His crucifixion and remains the lesson of the doctrines of Catholicism. If peace is the tranquillity of order, as it is, it is also the tranquillity of His order, not ours, not one that we constructed out of our own resources. This why we can only be sent when we are purged with His fire, when we are inflamed by His truth, when we realize that joy is given to us not made by us. Anything else will bring division, not peace. And it remains better to suffer division than to change what Christ has taught. This is why judgment is in God's hands, not ours, even when we can understand what Christ has taught us.

CHAPTER V

An Atheist in the Sacristy:
Why Does Faith Seek Intelligence?

I

The existence of Catholicism, in its own explanation of itself, is not due wholly to itself. What is characteristic of Catholicism is its sense of having received its substance from a beginning traceable to no human source. Yet, Catholicism is not a fideism, that is, not a position that maintains the transcendent things have no contact with normal human intelligence. If a major and constant issue in the history of Catholicism has been its relationship to intelligence, this is because it does address human intelligence precisely as intelligence — even when human intelligence does not recognize that it is being so addressed.

Normally speaking, we are rather surprised by the quite sophisticated level of thought and language we find in Scripture. St. Paul and St. John in particular have obviously profound depths of intelligence. The only way they can be taken lightly is not to read them at all. If there is a problem of intellectual infidelity, there is also an urge connected with belief to seek explanations of what it has received. If the teachings of Catholicism have caused divisions, it is because these teachings mean something in particular and reach to the very heart of life in its living.

Faith seeks intelligence, if I might put it that way, in order that light might meet light. The Scottish divine and writer, George MacDonald, whom C.S. Lewis so much admired, gave a sermon in the latter part of the last century entitled simply "Light." He suggested that we must first become "fit" for what we are to receive and have, but that our nature will indeed be completed. MacDonald, in a most beautiful passage, thus reminded us:

> There are good things God must delay giving until His child has a pocket to hold them — till he gets His child to make that pocket. He must first make him fit to receive and to have. There is no part of our nature that shall not be satisfied and that not by lessening it, but by enlarging it to embrace an ever-enlargening enough.[1]

Faith seeks intelligence in order to understand and be able to accept that we are given more than we can expect, that we must also make ourselves ready for what we can and will receive. One of the good things that God delays giving us is precisely Himself. Our individual lives, their narrative history, is the account of what we do with this delay, with this time, of what we do to prepare ourselves for the "ever-enlargening enough."

In Evelyn Waugh's autobiography, appropriately named for my purpose, *A Little Learning,* he included a chapter entitled, "A Brief History of My Religious Opinions," a chapter that hints at just why "a little learning" in its classical statement is "a dangerous thing." Waugh began by citing a passage of 18 June 1921, from his own diary. He gravely wrote — he was all of eighteen at the time — that "in the last few weeks I have ceased to be a Christian. I have realized that for the last two terms at least I have been an atheist in all except the courage to admit it myself."[2]

---

[1] George MacDonald, "Light," *Christ in Creation,* edited by Rolland Heim (Wheaton, IL.: Harold Shaw Publisher, 1986), p. 41. See *George MacDonald: An Anthology,* edited by C.S. Lewis (New York: Macmillan, 1978).

[2] Evelyn Waugh, *A Little Learning* (Boston: Little, Brown, and Company, 1964), p. 141.

When he wrote this self-confession, Waugh was in his last year at Lancing, an Anglican prep boarding school in the South of England. He went up to Oxford the following year.

In spite of his newly-found school atheism, however — he had gone to Lancing as a rather pious young man — Waugh still enjoyed being a sacristan at the school chapel. He even had a sort of atheist scruple about the impropriety of it all, a scruple prompted by his friend Drieburg who told him frankly that an atheist had no business "handling the altar cloths." So Waugh, with some atheist lack of logic, decided to consult the school chaplain about the matter. When Waugh arrived at his quarters, the chaplain and another master were just sitting down to have a smoke. Thus, with some embarrassment, he had to explain his strange perplexity to both chaplain and master. After soberly listening to his odd anguish — "adolescent doubts are very tedious to the mature," Waugh admitted — the two masters "genially assured" him that "it was quite in order for an atheist to act as a sacristan."

II

At the same time, moreover, Waugh had belonged to a school debating society called the "Dilettanti." During his last two years at Lancing, he found himself "eager to dispute the intellectual foundations of Christianity." The subjects of these school debates, he recalled with some amusement, were such propositions as these: "'Resolved: This House does not believe in the immortality of the soul'; 'This House believes the age of institutional religion is over'; 'This House cannot reconcile divine omniscience with human freewill', and so forth."[3] One wonders, on looking at this list, whether a school system that encourages such debates or one which ignores them is the more unhealthy one.

What is of interest to note about Waugh's account of his

---

[3] *Ibid.*, p. 143.

youthful atheism and doubts, however, was his state of soul that
resulted from them. He tells us: "I suffered no sense of loss in
discarding the creed of my upbringing; still less of exhilaration.
My diary is full of pagan gloom and the consideration of suicide."[4]
Gloom, boredom, and suicide, ironically, seem, more often than
not in intellectual history, to be the results of losing the joy that
Catholicism maintains itself ultimately to stand for. Indeed, it was
precisely into a world of gloom, boredom, and suicide that Catholicism was first born in the Roman Empire; hence we have the
abiding importance of Roman Stoicism, Cynicism, and Epicure-
anism as well as the insufficiency of their sober virtues.

These classic questions, which it is the function of faith and
intelligence to ponder even from the beginning of our intellectual
lives, even in school debating societies, are, to be sure, ones that
can make an atheist out of a Catholic, or, equally often, a Catholic
out of an atheist. This possibility is something that leads us to
suspect that our relation to God and to truth is not merely
intellectual, however much it is indeed intellectual. The immortality of the soul, after all, was advocated by no one less than Plato,
hardly a Christian, except perhaps *"naturaliter,"* as many of his
admirers ancient and modern have held.

Meantime, at least some institutional religion persists in all
ages, in spite of all academic predictions and Gates of Hell
prevailing to the contrary. Divine omniscience and freewill are
questions an Aquinas, for instance, with perhaps a little more
perception than the Dilettanti Debating Society in 1921, found
non-contradictory and therefore theoretically quite compatible
with each other. We could not even think of divine omniscience
without its including a free will that was really free.

The famous "dicta" that faith seeks understanding and that
understanding seeks faith are ideas that go back at least to St.
Augustine and St. Anselm, if not to Plato himself. Aristotle had
said that the human mind has a capacity to know or to "be" all

---

[4] *Ibid.*

things. *All that is.* Aristotle also had noted that politics would be the highest science if man were the highest being (*Ethics*, 1141a 20-23). But since he is not the highest being, he stands to it as a "contemplative," that is, as someone who must receive or behold what is not his to make or create. This conclusion is ultimately the real source of human freedom, that at its highest moment, it is not contemplating merely itself.

Thomas Aquinas also had argued that we can prove that God exists but we cannot show what He is like, not what His inner life consists in. Nevertheless, we continue to seek to know about God in His fullness. However little we can know about this First Being, Aristotle told us at the end of the *Ethics*, it remains worth all our efforts even in comparison to the admittedly important things of this world. We are curious about what this conclusion, that God exists, means. We cannot really let it go and remain content with ourselves, with our desire to know *what is.* For this awareness of divine existence leads our minds to establish the fact that finite being, including our own being, of whose limits we self-reflectively are aware, is not and cannot be the cause of itself. This is so even though, as we read in the Book of Genesis, we might be tempted to make ourselves, not God, the cause of the distinction of good and evil in the world.

Eric Voegelin, in a most provocative lecture given in Montreal in 1980, to young university students, told them that they must be open to something beyond themselves because "we all experience our own existence as not existing out of itself but as coming from somewhere even if we don't know where."[5] Such a question concerning our own being is one that immediately makes us realize that our very existence is a puzzle to us, that we cannot fully explain ourselves to ourselves by ourselves. This quandary leaves us either with dogmatically maintaining that there must

---

[5] *Conversations with Eric Voegelin*, edited by R. Eric O'Connor (Montreal: Thomas More Institute Papers, 1980), p. 9.

always be a puzzle or by wondering if some other source of answer is possible.

The late Allan Bloom caused quite a scandal by suggesting that the unhappiest souls in our society are not those of the ghetto dwellers, nor the dope addicts or peddlers, nor even the craftsman, the businessman, the poet, or the politician, if I might hint at the characters in the *Apology* of Socrates. Rather the unhappiest souls belong to those students in the twenty or thirty "best" universities. Bloom was once asked who was to blame for this situation. "I do partly blame the universities," he replied.

> One of the reasons for students' not reading seriously is their belief that they can't learn important things from books. They believe books are just ideologies, mythologies or political tools of different parties. . . . The golden thread of all education is in the first questions: How should I live? What's the good life? What can I hope for? What must I do? What would be the terrible consequence if we knew the truth?[6]

When such questions are not addressed, souls remain unsatisfied, empty.

No doubt it is also worth noting that Bloom did not specifically mention, and there is no reason to think he was hostile to it, the question of "Whether God has communicated to men anything either to do or to know?" The very fact that we experience ourselves reflectively as receivers of our own limited existences requires that we at least ask the question of the source of our particular being. We cannot, and still remain authentic to ourselves, close the question off as if the answer were not the most significant truth we want to know about ourselves.

---

[6] "A Most Uncommon Scold," Interview with Allan Bloom, *Time*, October 17, 1988, p. 74.

III

E.F. Schumacher, in his wonderful book, *A Guide for the Perplexed*, also recounted his own university days at Oxford. He was a perplexed modern young man there because the best university did not have a place in which the really important questions and their possible answers could be considered, or even presented.

> All through school and university I had been given maps of life and knowledge on which there was hardly a trace of many of the things that I most cared about and that seemed to me to be of the greatest possible importance to the conduct of my life. I remembered that for many years my perplexity had been complete; and no interpreter had come along to help me.[7]

Schumacher finally came to understand that the very nature of modern science methodologically excluded the most important questions that concern any human being. The heart and mind, consequently, will remain empty even at the highest and best of academic and cultural institutions because such education and culture simply will not deal, as they could and should, with what is most important to know and to do.

To find the truth, then, we must mostly go elsewhere. We must again look at the classics. We must again look at the mystics and the metaphysicians. John Senior wrote in this regard something that is very true that will even yet seem mysterious to most of us:

> The greatest contribution to the restoration of order in all human society would be the founding in every city, town, and rural region, of communities of contemplative reli-

---

[7] E.F. Schumacher, *A Guide for the Perplexed* (New York: Harper Colophon, 1977), p. 1.

gious committed to the life of consecrated silence, so that
silence would be present in our works and days ... to judge
and measure all our noisy accomplishments.[8]

The contemplation of our own accomplishments reveals, yes,
their grandeur but also their limits. We are a generation desperately
in need of the freedom of limits, the freedom of classic Catholicism
to know that the things of God, even in the city, come first.

In her penetrating essay, "Creed or Chaos?", which she
wrote in 1949, Dorothy Sayers spoke of running into a young and
intelligent priest who told her that one of the most hopeful signs
in the world was the growing pessimism with which many of us
viewed human nature. How so? "There is a great deal of truth in
what (the priest) says," Dorothy Sayers reflected.

> The people who are most discouraged and made despon-
> dent by the barbarity and stupidity of human behavior at
> this time are those who think highly of *homo sapiens* as a
> product of evolution, and who still cling to an optimistic
> belief in the civilizing influence of progress and enlighten-
> ment. To them, the appalling outbursts of bestial ferocity
> in the totalitarian states, and the obstinate selfishness and
> stupid greed of capitalist society, are not merely shocking
> and alarming. For them, these things are the utter negation
> of everything in which they have believed. It is as though
> the bottom had dropped out of their universe. The whole
> thing looks like a denial of all reason, and they feel as if
> they and the whole world had gone mad together.[9]

Those who think "highly" of the human race are those who do not
hold original sin, who do not think the errors and disorders found

---

[8] John Senior, *The Restoration of Christian Culture* (San Francisco: Ignatius Press,
1983), p. 198.

[9] Dorothy L. Sayers, "Creed or Chaos?" *The Whimsical Christian* (New York:
Macmillan, 1978), pp. 44-45.

among men are anything more than superficial, to be corrected by a proper political or economic agenda.

If the world we thought we wanted turns out to be a world that seems to have grown "mad," the world we produce by ourselves, that is, then we must begin to suspect the theories on which this humanly constructed world is built. When such theories fail, it becomes possible to look for other explanations. Some of these explanations may, indeed, be ancient ones, ones we thought we had discarded. If the reason contained in modern philosophy does not work, it may be because this reason is itself insufficient or itself distorted.

IV

Why does understanding seek faith? It is because understanding does not succeed in fully explaining what it sets out to understand. Things actually happen and take place in the world and in our lives that neither explain themselves nor are explained by our theories. There seems to be a continual flux between the theories that are based on the autonomy of the human intellect that admits no knowledge but what proceeds from the human will, and theories open to the kinds of things that actually happen apart from our own choices, things to which our minds as original sources ought to be open.

In other words, man is constantly searching but never finding. This "not-finding" is characteristic of modern thought not merely as a fact but as a principle. Somehow there is the fear of finding out that there is indeed something arising outside of ourselves, something we are obliged to do and hold, something that would require a change of hearts. Actions following on such ideas and choices leave their own empirical records in the lives and thoughts of our kind.

As the contemporary social record becomes more and more negative and corrupting, we begin to realize that the conditions of society and of soul are more accurately described by, say St. Paul's Epistle to the Romans, or by St. Augustine's *City of God*, or Plato's *Laws*, than by what we are taught in our universities, where we do little study of Paul or Augustine or even Plato because they find in things a right order. We are not academically allowed to suspect that these sources might indeed contain answers to our real problems. And if they do contain proper understandings and answers, we must wonder how it is that such a source can know more about ourselves than we, apparently the best of our kind, know about ourselves?

Why does faith seek intelligence? Lucy and Charlie Brown are talking over the stone fence. Charlie is clearly pretty bothered and down-in-the-mouth. Lucy with some uncharacteristic sympathy asks him, "Discouraged again, eh, Charlie Brown?" Charlie brightens up a bit at this show of interest as both he and Lucy gaze distantly over the fence. She continues, "You know what your trouble is? The whole trouble with you is that you're you!" Immediately, Charlie turns about, somewhat annoyed, to face Lucy, "Well, what in the world can I do about that?" Finally, he simply stares at her when Lucy responds cooly, "I don't pretend to be able to give advice. . . . I merely point out the trouble."[10]

The trouble, in other words, lies somehow not in our institutions, even though they can be better or worse as Aristotle understood, nor in the structure of the world, nor in the skies. The trouble lies in ourselves, in our freedom. No one tells us this except orthodox religion and the philosophy developed in an effort to explain it. In Sigrid Undset's biography of St. Catherine of Siena, we read: "Catherine's opinion was that politics are never anything but the product of a person's religious life."[11] The condition of our souls is anterior to the condition of our polities.

---

[10] Robert L. Short, *The Gospel According to Peanuts* (Richmond, VA: John Knox Press, 1965), p. 38.

[11] Sigrid Undset, *Catherine of Siena*, translated by Kate Austin-Lund (New York: Sheed & Ward, 1954), p. 262.

G.K. Chesterton once noticed an invitation in one of the London papers inviting general response to the set question: "What's wrong with the world?" Chesterton immediately sat down and wrote a letter to the Editor in which he replied quite briefly: "Dear Sir: 'What's wrong with the world?' I am. Signed, G.K. Chesterton." One of the main reasons faith seeks understanding is because from faith we learn that we are somehow fallen, that there is some disorder in our lives that we experience and need to account for, but for which we have no apparent explanation or solution. That there is something wrong is not merely a proposition of revelation. Aristotle himself often noted that man left to himself was the worst of animals. No one gives a more graphic description of human corruption than Plato. These classic philosophers knew that we were fallen, but they did not know of the Fall.

V

So faith seeks understanding. We have all encountered the young man or young woman, even the old professor, who informs us that he does not believe in God because of well, how could there be a God with all the poverty and pain and evil in the world? If we know of the Book of Job, of course, we are already prepared somewhat for the fact that what God ultimately requires of us is not the elimination of poverty or pain but obedience to His Will. Even those who are poor, even those who suffer, even those who are humiliated can reach that purpose for which each was primarily created. Some indeed think they can do so easier than those who are rich, intelligent, and well-made. The harlots and the publicans evidently go first into the Kingdom of God, a hard saying for us all.

But what about it? Could we not have had a better universe, one in which pain and evil were eliminated? Is not God responsible for the mess we are in? Of course, we know that other worlds are quite possible. We know about C.S. Lewis's *Perelandra* and his *Out of the Silent Planet*, that is, our own, in which he discussed other modes of salvation that God might have chosen. The question that more directly concerns us, however, is whether we ourselves are possible in other worlds? And if not, do we have any reason for rejoicing in this one?

There are, after all, some strange congruities. In spite of the fact that there is so much disorder in ourselves and in the world at which the enlightened mind rebels as if it were not its own fault or concern, some things do seem to belong together. If it is a mystery about why there is pain or evil, there is a much more subtle mystery over why there is joy than over why there is pain and evil. Hilaire Belloc once wrote a perfectly wonderful novel, or perhaps an allegory of himself, called *The Four Men*, about Sussex, the heart of England, of what happened on a walk on Halloween, and All Hallows' Day, and All Souls' Day in 1902. On All Saints' Day, All Hallows' Day, the four men found an old inn "brilliantly lighted," with small square panes and red curtains. They entered the inn, into a "pleasant bar" that opened out into a large room where about fifteen or twenty men were assembled to drink and sing.

Belloc continued:

> Their meal was long done, but we ordered ours, which was of such excellence in the way of eggs and bacon as we had none of us until that moment thought possible upon this side of the grave. The cheese also, of which I have spoken, was put before us, and the new cottage loaves, so that this feast, unlike any other feast that yet was since the beginning of the world, exactly answered to all that the heart had expected of it, and we were contented and were filled.[12]

---

[12] Hilaire Belloc, *The Four Men* (Oxford: Oxford University Press, 1984), p. 147.

How is it, we wonder, that we are so made that the things that content us are actually found in this world? How are we to understand this? Can it be an accident? Did the eggs and the bacon and the cheese and the inn and the appetite all just happen? Or are we indeed made for these things and are they made for us, even when, like the cheese, we make them ourselves?

Faith seeks understanding because we are "fit to receive and to have" such things, as George MacDonald implied. Yet, we must make ourselves ready to receive them. How is it that we are content and filled in anything? And must this completion be seen in the light of our experience that we did not cause ourselves either to be or to be human beings? We could never have guessed that things actually fit together. C.S. Lewis, in his usual way, put it well:

> Reality, in fact, is always something you couldn't have guessed. That's one of the reasons I believe Christianity. It's a religion you couldn't have ever guessed. . . . What is the problem? A universe that contains much that is obviously bad and apparently meaningless, but containing creatures like ourselves who know that it is bad and meaningless. There are only two views that face all the facts. One is the Christian view that this is a good world that has gone wrong, but still retains the memory of what it ought to have been. The other is the view called Dualism. Dualism means the belief that there are two equal and independent powers at the back of everything, one of them good and the other bad, and that this universe is a battlefield in which they fight out an endless war.[13]

This universe we could not have guessed, yet it exists. Faith teaches which of these two understandings is the correct one, either the good world in which something, something we find in ourselves, has gone wrong, or the endless war of the worlds.

---

[13] C.S. Lewis, *The Case for Christianity* (New York: Macmillan, 1943), pp. 36-37.

And if something has gone wrong, there must be some way to make it right, or else, again, even the world is in vain. But if there is a way to correct what is wrong, will we recognize it, even if it exists? And will it be the way we expected? Will we be among those who did not believe that any good could come out of Nazareth, because, well, where is this insignificant Nazareth anyhow? This Incarnation is not the way to repair a world, this baptism, this greater love than this, this body and blood. These ways are, as St. Paul said of the philosophic Greeks, intellectual scandals. We need something practical, some plan. Yet, we still find a Karol Wojtyla calmly telling a group of evidently hesitant bishops, in this case American ones:

> We are the guardians of something given, and given to the Church universal, something which is not the result of reflection, however competent, on cultural and social questions of the day, and is not merely the best path among many, but the one and only path to salvation.[14]

At the same time, there is present in the world a promise of personal salvation and a way to it that does not depend on anything arising from society, politics, or philosophy.

VI

Samuel Johnson, in his famous trip to the Hebrides in 1774, told of stopping in October at the Island of Ulva. Near Ulva was a small adjacent island called Staffa, about which a famous book had been recently written, but concerning which tome no one on the island seemed to be informed. Johnson continued:

---

[14] John Paul II, "I Confirm You to Truth," Address to Joint Assembly of the U. S. Archbishops and the Department Heads of the Roman Curia, March 11, 1989, *The Pope Speaks*, 34 (September/October, 1989), pp. 254-55.

> When the islanders were reproached for their ignorance,
> or insensitivity of the wonders of Staffa, they had not much
> to reply. They had indeed considered it little, because they
> had always seen it; and none but philosophers, nor they
> always, are struck with wonder, otherwise than by nov-
> elty.[15]

That we initially are struck by wonder, not need or want, was for Aristotle the foundation of all thought pursued for its own sake. But that we be struck even beyond the ordinary wonder, this was the classic purpose of miracles, of our being called specially to attend to certain events that we might otherwise not notice because, like the islanders on Ulva, we had always seen them or heard of them.

Why does faith seek understanding? In modern cosmological speculation there has always been fear that we would not find other intelligent life in the universe. We have now explored the last of the planets of our own solar system so that we can see pretty clearly that in this system we are quite alone. Neither radio astronomy nor space exploration has given us any indication that there is anything but us. To be sure, we read statistics showing that there are so many billions of stars in the universe that surely there must be, by the law of averages, other beings like unto ourselves. Other studies, however, hint that the specificity required that human life exist in the universe is so unlikely and rare that it begins to look like the formation of man was the very purpose of the universe.[16] The discovery of only ourselves is anything but exhilarating for most people, for if we are meant to exist in some specific sense, then we have a purpose that is not entirely a product of our own will or intellect.

---

[15] *Johnson's Journey to the Western Islands*, edited by Allan Wendt (Boston: Houghton Mifflin, 1965), p. 106.

[16] Stanley L. Jaki, "The Universe and the University," *Chance or Reality* (Lanham, MD: University Press of America, 1986), pp. 191-93.

No doubt mankind has some mission toward the physical universe. Even on earth, however, there begin to be Hegelian-type philosophers who now despair because evidently western liberalism has won the great battles and proved the ideologies designed to reorganize the world to be merely the tyrannies they are. Some find solace in the wars of religion that still rage on the planet, the Middle East, perhaps, because there at least something ultimate still seems to be at stake. But in essence intellectuals with a this-worldly perspective begin to speak a new kind of despair. This position is associated with Francis Fukuyama. *The Wall Street Journal* noted his "end of history" thesis, so reminiscent of Nietzsche, in a way pertinent to the problem of whether the world contains a purpose. Fukuyama "thinks that democratic liberalism has triumphed (a good thing), that ideologies are disappearing (also good, he feels), but that the new order may bring on 'centuries of boredom'."[17]

This thesis of boredom is, after all, not unlike the "gloom" that Waugh on losing his faith experienced as a young man in England after World War I. And indeed it probably stems from the same source. Faith seeks understanding. Let us suppose it is true, for the sake of argument, that the ideologies are dead. Voegelin had already stressed this fact:

> We have, since the mid- and late nineteenth century, since Comte, Marx, John Stuart Mill, Bakunin (and so on), no new ideologist. All ideologies belong, in their origin, before that period; there are no new ideologies in the twentieth century.[18]

If the twentieth century has exhausted the ideologies allowing them to work themselves out in practice so that we can see their

---

[17] Editorial, "About Neptune," *The Wall Street Journal*, August 29, 1989. See Francis Fukuyama, *The End of History and the Last Man* (New York: The Free Press, 1992).

[18] Voegelin, *op. cit.*, p. 16.

results, it does not follow that liberalism itself is not one of these ideologies, one of the successful ones. The fact, if it is a fact, that it has won, does not mean that it is not itself a man-made theoretical construct that is itself reductionist, that is, a method informing itself only of what its methods allow. It may well still cut man off from the true ends and issues for which he is made.

VII

In the revelational tradition, the purpose of the world is not some sort of perfect world order, nor is it a kind of unlimited freedom to do whatever we wish, though we may seek both. Rather, the world is a place of trial, a vail of tears, if you will. This does not deny that there may indeed be some kind of inner-worldly mission for mankind. But the drama of history and individual being relates directly to the ground of being, to God. The world exists for something other than itself. It exists in order that we might have time and space in which to choose what it is we are about. The drama of existence remains in the human heart; and the configurations of the world, its political and social orders, are merely, as Plato and Aristotle saw, reflections of these choices.

If faith seeks intelligence, as it does, it is to understand how the world might be seen as an arena for the action of God and the actions of men such that the very purpose of the world is achieved in the final actions of men with regard to that insufficiency that defines their very being. St. Thomas asked the question of whether the world was created in justice or in mercy (*Summa Theologiae*, I, 21, 4). He answered that it was created in mercy because it did not presuppose anything that God "had" to do. The order of the world, its diversities, inequalities, its vastness of time and space, are thus themselves good. We do not suffer any injustice in our being what we are. And if our existence as such is not "unjust," then it follows that it must come about from a source beyond justice. What is beyond justice is gift and generosity and love. If this is the source of our being, if this is what faith teaches intelligence, then we can begin to understand ourselves in a more lightsome way.

Josef Pieper, in conclusion, remarked that "Christian doctrine is primarily concerned with the doctrine of salvation, not with interpreting reality or human existence. But it implies as well certain fundamental teachings on specific philosophic matters — the world and existence as such."[19] Faith seeks intelligence because it knows that all things do fit together, that nothing will be "true" and contradict the particular path of our salvation that is founded in faith. It is not just any way, but "the Way," as the early Christians said of themselves.

When George MacDonald remarked "that there is no part of our nature that shall not be satisfied," he intended to include our intelligence. St. Thomas insisted, therefore, that the primary locus and act of precisely the beatific vision, of our final receiving of God as our end, was not found in our will by which we loved God but in our intellect in which we knew Him as He is, face to face, to use St. Paul's striking phrase.

We should, like the young Waugh, I think, be "eager to dispute the intellectual foundations of Christianity." If we dispute with that openness to all truth and to all sources which someone like St. Thomas insists to be required for its intellectual integrity, not reducing our attention by methods or prejudice or bad will or corrupt lives, we will discover, much to our astonishment, that there are indeed intellectual foundations to this faith. We will not, for the most part, find these considerations in the universities or in the culture except incidentally, in obscure books and in holy lives, in "consecrated silence," in our concern about the gloom and boredom into which the culture by its own confession seems to be evolving.

---

[19] Josef Pieper, "Philosophy Out of a Christian Existence," *Josef Pieper — an Anthology* (San Francisco: Ignatius Press, 1989), p. 165.

We will continue to be perplexed because the ultimate questions are never mentioned, never given a fair hearing. Yet, as in Belloc, there is the suspicion that there are feasts unlike any other feasts since the beginning of the world that are exactly answers to what our heart might expect, if it could be brave enough to believe that the mysteries are true. There are strange incongruities that we will encounter that no system will explain to us. Is it, to recall Lewis' alternative, a good world that has gone wrong or an eternal battlefield in which endless wars are fought in our fields or in our hearts?

When we think of these things are we, unlike the islanders of Staffa whom Johnson encountered, struck with the novelty of it all, struck enough to wonder as philosophers should about that "something that is not the product of human reflection," something not just the best path but the only path? Let us indeed like Waugh give a "brief history of our own religious opinions" to see what it is we are incited to think because of our faith. We can indeed remain atheists even in the sacristy. Belief is both a gift and a choice. But we all have the experience that our own existence "does not exist out of itself." We should not be either overly surprised or overly sad about the sad hearts in the best schools. Both the Greeks like Aeschylus and the just men of the Old Testament like Job knew that man learns by suffering.

There are indeed good things God must delay in giving us because of what we are, beings who know that they did not cause themselves to be. Yet, "there is no part of our nature that shall not be satisfied — and not by lessening it, but by enlargening it. . . ." If this is what faith teaches us, as it does, even if we be in the best universities in our time, or at Lancing in Waugh's time, or in Sussex on All Hallows' Day with Belloc, or in Siena with St. Catherine, or at Paris with St. Thomas, or at Corinth with St. Paul, we need to know what the world is like in which both faith and intelligence can and do exist.

This is why understanding ultimately arrives at something more it wants to hear because of what it has discovered about itself and the world. This is why faith seeks understanding, not merely itself. Catholicism is not merely a "faith" then, but a faith that seeks understanding, a faith that seeks *what is*, a faith that insists that the world asks the ultimate questions of itself so that it might know that answers have been already given in the world. Ultimately, this is what the Incarnation means for philosophy.

CHAPTER VI

The Strange Consistency:
Humanae Vitae After Twenty-Five Years

I

N o doubt, for many critics, the position of the Church on birth control or contraception seems the least necessary and the least defensible of all the doctrinal positions taken by the Church. If Catholicism is to exist in the future, it is said, it must "reform" this particular doctrine. Not very many people observe it anyhow, so that must mean, by democratic principles, that the people have spoken. Intellectuals, in particular, have had a great time with this position. No doctrine seems more contrary to modern secular life. The presumption is that if this one teaching is reformed, all will be fine.

On the other hand, the Church is strangely consistent and persistent here. No one can call this doctrine "popular" by standards of public opinion. On the other hand, the non-observance of something that is in fact not right for some reason does not make it right. Moreover, there has been a consistent understanding on the part of many couples that this teaching is close to the heart of marriage, that it symbolizes fidelity, love, responsibility, union.

To embrace a contraceptive mentality, Catholicism stubbornly maintains against all odds, strikes at something quite basic about human dignity and love. That the Church has been aware of this more profound level all along can be looked on in several ways. It can seem like the carrying out of the infallibility of the Church in a particular case. It can also be seen as the Church's way of warning about what will happen to family and society when some basic disorder, however popular, is set into the world at a most intimate and specific level.

In any case, the existence of Catholicism as a coherent and unified body of truths and practices, ones that both make sense and uphold the dignity of the human person, cannot be discussed without recognizing that some basic fault line is crossed by this widely attacked position. The teaching authority of the Church is not, however, required to be popular. It is expected to hold and teach what is consistent with its founding mandate. There is an authority within the Church that has the power to bind and loose, that it, to decide on an ongoing basis what is or is not consistent with this foundation, which the Church itself did not give itself.

If the Church is basically concerned with salvation and redemption, moreover, it seems fitting that issues in the life of each human person, even on a day to day basis, would cohere in involving each person in ultimate issues about the essence of life, love, responsibility, and purpose. Moreover, the violation of something basic will, even if there is ignorance and good will involved, have its consequences which, in the normal turn of things, will be capable of being observed. Thus, this issue has not seemed in the teaching of the Church to be one of minor consequence but one that really does involve the very purpose of mankind in its every day life and in its eternal life.

It is rare to hear that the Church has a common sense and intelligent case to be made for itself in these areas. One might even say that if the Church is right on this subject over against the almost universal testimony of the culture, it is a severe judgment of the culture itself and another uncanny challenge to human pride and self-sufficiency about what really does constitute its true good, its good in the very area wherein the culture claims to know this very good best.

We deal with something of a two-edged sword on the subject of the Church's strangely consistent position on the dignity and conditions of human sexuality, its glories and the abuses men and women make against it. On the surface, we would be led to expect that those who observe the Church's teachings would on the whole possess a deeper and more profound experience of human love than those who oppose it and do not practice it. Moreover, we would expect in some sense that the following out of the actions and ways of life contrary to this teaching would begin to manifest a growing social and personal disorder, one that would eventually, if unchecked, get out of control and undermine the very fabric of the physical side of human life and its spiritual reserves.

If Catholicism still exists, then, that is, if its understanding of itself in all areas, including that of family principles, is the truth of human things, we would expect both of these results to be taking place at the same time. We would expect that the deepest understanding of human sexual and family life is now available and understood by at least certain human beings willing to follow this teaching as the truth of their very being. We would expect a growing cultural disorder the proportions of which we can hardly fathom. As far as I can see, by any objective standards, both results are in fact taking place at the same time.

Humanae Vitae, the Encyclical on Natural Family Planning, was published on July 29, 1968. I was at the time teaching in Rome. I came to think, as I listened at the time to the almost frenetic criticism of the Pope, that something terribly wrong was behind the intellectual opposition to this teaching. To explain why I so thought, I subsequently wrote *Human Dignity and Human Numbers* (1971), and later *Welcome Number 4,000,000,000* (1977) and *Christianity and Life* (1981).

The stark logic of the papal teaching itself, it seemed to me at the time, was what was so powerful, a logic the denial of which has formed the basis of the anti-life and anti-family, yes, anti-eros atmosphere of our time. The "logic" became somehow prophetic, just as we might expect of it if it contained the truth. Though contrary to most of the presumably great minds of the time, this logic was still in conformity with revelation. We worried about the bedroom in 1968; we worry about civilization itself in 1993 because of what has happened there largely contrary to the teachings of the Church.

II

However, what I want to do here is to reprint, if I may, some paragraphs of a short essay I wrote in November, 1968, in the English Jesuit journal, *The Month* ("What Is At Stake? The Long-Range Significance of the Encyclical *Humanae Vitae*"). In retrospect, subsequent history has, it seems to me, pretty much demonstrated the dire consequences of denying something that the Church, for some unexpected reason of its own, insists on teaching. The long-range significance of the document is a testimony both to the wisdom of the Church and the courage of Paul VI.

That it is still a minority opinion, I know. But our social disorders arise, it seems clear, from disorders following from faulty teaching about human life and its nature. The confines of human life are becoming more out of control the more we deviate from the essence of the papal teaching in its own ordered reasoning. What practices they have been teaching even our small children in New York City, we can hardly bear even to hear of. Abortion is an established public policy, indeed, to the President, a "moral right." Homosexuality is held to be a "normal" way of life. A disease epidemic, perhaps the worst in the history of the world, can not even be spoken of frankly in its causes. All of these disorders and more are directly rooted, in a kind of divine ill-humor, in the denial of a principle and a practice found in this Encyclical.

I was talking to a young Jesuit priest one day, moreover,

about Janet Smith's forceful book *"Humanae Vitae": A Generation Later*.[1] He told me that his lately deceased uncle was an Augustinian priest, who gave this topic of the clerical response to this Encyclical considerable reflection. After watching religious life in its well-known crises during these past decades, he came to the conclusion that the major reason for the disruption of religious life was what followed from not supporting the Church on this issue. Communities divided themselves over it and agreed not to talk about the topic.

Meanwhile, the dissenters, always the publicly popular group, went right ahead teaching the dissenting view throughout the country, in practically every parish. This instruction spread the disorders that the popes feared into the very heart of Catholicism itself. This divisiveness, never fully addressed, effectively undermined religious authority within communities and its example spread to all areas of loyalty to the Church. Again here, the point is that the Church has understood that something fundamental to all walks of life was at issue here, including religious life.

Let me then re-present these remarks some twenty-five years after they were first published in England. The very language used then, which I will retain here, illustrates also the direction of the cultural changes that illustrate the papal logic. Politics has more and more come to dictate what things can be called right and what wrong, no matter what standards might be found in scripture or classical philosophy. At the time, as I do now, I merely tried to spell out against a system of reasoned standards what was happening and why. In one sense, the exercise is contemplative, that is, to observe clearly *what is*, what happens.

"The pressure on science welling up spontaneously from the demands of the sexual community," I wrote bravely in 1968, in language that sometimes is politically incorrect today, *"is to*

---

[1] Janet Smith, *"Humanae Vitae": A Generation Later* (Washington: The Catholic University of America Press, 1992).

produce a secure, safe method of birth control which allows the natural act to be the natural act. All scientific progress in this area has in fact been in this direction anyhow because what man instinctively, that is, naturally prefers in his sexual relations is either the natural act itself or, this lacking, something that approximates it as closely as possible. In essence everyone admits the natural superiority of the sexual act as it is received from nature.

"In other words, no one wants to use birth prevention means and in fact no one does (use them) except when constrained by some other (specific) reason. Birth control is in practice used only to prevent disease or birth when these motives are strong enough to overcome the natural desire not to interfere with the sexual act. All acts of contraception, then, are taken against what the participants prefer with regard to the consummation of the act itself. Contraception means the limitation of the act is preferred by many to nothing, but it is not preferred to the act as it is found in nature where this is available. The act as it is given by nature is always selected when the choice itself is given.

"This point can be seen better in this manner. If we list the known or proposed means of birth control according to their degree of deviation from... natural sexual activity — i.e., infanticide, abortion, sterilization, contraceptive devices (IUD's, condoms, jellies, diaphragms), the "pill," vaccine immunizations against the sperm, withdrawal, and rhythm — it is clear that the 'reason' for the invention or development of each new means was in some fundamental sense the unsatisfactory results with means that either attacked life, interfered with the act of intercourse, or made it inconvenient. The most 'desired' means seems clearly, if this kind of approach is valid, to be the one that allows and forms a normal female cycle that is both known, certain, and safe so that the natural act can be the natural act.

"Each new scientific improvement, then, seems clearly designed to foster the human desire to allow the unimpeded natural act, which is the essence of the papal position. The condom and the diaphragm were means (designed) to avoid the necessity of abortion or the distaste for withdrawal. The 'pill' was invented to avoid the inconvenience and interference of the condom and diaphragm. The injection, sterilization, and the

IUD *were invented or perfected to avoid the side effects and sophistica-
tion of pill usage.*

"*All of this seems to suggest that science is itself in fact headed in
the traditional direction and that the invention of a secure rhythm system
will not only prove immensely profitable but will be simply carrying to
its logical conclusion a scientific progress that began with the rejection
of infanticide as a legitimate means for birth control. Thus, it is strange
but science itself seems somehow to attest to the unacceptability of the
present preventative means. We can be practically sure that all the
present 'means' will soon be little more than historic curiosities because
mankind simply does not like them in its sexual activity.*

"*This way of setting up the problem, moreover, makes it clear that
human life is in some basic sense always involved in this discussion and
that everyone must draw the line somewhere at the means of birth
prevention in the name of man. Infanticide, as Will Herberg once vividly
pointed out to a very startled Protestant audience that refused even to
consider his most valid point, is still the 'best' means of birth control
because it at least allows society to take a look to see whether what is killed
is defective or not. Abortion on the grounds that a fetus 'might' be
malformed or it 'might' harm the mother is hardly so rational or even
humane. The line must be drawn somewhere, then, in a continuum of life
potential or actuality.*

"*That some connection between abortion and contraception exists
is strongly suggested by statistics in those countries where abortion laws
are very liberal. Here the curious fact presents itself that illegal abortion
still continues on a disturbingly large scale even among those who have
all the contraceptive means available and the knowledge about their
usage. This suggests that at the moment of intercourse such people, even
though they have no moral scruple about the subject, prefer not to use
preventative means and that, once conception has taken place contrary
to their desires, they have little hesitation in ridding themselves of what
is conceived as it was not desired in the first place and that the symbolic
meaning of the act did not include the mutual commitment to what was
its product. Not everyone who fails in contraceptive practice, of course,
automatically resorts to abortion, but this consideration makes it evident*

that a connection between life and responsibility to the fact of intercourse does exist.

"However, even broader issues are here at stake. To state this problem in its most extreme form: what is ultimately at issue is the very nature of a being in two sexes. This will seem a bit preposterous to the average person, but any familiarity with proposals for genetic experimentation and control or any analysis of the philosophical positions of homosexual and lesbian theory will soon reveal that it is precisely heterosexuality and its implications in love and the family that are at stake.

"The question is this: Is man a certain kind of being who was established by 'nature' so to speak in a better form (that is, in two opposite sexes) than man could produce himself? Can we, in other words, improve on sexuality and still keep it? These two issues — genetic control of human life and the meaning of perversion — lie behind the defence of the natural act in marriage.

"Too few people today are aware of the serious proposals being put forth in certain areas of the scientific community. Briefly, it is now possible at least theoretically to suggest — and let us not forget it is being suggested — that the two-opposite-sex marital relationship which does in fact produce children should be used only by the few for experimental purposes, that better genetic health could be produced by clonal generation rather than by sexual mating, that eugenic selection of offspring should replace the present system where every man and woman have a right to form his and her own family, that the same genotype or only a few should form the whole of the human race, that everyone should be his own 'twin', that children need no longer be conceived or developed in the womb of a woman, perhaps even that all people should be of the same sex.

"Implicit in many if not all of these positions and proposals is the notion that sexuality and its implications are the causes of the ruinous condition of the race and that it is not biologically necessary for the production and preservation of man, except perhaps as a kind of indifferent pastime that has no consequence in the empirical order. It is in defence of man as a being of two opposite sexes whose dignity rests in large part upon the 'naturalness' of man as he is received from nature that makes

this encyclical important. Man's natural system of reproduction is ultimately superior to any scientific or perverted alternative — the Magisterium has rightly, I think, taken its stand at this point.

"This same conclusion is also implicit in the scriptural and traditional rejection of perversion as a normal form of human life. . . , or as a superior way of life for man. What fundamentally distinguishes 'perversion' — that is, basically, homosexuality, lesbianism, and bestiality — from the two-sexed condition is its fundamental unrelatedness to the transmission of human life and its subsequent sense of natural frustration. In the broader context of these issues, together with some of the totalitarian implications of population theory which the encyclical rightly referred to, the papal document does do a basic service in suggesting that these are dangers in our intellectual and political environments that do strike at the very structure of man as we have known him. The issue, then, is somehow, as most of the criticisms of the encyclical have suggested, that of the nature of human love and its 'natural' exigencies.

"If we look only to the narrow terms of the problem as somehow only pertinent to the pill or to contraceptives, we will miss the real threats to human life that do abound in modern society. These threats cannot be totally disassociated from the theory and practice of contraception. Population fear, genetic control, and perversion do, furthermore, contain serious implications to the nature of man that we can no longer ignore. Perhaps the biggest weakness of the encyclical was its failure to note these broader problems and their relation to the nature of human life.

"Consequently, it seems to me that much progress can be made if we attempt to see this document in the larger context of the trends of scientific development of birth prevention, the meaning of genetic control of man, perversion, and population fear as a means to justify any action against human sexual dignity. Taken out of the narrower basis upon which it is read in Catholic circles, it becomes clear that serious life issues are here involved whether we like it or not and that the trend of the document is in conformity both with scientific development and the dignity of human sexuality which is really what is at stake.

"There is a serious danger to sexuality in the modern world and I

greatly fear that we are failing as a civilization to see its nature and proportion. It would be both sad and supremely ironic were an elderly pope to be the main defender of sexuality itself. I sometimes think God would like to play such a joke upon our pride and intelligence. What Paul VI has said is surely foolishness to the wise. The lesson of the next fifty years will be to see if the present wisdom of the wise turns to foolishness, for what greater foolishness would there be than to sacrifice sexuality itself in the name of sex? That we are in some danger of doing this is, paradoxically, one of the great realities of our time."

III

On re-reading this essay half-way to the "fifty years" it spoke of, we can notice that legally or socially we must call "perversion" just another form of normalcy today. Indeed, politically, we are not even free to use the term. We recall too the thesis of Joseph Sobran about why gay activists are interested in grammar schools and adopting children, that is, because they can have no children of their own.

Homosexual acts, furthermore, by definition are infertile and therefore constitute a radically different kind of reality than that created by heterosexual acts. We are not surprised to learn of the extraordinary numbers of "partners" that homosexuals often have. I once heard of the editor of a famous journal actually propose "homosexual marriage" precisely on the grounds that it was needed to curb such uncontrolled promiscuity. No doubt this changeableness and lack of permanence are because, ultimately, such acts on which homosexuality is based are, to recall some words of Aristotle, "in vain," contrary to nature. In order to prevent us from saying that acts can be "unnatural," we respond by denying that there is such a thing as nature.

We are well aware of the peculiar silences around AIDS and its causes, that we are spending billions of dollars on care and research as if somehow practicing gays have a natural "right" to their activity free of threat of such disease. We know too about RU-486 that kills invisibly as an afterthought. While we can no longer politically call homosexual acts "perverted," that is, turned away from their natural objects, we can, nevertheless, call nature itself "perverted" for allowing the disease to happen and thereby interfere with a "natural right" to be homosexual. We are not allowed, in any case, to call it a scourge of God, merely a sickness for which we are searching for a cure. Pointing out the fact that AIDS can be prevented in all cases simply by following what Christianity has always considered the only moral solution in any circumstances, that is, abstinence and self-discipline, results in an attack on Christianity for daring to say such things.

Furthermore, we allow born babies to die of starvation because of botched abortions or deformity, that is, we practice infanticide. We know that in several cultures girl babies are also aborted or even killed because of family preference. We see that euthanasia is with us, with generally the very same arguments used to justify abortion. We notice that the state controls more and more of the families, especially the poor ones, and the children, both in their begetting, in their early care away from their parents, and in their education.

We see that sex while still around, when completely protected against life becomes itself insignificant and sterile, as Paul VI emphasized. We are curious that the present Pope, in spite of all the intellectual and political opposition, says the very same thing that Paul VI did. We notice that what was once presented as "private" is now in the coercive hands of the state.

On the other hand, the concern I had twenty-five years ago with a more secure and simple rhythm or natural family planning method seems to have come about — I think of the program of the Billings Method or the Couple-to-Couple League. From many sides, from health to security, from aesthetics to fidelity, from the nature of love itself to its relation to children, natural family planning methods seem on every level superior to any of the other contraceptive or abortive systems. We practice and promote these artificial systems in our effort to avoid the basic understandings and principles that are really found in the commandments and the tradition.

IV

Let me conclude, as to the ultimate wisdom of it all, with the following remark of Flannery O'Connor, written about a decade before the publication of *Humanae Vitae* (June 27, 1959):

> The Church's stand on birth control is the most absolutely spiritual of all her stands and with all of us being materialists at heart, there is little wonder that it causes unease. I wish various fathers would quit trying to defend it by saying that the world can support 40 billion. I will rejoice in the day when they say: "This is right, whether we all rot on top of each other or not, dear children, as we certainly may. Either practice restraint or be prepared for crowding."

In retrospect, this spunky lady may have had it right — the most spiritual doctrine of the Church has to do with what at first sight appears to be one of the most material sides of creation, precisely where body, spirit, and life meet in their tininess.

Need we be overly surprised if this is really what the Incarnation is about, the way our spirit suffuses what we really are? Is it not shocking that *what we are* is really better, infinitely better, than any of the alternatives science or politics has come up with in the meantime to resolve issues really caused by disordered souls? Twenty-five years after *Humanae Vitae* the Church maintains the same spiritual teaching as it did in 1968 and as it did through another old pope in *Casti Connubii* in 1931, when the Church began first to treat the technical proposals in this area.

At the same time, the world falls more and more into familial and moral chaos by the logic of its disagreement with the Church on this very point. Never let it be said that the infallibility of the Church does not have its finger somehow uncannily fixed, contrary to the wisdom of the world, on the crucial point that alone, it now seems, will protect us in our very bodily being and teach us to remain *what we are.*

Yes, it is ironic, to repeat, that elderly popes are the main defenders of sexuality itself in the modern world. God alone would have it that way. Perhaps this is one of the reasons for which Catholicism exists, to keep the human, to keep those things that are most glorious and most vital to it. No doubt as our civil and personal disorders grow apace, He is trying to teach us something. If we continue as rapidly down the same "logic" that we did during the first twenty-five years after *Humanae Vitae,* surely not merely good human life will be in jeopardy but all human life itself. Some think the end of our civilization may come from nuclear weapons. It begins to look rather alarmingly, however, as if it may come because we refused to understand the long-range implications of *Humanae Vitae,* taught to us by old popes in their sober ways.

CHAPTER VII

On the Lack of Catholic Apologists

I

If there is a kind of intellectual and spiritual timidity in Catholicism today, a mood that makes every effort to conform itself to the spirit of the times, what might be the cause of this hesitation? Eric Voegelin had associated the origins of modern ideology with a loss of faith by precisely Christian intellectuals and politicians impatient at the transcendent answer that faith gave to ultimate questions.[1] The point is a subtle one because Catholicism is not unconcerned with the world or its well-being. We can never do evil unless we are doing some good, so that the ultimate disorders in human history will generally appear as goods concretely related to some understanding of a common good but one somehow in deviation from the good itself.

What is most lacking, then, is not a case for Catholicism but rather someone to make the case. The irony of recent times is that almost the only one making and capable of making this case has been the Pope himself. In a paradoxical way, modern media have made it possible for one man to witness to the core of truth even

---

[1] Eric Voegelin, *Science, Politics, and Gnosticism* (Chicago: Regnery/Gateway, 1968), p. 110 ff.

when it is difficult to discover at almost every other level. The irony is that the case is there to be made but those who should make it lack the moral vitality to make it.

Under the word, "apology," in Fowler's *Modern English Usage*, the following entry, itself a masterpiece of negative subtlety, is found: "It is perhaps the disuse of apology in the sense of 'justification, explanation or excuse of an incident or course of action' (*OED*), as Socrates and Newman used it, that has led to ALIBI'S unseemly occupation of the vacant place." We know, of course, that Plato's account of the trial of Socrates was called an "Apology," while Newman wrote the *Apologia pro Vita Sua*.

But neither Socrates nor Newman "apologized" in any pejorative sense for what he did and held. What each did was to justify and explain his thought and action. This rendering account, this testimony, as it were, is what a classic apology is about. Reality needs the illumination of words. Words say of *what is*, that it is. There is nothing negative or deprecating about it. It is in fact an act of the highest courage and human dignity, to state before the world that for which we stand. An apology thus requires in particular someone who articulates what it is that he maintains, even in an action that might result in death, as it did in the case of Socrates and Christ, or in a kind of ostracism, as in the case of Newman.

An excuse, based on the fact that one was someplace else at the time of an incident or course of action, however, is what is legally and properly called an "alibi." Under the word "alibi" in Fowler, we find that it is a Latin word that means simply, "elsewhere." An alibi is a perfectly good term that means in fact that when a crime was committed, the accused was literally someplace else, so he could not have been guilty of any crime.

Fowler tells us, however, that "alibi" is a "useful word — indispensable indeed in its proper place — with a precise meaning. That it should have come to be used as a pretentious synonym for excuse is a striking example of the harm that can be done by slipshod extension." For this untoward "extension," Fowler blames detective stories and their "ignorant readers"who have improperly come to use the word "alibi" for just "any means of rebutting a charge." Thus, "alibi," meaning merely any old "excuse," wrongly took the vacant place of the proper and noble meaning of that other word, "apology," and made any adequate and reasoned statement of one's position, formerly called an alibi, seem like a mere subterfuge.

II

At the risk of running afoul of Fowler's "slipshod extension," I want to suggest that we really have no "alibi," for our lack of real apologists for Catholicism. "Alibi,"meaning unfounded excuse, should not unseemly occupy the vacant place of apology, while apology should mean precisely an "explanation or justification," not any old excuse of not knowing what we hold. A case can be made for what we hold. What is not clear is whether a strong case will always be listened to. Will has replaced intellect as the organ of intelligence in much of the modern religious and intellectual world. We do not so much live in a time of lack of apologists, but in a time of a lack of listeners who seek *what is*. The spiritual problem is that we can refuse to hear the truth. The confusion is that there are many claims for our attention, of which the Catholic apologist's is only one. Meanwhile myriads of voices exist within the Catholic body, not all of which acknowledge the same truths.

Though He never wrote His own "apology," I have often thought Christ Himself was a rather good apologist. Take, for example, the scene in Mark (12:28-34), the scene where some Sadducees are debating the resurrection. The Sadducees bring up the loaded case of the widow who marries according to the Law the seven brothers who die in succession. Whose wife, they want to know, is she in the resurrection? Christ specifically answers this objection. An objection or confusion is answered as if this is part of Christ's purpose, that questions are to be answered or addressed.

Christ never lapses into obscurity. His legacy is a tradition that takes serious questions seriously. Almost the only question Christ did not answer is that of Pilate when, after a certain point, he proved that he no longer was interested in any answer (Matthew 27:14).

After listening to this discussion about the resurrection, we were told that one of the scribes "had listened to them debating and had observed how well Jesus had answered them." The man was struck by the answers. Jesus did not fall into a trap. The man in his turn decided to question Jesus also. He asked Him about the greatest commandment, no small question. Jesus clearly and directly answered this question with citations from Deuteronomy and Leviticus, that we are to love God and our neighbor as ourselves. "There is no commandment greater than these." The scribe did not learn this from Christ but from the Law.

The scribe, almost as if he is checking to see if Jesus also knows the Law, compliments Him, "Well spoken, Master; what you have said is true." It is important to note here that the scribe is testing Jesus, not the other way about. And he has a criterion that enables him to measure Jesus' claim. The scribe, not Jesus, goes on to affirm, "To love Him (God) with all your heart, with all your understanding and strength, and to love your neighbor as yourself, this is far more important than any holocaust or sacrifice." Jesus complimented the scribe on "how wisely" he had spoken. Jesus then said to him, "You are not far from the kingdom of God." In other words, there can be those who know the Law or reason quite well, who understand. They are not yet believers, but they are close.

But what I find of great interest here is the conclusion to this passage in Mark. It says simply, "And after that no one dared to question him any more." "Why?" we might ask. Can the answer be that the questioners sensed what would be implied if their subsequent questions were to be answered as well as the ones answered thus far? The problem was not that there were no answers, nor that there was no one to answer them but that there was none with the courage to listen to them because "he did not dare." Perhaps truths that men could not bear to hear were in fact true. Like Pilate, in asking "what is truth?", they went away about other things rather than know the answer (John 18:38).

Rumors that there are no Catholic apologists are thus, as it seems to me, greatly exaggerated. The frightening thing about the faith today is not that there is little to be said for it, but that there is so little to be said against it or in behalf of anything else. This situation is "frightening," I say, because it suggests that the reason why the truths of faith are not heard is the same reason that philosophical truths are not heard, namely, that we do not want to hear them. Will has replaced reason as the criterion of what we accept as true. We will maintain that all truths are relative rather than listen to any argument that suggests that they are not.

This situation, it would appear, is nowhere more evident than in the universities, where the very word truth causes some considerable intellectual embarrassment. A student of mine, for example, with some amusement, showed me a term paper of his, submitted to another professor, that persuasively argued the case for the fact that truth exists and that it transcends time and space. These are not, after all, such novel views. They are in fact our tradition.

On this term paper, however, were written the following remarks by the professor, remarks typical, I fear, of the difficulties many intelligent students confront today in academia:

> I would suggest that the views (of the philosophers) tell us (only) about the philosophers and the times they lived in, that's it! I completely disagree (that philosophy has any element of the permanent). Philosophy as a discipline and practice is not immune from cultural context. It is not timeless and transcendent, and it *never* transcends boundaries of cultural specification.

Fortunately, this perceptive student could see that the professor contradicted himself in his very objection. The principle that something "never" transcends boundaries is already a timeless principle as stated. The point is that these politically correct things are demanded in the schools and are expected to be employed by students as principles, no matter how contradictory. Once relativist premises are chosen by students, professors, or whomever, there can be no listening to truths that do transcend, the truths the apologist seeks to "explain and justify."

The young men in the *Republic*, the potential philosophers, also wanted to hear Socrates tell them whether justice was worth doing for its own sake. They wanted to hear Socrates, the philosopher, explain it to them, even if they could state the reasons against its truth. In this sense, the apologist exists to address those who will to listen, though he must be ready like the fishers of men in the Gospels to find them almost anywhere. He must be ready to confute, with true argument and explanation, those who write to students on their academic papers in terms that contradict reason.

III

A colleague of mine sent me a cartoon in the *New Yorker* (Richter) that puts us in an elegant Fifth Avenue apartment during a sophisticated party. We see the guests down below in the parlor chattering, while we look up the staircase to paintings on the wall behind. Two earnest and somewhat somber men are sitting on the lower steps drinking. The professorial type with a beard and a slight frown is listening to the confused modern gentleman who tells him, "My feeling is that while we should have the deepest respect for reality, we should not let it control our lives." These very words sum up better than anything, I think, the main problems that Catholic apologists run into today. For they encounter people who think that there is some other source for the guidance of their lives besides reality, besides *what is*.

The Washington Post carried a controversy about whether *New Yorker* cartoons were funny. The very notion that *The Wash-*

ington Post published an article admitting problems seeing the humor in the *New Yorker* is, I confess, itself rather amusing. It also portends the end of civilization, of a certain kind, the one that is based on reality and that sees the humor in articulating it. And we should thank God for this particular inability to understand each other's humor. Let's admit it, New York and Washington have always thought, with considerable justification, the other to be quite funny. But now suddenly they cannot understand each other's jokes. It is not that the jokes, like truth, become less humorous or intelligible. It is because we choose not to see the relationships that we might draw from a reality for the grounding of which we rely on the principle of contradiction.

Of course, I grant that not all *New Yorker* cartoons are inevitably funny. But a massive failure to see the humor in things is not unrelated to a massive failure to see the truth in religion. To understand both religion and humor, we need to understand relations and analogies. Aristotle said that our ability to see wit was a sign of intelligence, a sign that we could see relationships in *the things that are,* which is what intelligence consists in.

The late Walker Percy was often asked why he became a Catholic. Rather than go into a long discourse, he told us that he would much prefer simply to say something brief, something like, "I am a Catholic, or if you like, a Roman Catholic, a convert to the Catholic faith. The reason I am a Catholic is that I believe that what the Catholic Church proposes is true."[2] But Percy figured that it was sometimes better to be even more direct. "When it is asked just so, straight out, just so: 'Why are you a Catholic?' I usually reply, 'What else is there?'" Percy was the epitome of a great apologist. Though he could explain himself in more lengthy discourse, this brief retort comes pretty close to the heart of the matter. The best kept secret in the modern intellectual world today is precisely that, when we take a serious look around, there is nothing else.

---

[2] Interview with Scott Walter, *Crisis,* 8 (September, 1990), 14.

Of course, the quip, profound as it is, "What else is there?", does not exempt us from going about to take a careful look at "what else." Percy did that. We often only see *what is* when we realize what is not, what might not exist. In that sense, Percy did what St. Thomas did, namely, he stated clearly the essence of the "what else" and asked, "Is it true, even if, for personal reasons, I want it to be true?" That we wanted something to be true did not make it so. The right order of things always included, finally, the wanting what was true.

Apologetics is validly rooted in Catholic thought itself because, unabashedly, gently, Catholicism is intended for all men, everywhere. It is intended for their lives; it is directed to their understanding. It does not claim just to be another "religion," but a truth and a way. It says frankly to everyone, "Look, there is something you ought to know about." Apologetics presume at their best, that wonder, that desire to know that characterizes the human being in its flourishing, in its completeness.

The Holy Father's Encyclical on the Missions is an amazingly strong reaffirmation that Catholicism is intended for everyone, in every culture and time.[3] And Catholicism is intended to be known for what it holds about *what is*, in the light of which it is intended to guide our actions. Making the contents and the truths of the faith known to all, John Paul II wrote,

> is the primary service which the Church can render to
> every individual and to all humanity in the modern world,
> a world which has experienced marvelous achievements
> but which seems to have lost its sense of ultimate realities
> and of existence itself (#2).

Whatever else needs to be known, what Catholicism teaches about "the whole truth about man" needs to be explained, even when civil laws, as they often are, even in this country, are deliberately

---

[3] *Redemptoris Missio*, (December 7, 1990).

designed to prevent any serious teaching of these truths (#35). Perhaps the least studied discrimination in the modern world is the legal and social discrimination practiced against Catholics both in their own and in non-Catholic lands. Not even many Catholics study or know about these things. The Church as an institution is surprisingly inattentive to the legal and cultural restraints that are practiced against its members and its mission.

IV

A second characteristic of Catholic apologetics is simply that the faith itself requires us to give reasons for, some account of its truth. This aspect will seem strange at first. But it is one of the most extraordinary things about Catholicism. Whether in persecution or in controversy or in curiosity, its characteristic is to give reasons for its truth in the light of any truth *that is*. Catholicism is not designed to be a myth for the people to substitute for their intelligence when, supposedly, they are not bright enough themselves to know by their own reasoning power. This latter is the function many philosophers claim to be the essence of religion. Rather Catholicism is designed to be a true doctrine directed to minds that can know if they choose to do so.

In Nietzsche's *Antichrist*, he brought up the famous argument that there was only one Christian in history and He "died on the Cross." This is a clever witticism, no doubt. Nietzsche went on to say that Christianity should be about doing and not about teaching. Well, of course, it is both a doing and a teaching, a truth and an action. It never claimed to be anything else — "the Way, the Truth, and the Life," all three. The fact that for two thousand years there was only one Christian is no argument against Christianity's truth or its action. It is merely an affirmation, as Catholicism has always maintained, that it is meant for real people who are not going to be able to look exactly like Christ in every detail.

C.S. Lewis is the model of a great apologist in our times, a man whose books remain marvelously pertinent and widely read. On April 18, 1944, Lewis was invited to, of all places, the Head Offices of Electric and Musical Industries, Ltd., at Hays in Middlesex. He was simply asked to answer questions of the employees about faith. He was asked about everything from the Devil to whether "a factory worker could find God." To the latter question, Lewis did not see why it was any more difficult for a factory worker to find God than for anyone else, and to the former questions he suggested, à la Screwtape, that the less we know about his existence, the more dangerous it is.

But the function of the apologist is to take the objections and respond to them, to give an account. People give reasons for disbelief. Do these reasons hold? Whether they do or not is the apologist's vocation. With regard to Nietzsche's problem with the "only" good Christian, Lewis was asked how to "define a practicing Christian" and whether there were any varieties of them. "Certainly there are a good many other varieties. It depends, of course, on what you mean by 'practicing' Christian," Lewis responded.

> If you mean one who has practiced Christianity in every respect at every moment of his life, then there is only One on record, Christ Himself. In that sense there are no practicing Christians, but only Christians, who, in varying degrees, try to practice it and fail in varying degrees and then start again. A perfect practice of Christianity would, of course, consist in a perfect imitation of the life of Christ. I mean in so far as it was applicable to one's own circumstances.[4]

I cite this random response of Lewis to a question of some unknown worker in Middlesex in 1944, because it illustrates more than anything how the severest charges against Christianity, to

---

[4] C.S. Lewis, *God in the Dock* (Grand Rapids, MI: Eerdmans, 1969), p. 50.

wit, that there has only been in history one Christian, are not really charges against Christianity at all when explained in their full scope and context. Inevitably, however, the most profound problems of the philosopher several decades later show up in the factories. The need for Catholic apologists occurs everywhere.

Another of the great apologists of our time was Malcolm Muggeridge. Though its force is rapidly receding under the impact of logic and evidence, evolution has been in recent times one of the main arguments against the truth of Catholicism. Even yet, many folks are scandalized to hear it even questioned. No one wants to appear, well, anti-modern. Muggeridge was not deterred by such prejudices.

In 1978, Muggeridge gave a lecture at the University of Waterloo in Canada. After the conference, he agreed to answer some questions, not unlike Lewis in Hays in 1944. I keep repeating such instances to insist that the apologist is in fact to answer questions, that there is a "case for Christianity," to use the title of one of Lewis' books. This effort to take real confusions and difficulties, to show how they are to be understood and how the faith responds to them, with intelligence, is most important for faith itself. It is also important to insist that reason and intelligence and logic are not solely on the side of those who oppose faith. More and more, the opposite is true. We Catholics are often the last to know this.

The greatest apologist in centuries is on the Throne of Peter. It seems almost uncanny. Very few can bear to listen to him because he might just be right. Much is done to prevent his words and examples from being published or discussed. He reasons cogently. Better not to listen. This suspicion that he might be right after all, that both faith and philosophy do go together as he suggests, is the real source of opposition to John Paul II.

But to return to Muggeridge, "What are your views on evolution?" he was asked. "I myself am convinced," he replied,

that the theory of evolution, especially the extent to which
it's been applied, will be one of the great jokes in the
history books in the future. Posterity will marvel that so
very flimsy and dubious an hypothesis could be accepted
with the incredible credulity that it has. I think I spoke to
you before about this age as one of the most credulous in
history, and I would include evolution as an example.[5]

Again I repeat this observation of Muggeridge — Lewis made
similar remarks as did E.F. Schumacher — to emphasize the fact
that the problem of Catholic apologetics today is not about the
truth of its teaching, but in the politicization of reality that takes as
its criterion what we want, not what is true.

Sally is giving her report on religion to the Sunday School
class. She has decided to learn something about theology. In her
church history class, she discovered that her pastor was born in
1930. "My topic today is the purpose of theology," she begins
earnestly. With her hand in the air, she continues, "When discuss-
ing theology we must always keep our purpose in mind." Now
into the topic, she explains to the class, "Our purpose as students
is understandably selfish." And with great triumph she explains
the reason for this selfishness in theology class, "there is nothing
better than being in a class where no one knows the answer."[6]

But actually, there is nothing worse than in being in a world
in which, it is claimed, that there are no answers. The purpose we
have in mind as apologists is precisely to challenge the idea that
theology and religion provide no answers, when they appear to
have only alibis, excuses, and not the reasons they in fact do have
to the questions about the highest things that we are asked.

---

[5] Malcolm Muggeridge, *The End of Christendom* (Grand Rapids, MI: Eerdmans,
1980), p. 59.
[6] Charles Schulz, *When the Beagles and the Bunnies Shall Lie Down Together* (New
York: Holt, 1984).

V

I have suggested that the major problem for apologists today is not the truth of what is to be held but the inability of the hearers to listen. I suggest that a major justification for this inability or unwillingness to listen is the multiplicity of divergent and often contradictory voices, some even from bishops, that come from those who claim to believe. Take for example the advertisement that the University of Notre Dame Press uses to promote Charles Curran's book on higher education, which this press published. The promotion uses a citation from a *Commonweal* review. "The story of the Rev. Charles Curran's 1986 removal, at the Vatican's order, from the Catholic University theology faculty for his 'liberal' but widely held views on sexual morality and of his losing fight for reinstatement . . . is one of the great stories in American Church history." Indeed.

What is someone to think on reading such a review? Notre Dame, Catholic University, surely what is Catholic is known and promoted in both places? Add the *Commonweal*. Is such a removal by the Vatican really a "great story" in American Church history, or is it a kind of embarrassment, an epitome of what is wrong? We have in addition certain "liberal" but "widely held views," as if there were another source of knowledge or rule for Catholics, but not the Vatican which was apparently pictured in certain circles at Notre Dame or Catholic University to function as a kind of alien force. Perhaps one might argue that this is one of the great stories in American Church history because finally the Vatican decided to exercise some authority in lieu of episcopal action, so it is a sign that there is still some integrity and life left in the Church?

Thomas Molnar's book, *The Church: Pilgrim of Centuries* is a depressing study of the degree the Church has become itself liberal in dealing with civil society. In so doing, Molnar holds, it has lost its own voice to civil society and has become itself something modeled on any other voluntary group. But what interests me here is the last sentence of Kenneth Craycraft's review of this book for *First Things* (June, 1991): "*The Church: Pilgrim of Centuries* is a worthy assessment of why, at least at the present, this truth ("that sacred history obstinately accompanies profane history and comes to its rescue") is difficult to see."

The difficulty of seeing Catholicism as true is also rooted in an unclarity about what exactly the faith is. To write an apology for it is to clarify this truth of the Church. But when every statement of the Church is controverted and obscured in civil society or media or academia by Catholic clergy or intellectuals themselves, it will mean that for many people today, the problem of faith is reduced to finding what it might mean (see Chapter VIII). Among the discordant voices are those, suggested by the University of Notre Dame press release, that simply make it confusing to determine in any clear fashion what Catholicism might say of itself.

Perhaps the finest work of apology in this century is still Chesterton's *Orthodoxy*, written initially in 1908. The "Introduction" to this book is entitled, "In Defence of Everything Else," as if to say that somehow the defense of the faith is at the same time a defense of everything else. Chesterton realized that everything else needed defending. The word "defense" here is perhaps more accurate than "explanation" or "justification" because in many ways Catholicism is an attacked thing. It is not always enough to affirm the goodness of everything else, to justify the position by dispassionate argument. It is necessary to defend it against specific attacks that come from no neutral source, attacks that would destroy the thing defended if possible.

However, Chesterton is always amusing even in defense. In games he would see that the skills of the defenders were perhaps more to be appreciated than those more dramatic feats of the scorers and shooters. *Orthodoxy* was written as a result of a "challenge." "Even a bad shot is dignified when he accepts a duel." It seems that Chesterton's previous book *Heretics* had been a marvelously incisive attack on several modern authors and their positions. A gentleman by the name of G.S. Street had accused

Chesterton of challenging others to state their "cosmic" theory, but that he neglected to do so himself.

Chesterton, as he tells us, was delighted to be challenged to do what he loved to do anyhow, namely, to write books. In the beginning of *Orthodoxy*, Chesterton, as he explained it,

> attempted in a vague and personal way in a set of mental pictures rather than in a series of deductions, to state the philosophy in which I have come to believe. I will not call it my philosophy, for I did not make it. God and humanity made it, and it made me.

What is to be noticed here, I think, is that Chesterton displays the marks of an apologist in the best sense. He explains what he held and how he came to hold it after he explained what he did not hold and why he did not hold it.

But even more importantly, Chesterton acknowledged that his philosophy was not simply a product of his own will. His philosophy was one that could acknowledge something as true that he did not make, something that is not bound to place or time, even when it appears in time and place. That is to say, he can recognize a truth even if it happened long before his time and in a place he would only come to visit later. Behind any apologist, I think, must stand, implicitly at least, this intellectual assumption that truth is possible, that it can be known, and that explanation and justification, defense, are the duty we owe to it. If truth is possible, many theoretical positions and arguments are not wholly true. An apology, in this sense, is also an intellectual account. Men may or may not want to engage in controversy. But they cannot pretend that what they do hold does not need to be explained.

VI

What is characteristic of Catholicism is precisely this endeavor to explain itself, both to oneself and to the world. When

John Paul II hinted in the Encyclical on the Missions that perhaps this explain-the-faith-to-others endeavor was not adequately going on, he also emphasized the reason why. Some theories of philosophy and culture maintained that it was not necessary, that Catholicism had little or nothing to tell anyone other than a kind of cultural relativism in which everyone is saved simply by being what he already is.

Do we lack apologists then? I have suggested that we lack those willing to hear. I have suggested further that even those who are willing to listen hear a multiplicity of confusing voices about what it is they are to think about and believe. Finally, I have suggested, that there are certain philosophical theories that make it impossible to hear anything at all. To the first, what is needed is not so much an argument or an explanation but a change of heart. The fear is that Catholicism might be true so that many cannot safely listen. All Catholic explanation, it is intimated, is distorted and confused. No one would want to listen to it.

To the second, the disorder within the Church itself in almost all its institutions, we have both Newman's realization that there could be and in fact were heretical bishops, and parish priests and professors. Within this confusion, we still must ask whether the faith is related to the Rock of Peter, and whether to hear it, we need not go there? *Ubi Petrus, ibi Ecclesia,* to repeat the classical words ending Chapter I.

And finally to the third, we need to think. We have given up most serious study of philosophy and argument. When we have taken them up, we have imitated the sorts of philosophy that lead to St. Paul's foolishness. Perhaps it is not out of place to suggest that St. Thomas will remain a godsend precisely in this age when the capacity of the mind to know and to know *what is* is what is denied, even on term papers handed back to our students by their professors in Catholic universities.

"Belief in eternal life," Josef Ratzinger remarked sadly in an Address in Vienna (May, 1989), "has hardly any role to play in preaching today" (see Chapter XII). The apologist has no "alibi," no excuse if the faith or intelligence he explains or justifies is not that of the revelation itself. Too often, we hear preached fundamentally "this world," not Catholicism. Ratzinger went on:

> Here is the final deception inherent in the idea of the "better world," which nonetheless, appears today even among Christians as the goal of our hope and the genuine standard of morality. The "Kingdom of God" has been almost completely substituted in the general awareness, as far as I can see, by the utopia of a better future world for which we labor and which becomes the true reference point of morality — a morality which thus blends again with a philosophy of evolution and history, and creates norms of itself by calculating what can offer the better conditions of life.

No doubt it is true, in conclusion, that certain forms of "faith and justice" theories have come to be preached in the name of Catholicism. This is not eternal life.

The true "apology" for the truth of revelation continues to exist. We can explain and justify what it is we hold and maintain in the light of revelation. It is well that we are "elsewhere," "alibi," when the faith is presented as a utopia and not eternal life. Yet, in the end, we need no excuses or alibis. "Eternal life cannot be prepared for otherwise than in our present existence," Ratzinger observed. This "preparing for" is what the apologist does. It includes explanation and justification. It includes the truth *that is*. Walker Percy was right, "What else is there?"

PART TWO

THE REVOLUTION THAT IS CATHOLICISM

CHAPTER VIII

The Meditating Mole:
An Underground Catholicism?

I

In the first part of these considerations, I have been concerned primarily with the feeling that organized Catholicism is in some considerable difficulty. No doubt it is since any religion or philosophic system depends on the adherence of human beings to its premises. This difficulty has arisen, however, in a curious way because it does not immediately take into account the whole of what Catholicism says of itself. Catholicism is a deeply intellectual religion of its very nature. It is not a fanaticism nor an enthusiasm.[1] On the philosophic side it originates with considerations found in Aristotle and Plato about the highest things. On its revelational side, it contains a logic or consistency that seems directly challenging to philosophy not as rejecting it but as completing it.

In this second section, I want to take some essential issues in which Catholicism speaks for itself. In a broader sense, I will call it "the Revolution that is Catholicism," because this original newness remains by human standards still the most unexpected

---

[1] See Ronald Knox, *Enthusiasm* (Westminster, MD: Christian Classics, 1983).

and surprising doctrine ever addressed to the human intellect on the grounds that it was true.[2] What is peculiar about Catholicism is a claim to present the truth about God and, as an overflow of this, a claim to present the truth of man. But the truth of man, his ability to be and remain himself, in some sense relates to his supernatural destiny. If we get that wrong, we will undoubtedly get the human city wrong.

There is a passage from St. Maximus the Confessor that seems to put this relationship correctly, though we can easily find things similar in St. Augustine or in St. Thomas.

> Charity is a right attitude of mind which prefers nothing to the knowledge of God.... For God is far superior to all his creation, since everything which exists has been made by God and for him.... But the Lord himself reminds us: "Whoever loves me will keep my commandments. And this is my commandment; that you love one another." So the man who does not love his neighbor does not obey God's command.... A charitable mind is not displayed simply in giving money; it is manifested still more by personal service as well as by the communication of God's word to others.[3]

A kind of steady wholeness exists between the things of God and the things of man that implies that a disorder towards man is a disorder towards God, whereas a disorder towards God will result in a further disorder towards other men.

Perhaps it must be asked in the beginning about the title of this chapter — what is this "meditating mole"? In a way, the title

---

[2] For two discussions of the grounds for truth, see especially Yves Simon, "The Search for Truth," *A General Theory of Authority* (Notre Dame: University of Notre Dame Press, 1980), pp. 81-132; Josef Pieper, *The Truth of All Things* (San Francisco: Ignatius Press, 1989).

[3] St. Maximus the Confessor, *On Charity*, PG 90, 962-67, Breviary, Seventh Sunday in Ordinary Time, III, pp. 229-30.

is a gift from the dead, if it can be put that way. A former teacher of mine died at Georgetown several years ago. According to good monastic custom, I inherited his books. On death, things become common, only to be reacquired again for a time by someone else. The day will come, no doubt, when someone will inherit my crumbling and marked-up books. I wish him well; I have some good books. In the monastery, those members in more or less the same academic field usually get first crack at the deceased's loot, which turns out to be not pounds and crowns and guineas, but, as I intimated, mainly the contents of the dead monk's fondly accumulated library. Indeed, it is a fair system among those whose progeny is the spirit.

This strange, to the world, unnatural system, is fine by me, of course, because one of the books I spied in my friend's collection was Albert Camus' *Lyrical and Critical Essays*.[4] Almost nothing in this world do I love better than good — even bad — essays. Give me a Belloc or a Samuel Johnson or a Hazlitt or a Joseph Epstein and I am content for hours. Publishers, I know, say that essays have fallen on hard times. But I do not believe a word of it. And I had no idea how good these particular essays of Camus were. So, at a distance of a few years, I owe a debt to my friend even in death.

I have, moreover, found myself reading these essays aloud to a friend patient enough to put up with me. One year, I even read the one I will talk about here to the first autumn class of new graduate students. They were perplexed, to be sure, because they still suspected the world could be made perfect by a few minor adjustments in economics or regime. They only began to suspect, but not admit, what is in their own hearts. The act of reading a good essay, furthermore, is not completed until we read it aloud to some friend. Some things, read first in stillness, are meant also to be spoken in quietness.

---

[4] Albert Camus, *Lyrical and Critical Essays*, translated by Ellen Conroy Kennedy (New York: Vintage, 1968). See also James V. Schall, *Idylls and Rambles: Lighter Christian Essays* (San Francisco: Ignatius Press, 1994).

"Yes, but what does the title of this chapter, this 'Meditating Mole,' mean?" Some patience will be in order, for it is about Catholicism. The topic is self-revealing. Except in children's stories and spy novels, moles are not very engaging creatures, after all. And we will presume the little critter that eats gladioli and tomato sprouts is probably not an apt symbol of divine contemplation, but one never knows.

II

In 1948, Camus, who loved to write of the cities that surround the Mediterranean — Palma, Constantine, Oran, Ibiza, Florence, Pisa, and, of course, his native Algiers — wrote an essay in *Cahiers du Sud*, called enigmatically, "Helen's Exile."[5] Yes, Helen was the same lovely lady whose face launched a thousand ships. For Camus, she came to symbolize the Greek sense of reason, of limited reason, that modernity was systematically exiling.

In "Helen's Exile," in fact, were already foreshadowed the disturbing themes of Camus' great book, *The Rebel*, the realization that our times have "ended by placing the impulse of the will at the heart of reason, and reason has therefore become murderous." We have learned about iron will in the service of soft reason from men as diverse as Lenin and Pol Pot and the abortionists. This same theme, to be sure, the lethal nature of tenderness of the mind, is also found in Flannery O'Connor's famous "Introduction" to *A Memoir of Mary Anne*, in the late Walker Percy's novel *The Thanatos Syndrome*, and especially in Eric Voegelin's *Science, Politics, and Gnosticism*. A hint of it can be found in Allan Bloom, with more than a hint in Leo Strauss. Chesterton had already, in 1908, found the phenomenon in the modern habit of making self-doubt a quality of intellect, not heart.

---

[5] *Ibid.*, pp. 148-53. See also the essay on Camus in James V. Schall, *What Is God Like?* (Collegeville, MN: The Liturgical Press, 1992), pp. 80-100.

The passage in Camus that struck me most, however, was this:

> History explains neither the natural universe which came before it, nor beauty which stands above it. Consequently, it has chosen to ignore them. Whereas Plato incorporated everything — nonsense, reason, and myth — our philosophers admit nothing but nonsense or reason. The mole is meditating. It was Christianity that began to replace the contemplation of the world with the tragedy of the soul.

Here, of course, is my "meditating mole." Those specters that could not be accounted for by pure intellect, itself bent on creating by itself all that is, were left aside to go underground. They did not disappear but could be found still rooting about the human condition like an annoying mole disturbing the smooth surface of our own carefully planned gardens in which we allow to be planted only what we want there. We alone, we think, are the movers and shakers, the planters and the planted. But the mole continues to disturb our rationalist schools.

Yet, if we know the account of the origins of theoretical science in Aristotle's *Metaphysics*, we who call ourselves Catholics, that minority of them who still hold to the rocky strength of the Creeds, find Camus' reading of the intellectual origins of modernity somewhat surprising. According to Aristotle, it was Socrates who first began to turn away from the impasses of cosmological speculations towards ethics and the inner activities of the soul.

And there is some question about whether the word "tragedy" in any sense can be properly used of classical Catholicism. Christ's death, after all, was called in the medieval liturgies a "felix culpa," because of which we are, evidently, redeemed from ultimate tragedy. The debate, I know, is with those who maintain stubbornly that we need to be redeemed in the first place, or that if we do, we redeem ourselves.

Not a few Catholics and Christians now belong to this latter school done over on the model of modernity wherein salvation is indistinguishable from some sort of social activism or societal restructuring (see Chapter X). Josef Ratzinger has persisted in finding Pelagianism, the thesis that we could redeem ourselves, to be the most dangerous of contemporary spiritual problems.[6] Those who resist this modern Pelagianism in whatever form do so because they do not want to maintain that we do know, by ourselves alone, all of what is best for us.

It begins to seem sometimes that this belief that we ourselves do not cause or make our own good is the wildest and most fascinating of all ideas. One of the strangest phenomena of the modern era is the reluctance to describe clearly just what it is Catholicism officially says of itself (see Chapter IX). Those called to explain this odd faith in public fora seldom are convinced enough to describe what it is. Rather they tell us what their ideology wants it to be.

III

I write these remarks in the context of contemporary intellectual analysis. For surely, to anyone beholding the near chaos that is presented by modern religion itself, ironically also in Catholicism, nothing seems clearer than that many in the intellectual elites of Catholicism and Christianity do not really believe in what this faith has historically and technically thought of itself and how this thought relates to reality.[7] It is dangerous to whisper this suspicion in public, I know, but the fact seems obvious.

Some have thought that Catholicism ought to be the religion whose time has come. But at the very moment that the world's need of it seems greatest, Catholicism no longer appears to know

---

[6] See "Exonerating Pelagius?" *Thirty Days*, 4 (February, 1991), 40-55.

[7] See Thomas Molnar, *The Church: Pilgrim of Centuries* (Grand Rapids, MI: Eerdmans, 1990).

itself or what once may have made it intellectually attractive. As I have said, many thinkers are not surprised by this. The tensions of faith and the public order are too much for most people who, in lieu of vision, would finally go off to seek strange gods.

What strange gods? Camus had it right. Let me recall Camus: "We (the intellectuals of modernity) extol one thing and one alone: *a future world in which reason will reign supreme.*" And this is the reason, he thought, that kills. It is not the ordinary tyrants we need to worry about, but the tyrants with ideas, the ones educated in philosophy. What is new to our time is that it is sometimes the intellectual dons of Catholicism and Christianity who are found to be proposing similar goals of modernity. The wars of the world are still fought first in the hearts of the monks and the dons.

This is why these reflections are self-revelatory, since I belong to that stubborn remnant that holds that the faith is not intended to be primarily an instrument to activate the images of the ideologies into this world. The Marxist Christians, once so influential in the churches, did in fact know "that which they did," however poorly their socialist visions have done in recent years and however attractive this statist vision remains to many. Evidently they are replaced from the same intellectual roots by a succession of feminists, ecologists, statists, and deconstructionists who have in common an order of the world founded exclusively in the mind. In the media, those Christians who are feted are invariably those who are alienated from the central strand of revelational thought. The words are Christian but the ideas originate from elsewhere.

The virtue of "courage" came to mean in somber ecclesiastical discussions of war, for example, bravery against those who would be brave. In retrospect, those who can now speak freely in Russia and Eastern Europe find religious anti-war groups implicit collaborators with the Soviet regime. The case for the poor, in much religious rhetoric, had come to embrace the methods of those socialist systems that cannot produce. Hence, the poor will always be with us, again, it seems, thanks in part to religion.

Those Christians, like Solzhenitsyn or Armando Valladares, locked up in actual prison camps, were read passages from Christians in free lands praising Marxism as a proof that all is lost for those in ideological prisons, that even the Church supported their captors. In retrospect, it seems almost bizarre. When real peasants became cardinals as in Nicaragua, they were insulted, even in free lands, because they rejected the revolution "designed to free the peasants."

Camus made his passionate plea in the name of beauty and friendship, in the name of limitation. This was the plea of Leo Strauss also, a return to the classics, to the Greek sense of finiteness. In this was such salvation as we might expect in this world. "The Greeks," Camus wrote, "who spent centuries asking themselves what was just, would understand nothing of our idea of justice. Equity, for them, supposed a limit, while our whole continent is convulsed by the quest for a justice we see as absolute." The City of God is looked for in this world.

Values now have become that which we want to put into a world with no intrinsic intelligibility either to the world or to man. Human nature, it is said, is not already given. We make it. And in our polities, we enforce those views of polis-made human nature that conform to our ideas of man, not to the metaphysical nature of man himself. The abortion clinics, those embarrassing realities, are legal, therefore right, because what is human, is defined by courts and legislatures and presidents, not by reality.

This is what we do. Who is to say otherwise without overturning our polity? The euthanasia clinics are already operative in Holland and we think of it here. Those oddities, like myself, who wonder about the legitimacy of these things, are seen, even in some parts of the churches, as enemies to the established order. We rely on grounds other than Camus' "will at the heart of reason."

We ought not to be astonished that the modern mind has come to hold these things, those of us in particular who are Catholics. Catholicism has never held that it is not also a religion of reason. This claim remains the most embarrassing thing about it to the modern mind, particularly when it engages it. A G.K. Chesterton is looked upon as an anomaly, whereas he stands even yet at the heart of that Catholic claim for a reasonableness not beyond reason, but in the service of reason.

Camus still belonged to the school of intellectuals who felt that the Greeks were enough. The early years of Christianity through and beyond Augustine were years in which Tertullian asked "What has Jerusalem to do with Athens?" The central answer of Augustine as of medieval Catholicism was, simply, "everything." But Camus was right, the sort of reason that evolved in modernity, the reason that the avant-garde of Catholic intellectuals use to explain the faith, ends up with autonomous reason, with will, not reason.

"Now that God is dead, all that remains are history and power," Camus continued.

> For a long time now, the whole effort of our philosophers has been solely to replace the idea of human nature with the idea of situation and ancient harmony with the disorderly outbursts of chance or the pitiless movements of reason.

The texts for what passes as morality in the schools are mostly "situation" oriented. All is excused except the political sins — discrimination, racism, sexism. Hell is reinstated as a place in which to expel the proponents of these latter crimes. And Hitler is not the sole occupant of this new receptacle for the damned. In this intellectual system, we must not change our world to conform to the morals of faith; we must change our minds. This is one of the main forms of contemporary social "action," of raising our consciousness.

Likewise, when we hear that we must have "values," we forget that this is a modern word that can mean exactly what the will wants it to mean. "For the Greeks, values existed a priori and marked out the exact limits of every action," Camus noted.

"Modern philosophy places its values at the completion of action. They are not, but they become, and we shall know them completely only at the end of history." The end of history will arrive when nothing contrary to our ideas exists or is allowed to exist in the world.

But if the utopians — militant, religious, atheist — will, in the end, murder us or coercively conform us to their models, can moderation save us? The passionate pleas for moderation, the sober liberal's fanatical anti-fanatical rhetoric, the insistence that no discussion ever ends, no argument is ever completed in truth, is this merely another form of skepticism? Eventually, I think, it is. The utopians are wrong, but their danger, their error, in a way, is more healthy than that of our contemporary intellectual cynic who dogmatically insists on the truth of nothing so that he can be free. Nothing is given in vain, not even our desires for absolute justice and truth.

IV

What the debate or argument is about, then, is not whether there is such a thing as a highest good, but its nature and location. This is why the debate over the moderation of Greek reason, limited as it was and should have been, cannot be complete without Augustine, without some effort to locate the City of God. Modernity, since the Enlightenment, does indeed, as Camus knew, "seek a world in which reason will reign supreme."

And the mind of modernity did want to locate this world of supreme reason in history, within some here and now frontiers. The terror of the twentieth century is to be found in no other place but the minds of the intellectual politicians who wish to bring about the end of history that will be the embodiment of their chosen "values." Humanism becomes our own creation, not our response to *what is*.

Where does this leave my concern for classical Catholicism,

now existing more and more underground? Perhaps it only exists in the words of the Holy Father, who remains reviled precisely because he understands that Catholicism is not the modernity that seeks to place its will at the heart of reason. "Nor is it difficult to show that in the last two decades," John Paul II remarked to several Brazilian bishops,

> many Christians allowed their beliefs to become gradually extinguished, and others took their distance little by little from the principles of truth, to the point that a sad confusion resulted as regards ideas and action. It was the result of following a model of Christianity and of the church that was as fanciful as it was utopian. . . .[8]

The mole, it seems, is meditating. All ideology is at bottom empty, even when advocated in the name of religion.

Camus, in his eloquent plea against modernity, longed for a return to beauty, to art, to the realization that "friendship is a virtue." It is, as Charles N.R. McCoy wrote in his *Structure of Political Thought*, the intellectual politician with the freedom of the classical artist that lies at the root of our dilemmas.[9] But for Camus, "the artist, through obligations of his very nature, recognizes limits the historical mind ignores."

The artist in his own order is free with regard to ends in a way that nature and through it, the politician is not. As Josef Pieper reminded us, the artist is imitative of nature in the very order of nature's making. But the politician deals with what is made already. That he should be so limited is our sole theoretic protection against the intellectual politician who murders to right the world of the evil he beholds in his abstract form, now taken to be reality, now put into reality.

---

[8] John Paul II, "The Bishop's Prime Role as a Teacher," December 7, 1990, *L'Osservatore Romano*, English, December 17, 1990, p. 9.

[9] Charles N. R. McCoy, *The Structure of Political Thought* (New York: McGraw-Hill, 1963).

But where do the limits of Camus meet the unlimitedness of religion now too often supportive of the modern project that would seek to render unto man solely according to man's own definition? In friendship, Camus reminds us, following again Homer, we refuse "to be fanatics, recognizing the world's limits and man's through the faces of those we love, in short, by means of beauty." In this way we rejoin the Greeks' understanding of limited reason.

But this proposal rests on unsteady grounds. The mole is meditating. For friendship is by no means the virtue that allows us to be content with the limited nature of our being. Indeed, it is precisely friendship that leads us to ultimate questions that may be, but by no means need be, the haven of fanatics. Perhaps it is no accident that the ideologues in our time have called one another comrades or brothers in worldly imitation of the monks.

The tracts on friendship are still found in the classics, in Plato, in Aristotle, in Cicero. And it was Aquinas who saw that this particular tract on friendship was the foundation of any possibility for eternal life. For it was Aristotle, after all, who realized that in so far as we could, we should set aside human things to devote ourselves to contemplating the orders of reality.

Yet, Aristotle emphasized that we would not want to be a king or a god, if that meant our becoming someone else, if it meant losing our friends. The vivid appreciation of the beauty of the particular faces we behold does not lead us to moderation, as Camus thought, but leads us through moderation to the highest things. The limits of Greek thought are still limits, and we should respect them.

To be sure, Camus knew that "the Greeks never said that the limit could not be crossed." Here, no doubt, he was thinking of hubris, of the scientific claim totally to reconstruct man, of the politicians or economists engaged in the same process by persuasion and coercion until the roots of worldly evil, as it was hoped, were eradicated. What has Jerusalem to do with Athens? That is, could the limits be crossed from above without violating the limits of reason?

V

The modern philosophers, even those who advocate a revival of the classics, think not. In other words, are the acknowledged, and defended, limits of reason themselves necessary before the question of revelation can be properly posed? Voegelin and Strauss were courageous enough to wonder if revelation might not be possible, or at least to realize that it could not necessarily be excluded. They were right in thinking that it could not. That is, they were right in realizing modernity had failed.

Yet, this very failure seems particularly lost on many articulate thinkers in the churches. This is the unfortunate tragedy of our era. The freedom of speech or thought, if it means anything, means that beyond the polis, in the hearts of the clerical and intellectual dons, there is room for higher order concerns that do not stop in this world. The young man or woman who arrives Sunday after Sunday in the churches, to hear a liturgy with little beauty and a word that is rather poor sociology, begins to wonder where to turn since he suspects that if this be "faith," it must be rather silly.

Likewise, this intrinsic problematic in the churches represents a political crisis of proportions we have yet to comprehend. For as Voegelin noted, the unlimited mind will turn on the world with a vengeance when legitimate questions arising from actual living do not have also the moderation of classic faith. The public order is jeopardized most by religion become ideological because there is no longer anywhere to turn for the limits of things but to the will at the heart of reason, and there is no limit in will as such, particularly at the heart of reason.

Camus, near the end of "Helen's Exile," concluded, "Oh, noonday thought, the Trojan war is fought far from the battleground!" That is, of course, quite right. The increasing attention to the inadequacies of our best universities, themselves often prisoners of will in the service of unlimited reason, leaves the battleground strewn with unacknowledged, unresolved intellectual crises. Camus thought the artist might save us, but we recall that one of the poets accused Socrates, and Socrates himself barely glimpsed the good. He died, executed by the state, because it saw his truth as subversive of its chosen order, its chosen will.

"The terrible walls of the modern city will fall, to deliver Helen's beauty, 'its soul serene as the untroubled waves'." But Helen is no more, her beauty as fragile as all finite being. The mole is meditating. What perplexes us remains the mystery of finite being, the actual friendships we have. In our polity, in our civilization, the universal civilization, as Strauss called it, something is missing that was once there. Incarnation and Resurrection, the doctrines most problematic in modern theology, are refused broader consideration in the light of the only questions really worth asking. The philosophers are off pursuing themselves and their distinctions, as both St. Paul and St. Thomas suspected would happen to them.

Josef Pieper, in his wonderful book, *Happiness and Contemplation*, wrote:

> Man as he is constituted, endowed as he is for a thirst for happiness, cannot have his thirst quenched in the finite realm; and if he thinks or behaves as if that were possible, he is misunderstanding himself, he is acting contrary to his own nature. The whole world would not suffice this "nature" of man. If the whole world were given to him, he would have to say, and would say: it is too little.[10]

What has Jerusalem to do with Athens? It is essential to any abiding political order that such questions be posed freely and responded to freely. The condition of our universities, the condition of our very polity, even the condition of our religion, unfortunately makes this sort of reflection on the higher things practically impossible.

---

[10] Josef Pieper, *Happiness and Contemplation* (New York: Pantheon, 1958), pp. 38-39.

"Oh, noonday thought, the Trojan War is fought far from the battleground." Camus was right that it is not on the battlefield where civilizations collapse. Nor do they die solely by claiming that God is dead, therefore, man rules. Beauty will not save us, though it can remind us both of our finiteness and of what Augustine called "beauty ever ancient, ever new." The silence that surrounds our civilization about the highest things comes not from exhausted battlefields, nor from inattention to the beauty of our friends. Rather it comes from the projection onto the world of abstractions, now sanctioned even by sundry clerics, so that even if the correct questions are posed by the Greeks, we can no longer hear the other answers of our tradition, posed to these very questions.

VI

The mole is indeed meditating, while the murderous will at the heart of reason in modernity remains voracious until we realize the location of those realities we do not experience, but whose completion are not of the order of our politics or of our world. These reflections are, as I say, self-revelatory because there are some of us who suspect that the answers we seek have, in fact, been spoken to us. We can suspect this revelation is directed to us, however, only if we pose the real questions that arise from friendship and limited polities.

When monks die, we should inherit their books. We should read them again. While they live, however, it is well to attend to the objects of their love. Our polity also depends on it, for an alliance of religious fervor and political ideology would encompass more tightly than ever before that murderous will at the heart of reason, of which Camus spoke, not merely with a plan, but with an enthusiasm to carry it out as if it were a pursuit of the highest things.

This intelligence is the battlefield, far from the Trojan War, that sees the struggles of our future already being waged, and evidently, lost because we cannot or will not consider all the answers to the questions that reality does pose to us. While the world goes on, during these past decades, Catholicism has, in its own inner resources, those identified with its central heart, independently engaged the world on its own terms. The intellectual character of our time, in this sense, more closely resembles a voluntary rejection, much like that of Callicles in the *Gorgias*, than a dialogue of those interested in the truth *that is*.

If I might speak, then, of the Catholicism as a "meditating mole," I would mean, contrary to Camus, that the contemplation of the world and the tragedy of the soul are not replacements one for another but both belong to the same world. The public world has been in large part contrived of human will and its structures that have been designed to explain man to himself. These explanations once put into the world by the intellectual politicians have little place for those rays of light and truth that come from revelation and classical reason, those which are willing to include *all that is* in their formulations.

What I mean by "an underground Catholicism," then, is the striking fact that the Church has not merely survived but has been able to make a coherent case for itself not apart from the world and its learning or its understanding of itself but precisely in reflection on this understanding. Catholicism thus is not closed to modernity but has its truths and its errors reflected in its very articulation of itself. Unnoticed, under the surface of things, perhaps, there has never ceased to be an articulation of the meaning of the world itself as reflected in revelation and in the philosophy incited by it. The human mind, the modern mind even, therefore, always has an alternative available to it, an alternative that explains what it is missing in the light of what it knows.

CHAPTER IX

The Church Explains Itself:
The New Catechism

I

Catholicism is essentially a gift, a gift of God that results in an understanding about which is organized a society with its own structure and its own forms of life. The Church has been told that it would last all days, even to the end of the world, for it was to keep present in the minds and hearts of mankind what God had revealed to them about Himself and about themselves, about the world. From time to time, the Church has felt it wise and necessary to explain itself, its coherence, its unity of thought, where its thought stood before the other religious and philosophic systems of the world.

Throughout the past half century, it has been clear that, in addition to the formidable work of Vatican II, there was need of something more systematic and coherent that would place in a single form the whole of the Church's understanding of itself. No doubt the considerable intellectual and moral chaos of recent times, the confusions and doubts on the part of many of the faithful and their ecclesiastical leaders, as well as of the general public, has prompted an effort to set down in a clear and concise manner just what the Church holds about itself, about God, about what man is and is to do in this world, itself coming from God.

Catholicism has always proposed that there are answers to mankind's ultimate questions but that the questions must still be formulated and properly formulated before its answers will be seen as plausible and possible. The Church's mind is perhaps best summarized in a passage from Saint Irenaeus, one of the earliest and most profound of the intellectual bishops. "With God," he wrote, "there is nothing without purpose, nothing without its meaning and reason."[1]

The Church understands that it is proper to its own mission and nature to articulate in words and arguments, themselves made as clear and as exact as humanly possible, what it holds to be true. "Today, however, it seems necessary to reflect on the whole of the Church's moral teaching, with the precise goal of recalling certain fundamental truths of Catholic doctrine which, in the present circumstances, risk being distorted or denied," John Paul II wrote in *Veritatis Splendor* (#5), in a document in which he often cited the *General Catechism*. These arguments themselves refer to realities and are not substitutes for them. On the other hand, the human mind is made to know. Thus, it should seek to know and ponder what is true, even of divine and revealed things.

After considerable study, in late 1992, then, John Paul II authorized the publication of a *General Catechism*, something that would endeavor to explain to anyone who wanted to know, whether they be believers or not, what the Church officially held and why it held it. In presenting this document, John Paul II wrote:

> A catechism ought faithfully and organically to present the teachings of Holy Scripture, of the living tradition in the Church, and of the authentic Magisterium, along with the heritage of the Fathers, of the holy men and women of the Church, in order better to know the Christian mystery and to revivify the faith of the people of God. It ought to take account of the explications of doctrine that the Holy

---

[1] Saint Irenaeus, Bishop, *Against the Heretics*, 4, 18.

> Spirit has suggested to the Church in the course of time. It
> is necessary also that it clarify by the light of faith the new
> situations and problems that have not yet been posed in
> the past.[2]

The existence of Catholicism is greatly clarified by such a statement, one that has been in considerable need, as I have tried to
show in these considerations.

A friend of one of my brothers, for instance, was at a Mass in
his local parish on the Feast of the Immaculate Conception. The
local pastor, known evidently for his own versions of the Liturgy
and doctrine, explained in his homily that there is considerable
difficulty with this doctrine of the Immaculate Conception. The
priest told the parishioners, furthermore, that there was too much
attention to Mary in the Church.

At this point, it seems, a local doctor stood up in the pews to
interrupt the priest. He explained to the pastor that the Catholic
Church did not teach what he had just said, that some of the
parishioners, at least in their own church, expected to hear what
the Church taught, however difficult it might be to comprehend.
They do not come to church to hear the priest's own private
opinions. Another man said the same thing. Some parishioners
applauded.

At this point the priest, realizing he had to say something in
reply, explained that it was important to make the doctrines of the
Church believable to the people of our time, which he was trying
to do. Applause for him. Clearly, here is a typically divided,
confused parish in which the pastor is going to make things
palatable and the parishioners want to know what the Church
actually holds.

Evidently, the Immaculate Conception was, in the priest's

---

[2] John Paul II, "Constitution Apostolique Fidei Donum," *Le Catéchisme de l'Église
Catholique* (Paris: Mame/Plon, 1992), p. 7. (Translations in this essay will be my
own from this original text.)

view, dubious to the Catholic people of our time, so it had to be minimized to protect them, an approach the very opposite of the intellectual tradition of Catholicism that has seen in such mysteries precisely something the human mind and world needs. The priest conceived his duty as a kind of filter to shelter the supposedly weak faithful from the full brunt of what the Church actually teaches. The doctor, on the other hand, knew what the Church taught and expected it adequately explained and defended by those responsible for the parishes. Sometimes today, it often seems, the clergy are the ones who are intellectually weak and need the laity to protect them from their own doubts.

What is usually called "modernism" is a heresy that proposes that only doctrines that are acceptable to the norms of a given time can be believed. The Church, in its tradition, thinks it must be faithful first to what is revealed. Having this information, accurately preserving its own heritage, it can then see why what the Church says of itself does not contradict reason. Modernism or gnosticism fashions the Church to what are said to be acceptable scientific or cultural possibilities of acceptance. These theories take precedence to faith and interpret it.

II

Roman Catholicism, at its best, explains firmly and clearly what it believes and holds. Though it recognizes how meanings of words can change in time or place, it seeks words and concepts that unerringly reflect the reality believed. The Church only then sets out very carefully to examine why what it holds is both consistent with its own teachings and not contradictory to reason. The Church is by no means hostile to the learning of a given time. It instigates in fact not a little of it. But this learning itself must stand some test of truth. Nothing is simply true because it happens to be produced in a given time, even in our time.

In his recent remarks on the Church's study of the Galileo Case, John Paul II remarked:

> There are two realms of knowledge, one which has its source in Revelation and one which reason can discover by its own power. To the latter belong especially the experimental sciences and philosophy. The distinction between the two realms of knowledge ought not to be understood as opposition. The two realms are not altogether foreign to each other; they have points of contact. The methodologies proper to each make it possible to bring out different aspects of reality.[3]

It is clear from these remarks, that, in the Church's own view, the exact knowledge of what the Church teaches is itself a contribution to reason. It is not an aid to the faith to imply that any of its essential teachings cannot be held because of some supposed conflict with what modern people might or might not be able to believe. The Church is in the business of examining any presumed conflict in the light of the reasons given for the said conflict. The Church is not anti-rational, but almost the very opposite.

On the other hand, there are points of contact between faith and reason that bring out different, more complete understandings of reality. We do not really know that revelation can make a reasonable case for itself until we know what questions reason itself is perplexed by, confused by. In other words, there are not two different "worlds," one of faith and another of reason, but one reality whose fullness is addressed both by our reason and by what God has revealed. Any notion that these are incompatible with each other is itself not Catholic. Indeed, refusal to consider the possible relationships existing between faith and reason is itself a sign of a refusal to face the full implications of *what is*.

---

[3] John Paul II, October 31, 1992, *L'Osservatore Romano*, English, November 4, 1992, p. 2.

I bring this incident of the Immaculate Conception up in the light of the Holy Father's remarks because I think it a good introduction to the *General Catechism*.[4] What this *Catechism* does is to give to the faithful an authentic, accurate statement of the essence of each teaching and practice of the faith. This effort is an organized whole so that the relation of each practice and teaching to this whole, including what we know from reason, is understood.

Thus, if a priest or anyone else confuses or misstates the teaching of the Church, as in this case, about the Immaculate Conception, it can be easily shown just what the Church authoritatively teaches on the topic. The doctor can check the pastor and the pastor need not rely on his own private views. Thus, #491 of the *Catechism* reads: "Along the centuries, the Church has understood that Mary, 'full of grace,' by God, has, from her conception, been redeemed. This is what the dogma of the Immaculate Conception confesses. . . ." The text goes on to cite the exact wording of the proclamation on the subject by Pius IX and gives a further enlightening account of its meaning.

Moreover, should a bishop or theologian teach the opposite or cast doubts on this or that doctrine, the faithful will know that it is the speaker or writer, not the Church, that is confused on this topic. If you will, this *Catechism* is a kind of long-awaited proclamation of intellectual freedom for individual Catholics, the freedom of the truth that makes Christians free, the freedom that revelation gives to reason, the freedom to be aware of the limits of intellect itself, the freedom from doubts about the faith originating in the disorders or confusions of individual priests, bishops, or theologians.

Probably no stronger or more complete document than this *General Catechism* has ever been given to the Church, to layman as well as cleric, about the overall teachings of the Church. In its own

---

[4] *Le Catéchisme de l'Église Catholique* (Paris: Mame/Plon, 1992).

way, the *General Catechism* is a gripping, exciting statement about God, man, and the world, the relationships existing between them. If, as it is popularly maintained, the modern and post-modern mind cannot understand or accept, say, the Immaculate Conception, it does not follow that we should cast doubt on the doctrine. Rather, while not denying the perplexity of its mystery to us, we should question the modern mind itself and the methodologies that prevent it from seeing the meaning and consistency of this particular teaching that has its place and truth in its whole of the teaching of revelation.

III

The *General Catechism* contains 2865 paragraphs. The book is organized into four general parts: the Creeds, what we believe about God; the Sacraments, the actions or signs given by Christ for the new life of grace; the Commandments, what we do, how we should live, and finally prayer, how we are to respond to God. The book is masterfully documented, indexed, presented. Because of cross references, it is easy to find any topic of doctrine, moral practice, or pious devotion, such as the Rosary, that is a part of the Church's tradition.

The importance and value of this book can be approached in many ways. The book is addressed to Catholics, particularly to bishops. However, it comes from that side of the faith that challenges and informs our intelligence. The faith addresses intelligence as such and supposes that intelligence has problems and unresolved perplexities the answers to which are at least proposed by revelation. In his formal presentation of the *Catechism*, John Paul II said of it, with regard to its audience, that it is

> a gift for everyone: this is what the new catechism is meant to be. In regard to this text, no one should feel a stranger, excluded or distant. In fact, it is addressed to everyone

> because it concerns the Lord of all, Jesus Christ, the one
> who proclaims and is proclaimed, the Awaited, the Teacher
> and the Model of every proclamation. It seeks to respond
> to and satisfy the needs of all those who, in their conscious
> or unconscious search for truth and certitude, seek God....[5]

Clearly everyone, bishops and clergy, as well as laity and non-Catholics, are, in understanding Catholic doctrine, bound to the same standard, that is, to what does the Church, like it or not, say of itself. Likewise, all are bound to the same searching for what human life itself is intended to be and mean.

The Catholic faith, thus, has a peculiar relation to intelligence. First of all, it does not fear intelligence but habitually assumes that faith not only is not contradictory to reason but that it makes intelligence to be, if you will, more intelligent. I sometimes suspect that this blunt claim to truth, including the truth of the particulars of revelation about the nature of God and the purpose of man, is the root reason why the Church is feared and increasingly hated in our times. The fear is that the Church is right on basic positions and that the modern world contains many serious errors which ought in humility to be acknowledged and changed.

This reaction of intolerance and hatred towards the Church's very insistence of stating the truth about itself, of its claim to be true, I think, is, likewise, what lies behind the remarkable statement of Archbishop John Quinn of San Francisco to a group of high school students, a statement worth repeating here at some length:

> If you want to be a Catholic today, you have to be prepared
> to be ridiculed, to see the Pope ridiculed, to see the Mass
> and the Sacraments profaned.... There is no longer room
> for ambiguity. We have to know where we stand and with
> God's help we have to stand firm in the midst of these

---

[5] John Paul II, "Catechism Is Truly a Gift to the Church," *L'Osservatore Romano*, English, December 9, 1992, p. 2.

increasing attacks. The Catholic Church, it should be clear, is the one thing in American society today which is exempt from the rules of fair play and which can be openly ridiculed and held up to contempt. This is no longer possible for any other group in our society: women, ethnic groups, the handicapped, or other religious groups. Only the Catholic Church can be freely and without recrimination made the object of public contempt and ridicule.[6]

This hatred is rooted in the rejection of the order of right living that the Church is bound to uphold against the political enactments of its opposite.

Because the Church claims its teachings to be precisely true and makes a strong, consistent, and intelligent case for itself in all the particulars of life and reason, it challenges at their very core the counter ideologies, religions, and philosophies of our time, particularly the ones that would deny the possibility of truth at all. Whatever be their proper limits, tolerance and compassion have led us to a position where nothing seems true and nothing disordered except the claim to truth itself.

IV

The fact that someone is not a Catholic in belief, moreover, does not mean that he cannot, in any sense, understand what these 2865 articles mean. Anyone can read them and repeat intelligibly what they signify. It is true that stating their meaning as the Church presents it is not the same as belief in them, no more than a correct statement of what Marxism believed or Hinduism held meant that someone, so stating, was a Marxist or a Hindu. The words defining what Catholicism holds are neither unintelligible nor unmeaningful.

---

[6] Archbishop John R. Quinn, Homily to Catholic High School Students, October 7, 1992, *Lay Witness*, 14 (January/February, 1993), 9.

From now on, no one can honestly claim that what the Church teaches about itself on essential points is not known. To state the truth about what Catholicism holds is a matter not of faith but of simple justice and intellectual honesty, binding on everyone, not merely Catholics. The fact that someone thinks that this or that doctrine of the Church is false does not justify an inaccurate statement of this presumably disbelieved teaching. This is elementary, but needs to be emphasized in this context.

The importance of this *Catechism* in this sense, then, its official status, is that it is no longer permissible to misunderstand or misstate what the Church teaches on fundamental points. It is perfectly legitimate to state accurately what the Church says of itself and then to acknowledge one's own failure to comprehend its whole meaning or truth. In its doctrinal and disciplinary canons, the Church has tried to state accurately the position of its own critics and opponents. What is not morally defensible is to state, say, that the Church does not hold the doctrine of purgatory, or the divinity of Christ, or the Assumption of Mary, or the illicitness of contraception, or that only males can be ordained priests.

On an academic level, then, it may be possible for someone to disagree with such positions if he can logically and honestly do so after honest examination. But the reasons given for such disagreement remain public. Consequently, they will be respectfully and carefully tested and argued, in fair intellectual discourse, by the Church itself on grounds of reason. Simply because someone with good or bad will disagrees with a position within Catholicism does not mean that the issue cannot be taken up by Catholic thinkers and examined before the bar of reason common to all men, including those in the Church. The Decree on Religious Liberty of Vatican II meant the freedom to state and present religious and philosophical positions within a society. It did not mean that one is exempt from seeking the truth nor that the Church is not free to respond intelligently to a position contrary to its own.

But it is not all right, not morally all right, for Catholics themselves, particularly for clergy, nor for any one else, for that matter, to maintain that the Church does not teach these things that it does teach, however outrageous they might seem. Someone can be quite embarrassed that the Church might find any given tenet within the body of what it has received to be what it is. So be it. What is not valid, on the basis of this presumed embarrassment, is to suggest that the Church does not teach it.

Looked at from the side of the believer, however, such clarity and order of teaching serve a most valuable purpose. No one today, to recall Archbishop Quinn's remarks above, can really be unaware that the Church's own teachings and doctrines are under severe and increasingly intolerant attack both from within and without the Church. This compendium was intended primarily to take care of the problems within the Church, of problems presented by the preachers and teachers who do not in fact give to the people what the Church teaches, the doctrine that will make them free.

Indeed, reading between the lines, perhaps, I would almost argue that this compendium is primarily intended for those teachers and intellectuals within the Church who have so often been a source of scandal among the faithful and confusion among the non-believers, who have not really themselves accepted the truths contained in the Church. The first line of its own defense for the Church is the effort, made brilliantly here, to be sure that every member of the Church could have the means to know exactly what the Church said about itself on each point on which the Church has taken a stand.

Bishop Christoph Schönborn, the Secretary of the Drafting Commission for the *Catechism*, said of its structure:

> We therefore started with the bases of the faith: what God has revealed, what he himself said, what we cannot know without his revealing it to us. We spoke about the sacred Scriptures, which is the chief source of what God commu-

nicated to us about himself, and about the Tradition of the
Church, which transmits to us what God has revealed.
Finally, we address the faith as man's response to God.[7]

The importance of this statement is that it explains the central
approach of the *Catechism*, its effort to state what the Church
teaches about each of its doctrines, sacraments, or human practices.

V

The *Catechism* is not primarily apologetic or argumentative.
It does not start, like philosophy, from what is most familiar to us
in our experience. What it does is to state clearly what is found in
the deposit of revelation about God. First of all, the inner life of
God, the Trinity, is discussed as we know it in our Creeds. What
is taught about God in the Creeds — the *Catechism* follows the
order of the Apostles' Creed — is itself based on the words and
actions of God found in Scripture.

Next to be treated is the Church and its duties, its sacraments. What flows from what we know of God and our life of
grace is man and his personal response to God in man's own
words and deeds. Thus, the *Catechism* shows why human liberty
and knowledge lead to a consideration of the right ordering of
human life as described in the two great commandments of love
of God and neighbor. This love is made more concrete and
particular in the Ten Commandments and all their ramifications.

Finally a section on prayer completes the book. Prayer is
itself an object of revelation. That is, we are taught how to pray as
if whatever we already know, and this is something, is quite
inadequate when we discover what God is like in His inner life of
the Trinity. We are taught, in other words, how the kind of

---

[7] Christoph von Schönborn, O.P., Interview, *The Catholic World Report*, 2
   (December, 1992), 57.

creatures we are, finite but rational and free, are to respond to God. God takes our own inner lives seriously. The final section of this *Catechism* on prayer is a gem of instruction and reflection on the completion of man's interior life and acts.

Though the Church maintains over and over that Catholics are to live the life of faith in all its particulars, both in word and deed, it does not forget man's fallenness, his sinfulness. Christ came to call sinners. He is not overly surprised that, even with grace, such is what they are, sinners. The fact of continuing human disorder over the centuries and in our own time and lives is not, for the Church, an argument against its truth and necessity, but an argument for them.

While it is true, then, that we can be examples to others if we practice what we believe, we may also, by actually being just and worthy to the best of our abilities, be simultaneously occasions for scandal and rejection to those who will not believe or who do not accept the grace to believe. The lesson of Christ's own life was not that by being incontrovertibly good, everyone immediately chose to imitate Him. Not a few chose to crucify Him. We might be astonished by this, but we cannot deny this was the case.

With some exaggeration, but still with truth, then, we can say that even if no one practices what this *Catechism* teaches about the Church, about what we are to believe, about how we are to live, this personal sinfulness does not change or impugn the truth of what is taught. Indeed, since the consequences of human disorder are generally themselves records of fact and history, we can use this record to show the strong case for the validity of actions or words that do not result in such disorders.

This teaching about truth, about the truth about God and man, is meant for everyone, even for those who do not receive it. It is meant for them as that for which their minds and hearts search. Again without denying the fact that we need God's grace to believe, this body of teaching is not an exclusive possession. It is public knowledge — meant to address every human being, but especially every Catholic. However much or little one may believe some or all of these teachings, still the whole body of doctrine remains a call and a challenge to complete what has been begun. Truth is a whole and cannot be full without the coherent articulation of all its parts.

I read this *Catechism* in light of much criticism, even within the Church, of its particular teachings, criticism that finds these teachings contrary to the modern mind. The main thing that strikes me, however, is the Church's quiet courage in reaffirming what it feels obliged to maintain. Thus, we find the doctrines of angels, hell, and the existence of the Devil to be taught by the Church and to be feasible, plausible teachings not contrary to reason. We find that robbery and divorce are still wrong, as are homosexual acts, however much we might seek to understand why people might indulge in them. We find that Christ is true God and true man. We find He died and rose from the dead. We find a complete treatment of Mary, her place in the Church and in our devotions.

VI

A *Catechism* is also to deal with possible perplexities that have arisen in modern times. Thus, there is a section on the social doctrine of the Church. The family, the state, the economy, war, the international community, and voluntary institutions are treated as intelligible matters of justice, order, and charity. The *Catechism* talks about the state and politics. It leaves great freedom for the different kinds of legitimate states and recognizes that its own task is not political.

Yet, Catholicism also recognizes that the political can touch on many things that reach the essentials of belief and practice. We know that there are states in which Catholics are not allowed freely to practice their religion. This social doctrine recognizes that there are ill-organized states. We know that there are recommended forms of government. Some forms are better than others. The *Catechism* implies that imperfect or oppressive forms ought to be changed, preferably peacefully, but not replaced by something worse.

On the other hand, change in society generally begins not in changes in state structures but in changes in heart and mind. This is why belief and commandment are the first line of defense not only of personal and eternal life but also of political life. The Church has something to say even in the worst states and knows that human souls can be saved in the worst as well as the best states. In other words, what the Church is essentially about is not politics, but the salvation of souls.

No doubt this salvation takes place in existing societies that are not themselves and never will be holy kingdoms. "In a discernment according to the Holy Spirit," we read,

> Christians should distinguish between the growth of the Kingdom of God and the progress of culture and of society where they are engaged together. This distinction is not a separation. The vocation of man to eternal life does not suppress but reinforces man's duty to put into practice the energies and the means received from the Creator for serving justice and peace in the world (#2820).

This statement has the relationship right.

The *Catechism* leaves one with the impression that there is a whole understanding of reality and a whole drama of soul that take place within oneself and in one's immediate world that will not be seen above the surface of politics or economics except perhaps in disordered acts and lives or in unaccountably generous deeds. This interior life is where the real drama of existence takes place. Chances of acting rightly are, for the most part, dependent on believing and understanding rightly.

On the other hand, believing rightly is often a function of acting rightly. So if this *Catechism* takes great pains in dealing with the specific questions of what it means to believe and act rightly in terms of specific actions, intentions, and understandings, it is not because it is trying to "impose" some alien doctrine on us, but because what it is we really want is the truth, even if we reject it. We must be prepared both to understand and receive the truth.

Let me conclude by again stressing the overall consistency that this *Catechism* reveals. We should not underestimate either in ourselves or in others the difficulties we might have with thinking rightly and acting rightly. God exists and has created us for himself. This fact explains the prohibition of false gods we find even in the Commandments. We are reluctant to believe that we can be so important as to be offered precisely eternal life with the Triune God. The alternative to the truths proposed to mankind in this *Catechism* is not something greater but always something less.

Whether God exists and if He does, what is His inner life like, these must be questions each of us ask ourselves. How are we to live? Do we have any guidance in this living? These are becoming ever more pressing problems in the light of the disorders of society and of philosophic trends that insist on basing all human life on our own autonomous wills that are subject to nothing other than themselves.

The *General Catechism* is an alternative to the sort of public and private doctrine we have formed for ourselves without the guidance of revelation and the reason on which it is firmly based. The life and dignity of man found here may be the only real and certainly the most exciting alternative to what exists in the public forum. Catholicism continues to challenge the heart of man with a claim to truth. This claim is no vague or mindless velleity, but an articulate and coherent whole, consistent in each of its parts, not denying reason but inviting it, thriving on it.

This *General Catechism* is then a charter of freedom for individual Catholics seeking to know with clarity what it is they believe about the major issues of time and eternity. But it is also a challenge to all other alternatives, a challenge for them to reexamine their own beliefs and test their consistency and coherence against the results of life itself as well as against the ordered truths found in the Church's remarkable presentation and explanation of itself.

CHAPTER X

The Person From Within:
The Foundations of Social Teachings

I

In the modern world, the alternatives to Catholicism almost always take the form of a social theory or program that promises a radical improvement in the human condition. This projected improvement is to come either through the reform of something outside of the inner soul or will of man, in his institutions or his environment, or through a change in his subjective will with no relation to any objective order. As I have pointed out, there is something logical in such social proposals, both because religion has some particular effect in the world these counter-proposals seek to replace and because the most subtle alternative to God is a counter-city, a City of Man, as St. Augustine called it, something that at first sight will claim to have the power to correct mankind's ills.

John Paul II in his major Address in Santo Domingo quite clearly has understood the import of this issue:

> These days are witnessing a cultural crisis of unheard-of proportions. It is certain that the cultural substratum of the present has a good number of positive values, many of them the result of evangelization; however, at the same

time, it has eliminated basic religious values and introduced deceptive ideas which are not acceptable from the
Christian viewpoint.

The absence of these basic Christian values from modern
culture has not only obscured the transcendent dimension
. . . at the same time, it is a major cause of the social
disenchantment in which this crisis of culture has developed. In line with the autonomy introduced by rational-
ism, today there is a tendency to base values most of all on
subjective social consent which frequently leads to positions which are even contrary to the natural moral law.[1]

The religious values that remain have been cut off from their
spiritual roots. Alternative structures of life come from an
autonomous reason and will subject to nothing but itself.

These types of proposed correction, either restructuring
society or leaving the will no criterion but itself, however, will
always have something mis-placed about them. They will miss
the heart of human dignity and the drama of human choice and its
object wherein all real change in the world ultimately originates.
Here, I want to suggest in general why Catholicism insists that
man does not live by bread alone, even if he needs bread. I want
to show how, in the latest statement of the Church on this issue, the
Encyclical *Centesimus Annus,* this priority is consistently formulated
to take into account both the spiritual and the political and
economic dimensions of man.

During the years I was in Rome, I had the pleasure of
knowing a fellow Jesuit, Roger Heckel, whom the Holy Father
appointed to be the Secretary of the Pontifical Commission on
Justice and Peace. He was an Alsatian, a man who later became a
bishop in Strassbourg. He was unfortunately killed in an automo-
bile accident at a relatively early age. He wrote a number of
brilliant things for the Commission. To begin these considerations

---

[1] John Paul II, "Address to the Bishops of Latin America," October 12, 1992,
   L'Osservatore Romano, English, October 21, 1992, pp. 8-9.

on how we should live, which I think flow naturally from the implications of the *General Catechism*, that is, from a coherent presentation of what the faith holds, I want to cite something from Bishop Heckel as I think he comes close to the heart of how Catholicism looks on the political and social life of man.

"What is true in the reciprocal interaction between the quality of human person and that of institutions is all the more fruitful when we are able to recognize the priority of the ethical and spiritual dimension, human transcendence," Heckel wrote.

> The development of the moral and ethical life, however "seems unfortunately always to be left behind" (*Redemptor Hominis*, #15). This gives rise to the practical urgency, the permanent and fundamental necessity to *strengthen the human person from within*. This is the proper task of the Church whose "social doctrine" takes on life only when it is presented by morally and spiritually mature consciences.[2]

Already here is stressed the emphasis that will be found in every historical document and teaching of Catholicism that the inner life of man causes and shapes the exterior life, including the economic and political life. And there is a "reciprocal" relationship. Good polities will assist this same inner life; bad ones will cause harm. But in no case is man determined by these external orders.

Religion has been called, in a famous phrase, the "opium of the people." But it has also been held to be the "foundation" of public order. In the first case, religion is depicted as a distraction of men from the "important" things that they were called on to do. These important things, it was said, had to do with the construction and reconstruction of the worldly city to be a fit place for human living and habitation. The sources of this fashioning of the human city were said to belong exclusively to man and his own powers. Anything from outside man, including any divine influence, was said to be "alienating."

---

[2] Roger Heckel, S.J., *General Aspects of the Social Catechesis of John Paul II* (Vatican City: Pontifical Commission on Justice and Peace, 1980), p. 19.

In the second case, religion was itself a civic project. It had no transcendent purpose in itself but was seen to be a necessary way to maintain order among those citizens who could not be expected to understand the need for law and order from their own resources. To propitiate the gods, religion substituted among the people for the knowledge of how to rule among the philosophers. Religion in the case of the non-philosopher filled in for what thought or virtue could not do for them. In this sense, religion did not "distract" men from their earthly duties, but incited them to fulfill such obligations even when they did not understand them. The philosophers themselves did not believe in the civic religion itself, but they recognized its civil utility.

II

Political philosophy has long wrestled with its most central question — namely, what is the best regime? But in the best authors, this question was seen to be resolutely answered in a negative fashion. The best regime did not and could not exist as an actual state without refashioning man or submitting him to such a control that human life would be practically impossible. The impossibility of the best city led to the actual or imperfect cities as the real situation of mankind. The most important result of philosophic reflections on the best regime was that politics was essentially "limited." There were things that could not be achieved by politics. There were aspects of man, indeed the highest ones, that transcended the political order. Freedom, in its highest sense, meant the possibility of pursuing these higher things without necessarily neglecting the ordinary things.

The note of all healthy political thinking, consequently, is its abiding awareness of this sense of limitation. Politics ought to be politics, but it ought not to be anything else but itself. Certain things could rightly be done in the political and economic orders, but there were things that could not be achieved. And this implied no defect in politics, but rather implied that it knew its own limitations, knew what it was. When in the Acts of the Apostles (4:19-20), Peter and John were forbidden to preach the Good News, they politely replied that this was one prohibition that the civil authorities did not have within their competence because their message was not limited to nor did it originate in the category of politics.

The uniqueness of the New Testament in political philosophy is not its attention to the things of God. All classic religions and philosophies, all ancient cities, both Jerusalem and Athens, recognized some sort of public due to the divinity, usually manifested in the form of civic liturgies or ceremonies. The New Testament is not, moreover, a treatise in political science or economic doctrine. No doubt, there are things in the New Testament that would cause special attention to be placed on political or economic affairs — we recall that Christ had the apostles pay taxes to Caesar, that St. Paul did not hesitate to use Roman judicial proceedings to defend himself, that the poor were always to be with us.

However, the New Testament is not primarily a teaching about the structure or constitutions of the civil order. It is a teaching about salvation in any political order. St. Paul himself was probably executed under Nero, certainly one of the world's most unlovely rulers, yet he admonished the Romans that all authority, even Nero's such as it was, came from God (13:1-7). We can assume, of course, that St. Paul did not think that Nero was some sort of Platonic philosopher-king. If we wish to examine rule and the forms of rule, the relation of the ruled to the rulers, the nature of citizenship and authority, we do not go to the New Testament, but to the philosophers, to the lawyers, to the experience of men of wisdom, and to practical knowledge.

The purpose of the New Testament then was not to explain the things of Caesar, even while it acknowledged that there were indeed such civic things that it was the purpose of thought and experience to discover. The New Testament did not intend to substitute itself for what man could figure out by himself, though it did imply that there were things even perhaps political things like the true nature of reward and punishment, that men could not ultimately figure out for themselves. The fact that the New Testament does recognize things of Caesar is, indeed, one of its chief claims for its own credibility. But its religious purpose did have the effect of limiting Caesar to those things only that belonged to Caesar, which things were learned primarily from experience and the philosophers.

If the purpose of the New Testament was to teach man about his ultimate, not political, destiny, it did not imply that there was no connection whatsoever between these two purposes. The New Testament treated man as a whole in which all human actions and deeds fit together, including man's relation to God and to the polity. Aristotle had already distinguished between contemplative happiness and political happiness. For Aristotle, the civil society did have a legitimate purpose and form, the ultimate purpose of which was to enable men eventually to participate in those things that belonged properly to philosophy.

The active virtues were required, moreover, for the contemplative ones, but both were proper to man's condition. It was in this contemplative life, that Aristotle held was more divine than human, however, that the higher questions of the immortality of the soul and the transcendent nature of man resided. It was to these questions that revelation primarily addressed itself so that in defining their proper nature, man was freed from the temptation of building his own heaven on earth by his own powers. In this sense, the doctrine of the resurrection of the body completes questions asked but unanswered by political living and philosophy.

"One cannot revolt against God without revolting against reason," Eric Voegelin has written.[3] It has been the Catholic

---

[3] Eric Voegelin, *Autobiographical Reflections*, Edited by Ellis Sandoz (Baton Rouge: Louisiana State University Press, 1989), p. 76.

tradition in social thought, following Aquinas, that there is a right order of things that includes revelation and reason, the one supports and understands the other. The disordered political society — and there are many forms of disorder of soul and polity — may in fact be the sort of actual state in which most real men, most of the time, have ever lived.

Utopia, as St. Augustine realized, is not a Christian concept, yet it brings up the question of the exact location of the highest things even when they cannot be achieved in this world. We will never have perfect political order, though, to be sure, some political orders will be better or worse than others. It is important, even religiously important, to know these differences and their consequences.

Salvation in the Catholic sense can be found and achieved in any existing political order, even the worst one. Likewise, it is quite possible to lose one's soul in the best and most just of historically existing political societies. Catholicism is not "individualistic" in the rigid philosophic sense, but it does teach that we are responsible for our souls even when salvation is a gift. Political and economic life in this sense is not therefore frivolous, not something that makes no difference to our ultimate good and goal.

Moreover, there is no "collective" salvation that ultimately would place our transcendent fate on the shoulders of some corporate being. The great modern political heresy from Rousseau is to postulate that our ills lie in the structures or systems and not, as St. Augustine following the teaching of Genesis, knew, in our souls, in our wills. E.F. Schumacher has written in this regards:

> Some people are no longer angry when told that *restoration must come from within*; the belief that everything is "politics" and that radical rearrangement of the "system" will suffice to save civilization is no longer held with the same fervor as it was even twenty-five years ago.[4]

---

[4] E.F. Schumacher, *A Guide for the Perplexed* (New York: Harper Colophon, 1977), p. 138.

This abiding truth that the reform of the polity attends the reform of the soul was found in the *City of God* and remains a basic truth for the understanding of Christian thought about the greater public order. It is also the ultimate grounding for the familiar Christian teaching that even in economic or social matters, everyone should seek to do what he is capable of doing.

In his Puebla Address, John Paul II wrote:

> The Church's action in earthly matters such as human advancement, development, justice, the rights of the individual, is always intended to be at the service of man; and of man as she sees him in the Christian vision of the anthropology that she adopts. She therefore does not need to have recourse to ideological systems in order to love, defend and collaborate in the liberation of man: at the center of the message of which she is the depository and herald she finds inspiration for acting in favor of brotherhood, justice, and peace, against all forms of domination, slavery, discrimination, violence, attacks on religious liberty and aggression against man, and whatever attacks life.[5]

What John Paul II said here was that Catholicism at its center contained its own revelational resources for dealing with what man is in his dignity, for understanding what violated this same dignity. However much reason and experiential politics may go wrong, these revelational sources remain true and intact for their own purposes, purposes that indirectly at least also serve the order found in reason.

III

That there is an ultimate correspondence between this revelational teaching in so far as it touches human conduct in this

---

[5] John Paul II, Puebla, January 28, 1979, III, 2.

world and what good men have learned is the classic doctrine that faith and reason do not contradict each other. On the other hand, these are not exactly the same sources except in the sense that both arise, though in different ways, from the same transcendent source. It is quite possible to have religious presence in quite disordered societies, to draw even in such dire places order and inspiration from prayer, suffering, and penance. Change in disordered societies will seldom be easy or rapid, and must begin and continue at the deepest levels of human personhood. This is also the teaching of the best philosophers like Plato and Aristotle who do deal with both the order of the soul and the order of polity.

For Catholicism, freedom of religion has meant, among other things, the freedom to teach its own doctrines and receive its own sacraments in any civil polity. The twentieth century has been unique in that it is the first century to develop political systems that claim and enforce complete control of man including control of his beliefs and his thoughts. Catholicism has seen, as have many philosophers and men of common sense, that this claim implies that politics is its own justification.

This position means that in modern thought, there is a claim to be able to explain all the disorders in society and establish a perfect order depending on nothing other than man's own powers. From the very beginning of its existence, Catholicism has been confronted with the idolatry of the state. What is unique in modern times is both the powers available to the state to enforce its idolatrous claim and the intellectual apparatus to make it plausible.

The practice of Catholicism, thus, finds itself involved with the modern state at two levels. On the one level, it is a teaching of the limits of man, limits that conform with his being, but limits that do not deny man's essential goodness or his mission to use all his powers, including his political ones, to establish a more human civilization. Secondly, there can be and are many civil orders that display a wide variety of form and ethical priorities. In itself, this diversity is not bad but something to be expected and encouraged.

While Catholicism is realistically concerned with the right ordering of the civil order, this right ordering is not its basic task. Its primary task concerns those things that are revealed to it about man's nature, destiny, and the spiritual ways to reach his salvation. Politics in this sense can utterly fail, while man can succeed. The members of the ultimate City of God or City of Man, as St. Augustine taught, can come from any existing civil society.

The basic Catholic teaching about politics lies in the phrase in the New Testament that admonishes men to "seek first the Kingdom of God." This priority is by no means in conflict with the love of neighbor. But it is a priority that limits politics. A politics that is not limited to its own competency is a politics that rivals the Kingdom of God and offers men a choice between itself and God. The seriousness with which we must take this possible claim of the state to substitute itself for God is manifested in many areas —in law, in attitudes to life, in understanding human enterprise, in the undermining of the family.

The great Protestant theologian Oscar Cullmann wrote in this regard:

> The Church's task with regard to the State, which is posed for all time, is thus clear. First it must loyally give the State everything necessary to its existence. It has to oppose anarchy and all Zealotism within its own ranks. Second, it has to fulfill the office of watchman over the State. That means: it must remain in principle critical toward every State and be ready to warn it against transgression of its legitimate limits. Third, it must deny to the State which exceeds its limits whatever such a State demands that lies within the province of religio-ideological excess; and in its preaching the Church must courageously describe this excess as opposition to God.[6]

---

[6] Oscar Cullmann, *The State in the New Testament* (New York: Scribner's, 1956), pp. 90-91.

The limits of the civil society, therefore, are precisely that, "limits." That is, there are legitimately things that belong to the state and things that do not.

Finally, neither the state nor the Church exist for themselves. Each has its own dignity and organizational structure. Yet, each is designed to serve its own defined purpose. The state is in this sense natural; it is something that arises out of man's very being what he is. The Church is established for a supernatural purpose, to achieve in each person what cannot be achieved by man's own powers. While the state can and has posed as a substitute for the divine, this is an aberration, not the normal face of the civil power; but both state and religion minister to man's destiny, to his individual destiny that is a dramatic relation to the divinity, to God.

Catholic thought about politics, then, places man within the normal institutions of human life, family, state, society, religion. Each of these minister not to himself but to God. Each member of any polity is ultimately to choose to be a member of the Kingdom of God or to refuse so to choose. No civil power can change this deep drama that goes on in any and every civil order. The foundations of Catholic social teachings, then, "strengthen the person from within" both for the civil order and for that Kingdom of God to which each person is called in whatever civil society he might happen to live, in whatever era of human history.

IV

How does this position about the primacy of the spiritual fit into the latest understanding of Catholicism about itself and the social condition of the world? When the 1987 social Encyclical, *Sollicitudo Rei Socialis*, was published, I was very concerned about it. I felt at the time that the Holy Father had missed one of the great opportunities of the century. Finally, at a crucial moment, he had the occasion to remedy what was most lacking in Catholic social thought, namely, its failure to recognize the relation between wealth-production and the sort of basic social disorders the Papacy had criticized since the beginning of the modern era, since *Rerum Novarum,* in fact.[7] But, as I saw it, *Sollicitudo Rei Socialis* failed to meet this challenge and in fact seemed to be a step backward.

Fundamentally, as Lord Bauer had pointed out in a biting essay on the dangerous inadequacies of "ecclesiastical economics" at the time of Paul VI, the apparent re-distributionist bias of the thinking in papal social doctrine should have been rejected on empirical as well as on moral grounds. Redistributionism is the theory that a finite amount of goods exists in the world so that what one person or country has implies that someone else must lose by the same amount. The theory is in many ways attractive, but it is quite false as a fact. To solve the modern problem of poverty, it is said, we must redistribute existing wealth politically, not create new wealth.

But in fact, this re-distributionist theory was not the solution to dire problems but the cause of further poverty and, in addition, of much tyranny, however good may have been the subjective intentions of those who promoted it, including the papacy.[8] Rather than seeking to understand how and why wealth is produced, papal thinking seemed rather to suggest that the problem was one of greed and the failure of the political order. The ecclesial analysis, in other words, seemed to embrace modern theories of world order that were anything but solutions to the problems the papacy itself wanted confronted.

In contemporary ideological analysis, the so-called maldistribution of the world's goods seemed to be explained in terms

---

[7] See James V. Schall, "John Paul II's *Sollicitudo Rei Socialis,*" *Religion, Wealth, and Poverty* (Vancouver, BC: The Fraser Institute, 1990), pp. 149-70.

[8] Lord Peter Bauer, "Ecclesiastical Economics: Envy Legitimized," *Reality and Rhetoric: Studies in the Economics of Development* (Cambridge: Harvard University Press, 1984), pp. 73-89.

of envy by the poor alongside the moral corruption of those economic systems that did in fact produce existing wealth in the modern world. The result of such a theory was that instead of examining the many cultural, political, economic, and especially religious causes of why the poor were poor, the poor were told that they were poor because they were exploited by the rich, by those who knew how to produce wealth.

As a result of this analysis, the poor need not learn how to produce wealth but instead they should insist, even violently, that what was rightfully "theirs," on the basis of some exploitation theory, be "returned" to them. Such theories not only proved statistically impossible — the world needs more wealth, not a redistribution of existing wealth — but justified decades of wasted energy and effort by the poor peoples themselves seeking a false solution to their own problems and blaming theories that did work to solve their own problems.

The world was seen, furthermore, to be divided between North and South, the rich and the poor. The most important thing was the "gap" between rich and poor and not, as in fact is the case, the gradual increase of wealth on the part of everyone. The solution to this problem of poverty, however, was not through the ideological systems often chosen by the poor nations themselves to be their models of development, rather it was to be found in the success of the rich.

But this success was not primarily an exploitation or an injustice. It consisted in learning new ways of production and distribution that depended on intelligence, enterprise, and work, methods that did not in principle take away anything from anyone. These new methods proceeded from what exists, through the most basic of resources, human knowledge and skill, to fashion new wealth. This approach was the real key for helping the poor, a key that often seemed to be understood everywhere better than in the Church.

Many activist tendencies in the Church, such as liberation theology, "gapism," and the newly present and worrisome uncritical appearance of ecological rhetoric in ecclesiastical circles seemed to reinforce this suspicion that the Church was going in the wrong direction. But if the Church really wanted to achieve what it claimed that it wanted, namely, a free, limited society that was guided by principles of justice and generosity, it needed to understand and support a productive, expansive, and efficient economy that could actually make the poor rich, if given a chance.

It is not that John Paul II himself did not at times show great sympathy for certain elements of the free market system. But such rather uncritical notions as "options for the poor," or "consumerism," or a kind of bias against profit in his writings and speeches seemed to strike at the very roots of any positive system that might be able to meet the needs of mankind in behalf of which the Pope so eloquently witnessed wherever he travelled.

Much attention thus was given to the poor countries, not to the successful economies after World War II. The so-called "Fourth World," the least developed countries, received more sympathy than these oriental countries like Japan or Taiwan or Korea, lands with far fewer natural resources than many of the so-called poorest countries. These Far Eastern countries graphically showed that nations could pass rapidly from poverty to wealth during the same period that concerned clerics and other secular idealists were complaining about the poor being exploited by the rich.

There is nothing wrong with calling attention to extremes of poverty, of course. John Paul II's important Encyclical *Centesimus Annus* (1991) did this as do all Encyclicals. But in this new reflection of the Church on its understanding of man's action in the world, the whole problematic and tenor of this attention were significantly shifted away from the re-distributionist context about which I had been concerned. The very meaning of "options for the poor" need no longer be ideological in overtones but directed instead to the real possibilities for a poor people to overcome their own problems with the intelligent aid of those who know how to produce wealth in the first place.

V

Before I remark on what is so right about this extraordinary Encyclical, an understanding of which seems essential to understand the insightfulness of Catholicism itself, let me first call attention to a number of points that I still have problems with, this in the name and spirit of what John Paul II has been trying to do. John Paul II is the most extraordinary and intelligent of men. There has been no one quite like him in the modern era, a holy, wise man who has spoken to more political and intellectual leaders in the world than any man in history, surpassed only by the numbers of ordinary and poor people who have sought out and listened to his words. It can be argued that the decline and fall of the Marxist states are due more to him than to any other man or source.

To acknowledge what the Pope did requires recognition of spiritual forces at work in the civil order. Thus, the spiritual and religious roots from which the Pope comes remain alien to the liberal premises of the modern era. These premises are at a deep level often the same ones from which Marxism arose in the first place. Many of these secular forces are also very present in the Church itself in a form that seeks to transform the Church into an instrument for the achievement of the ends of the remaining ideologies of our era.

These premises of modernity, just to put them on the table, maintain that the "whole truth about man," to use the Pope's memorable phrase in exactly the opposite way that he does, is that man is the cause of his own being.[9] Freedom is autonomy. There is no natural order to which man is subject. Freedom is creating one's own life, family, polity, world, on the basis of one's sole choices, themselves presupposed to nothing but themselves. Man is to take total control of what he is and makes. If there are some

---

[9] See *The Whole Truth about Man: John Paul II to University Students and Faculties*, Edited by James V. Schall (Boston: St. Paul Editions, 1981).

so-called "limits" in nature, these restrictions merely serve, in the ecological wing of this position, to justify the subsumption of man into the ongoing process either of state or of nature.

No individual purpose exists beyond this life that would question man's ability to refashion and reconstruct himself against any so-called natural standards or norms that would prescribe or guide him in his normal activities to the purpose of his existence. Any effort to claim that the human being cannot will what he wants is looked upon as fanatical. There are no norms to democracy or to human nature other than those that man gives himself. Needless to say, a Pope who maintains eloquently and persistently that this sort of understanding of human nature and freedom is not at all its "whole truth" will be seen as anything from a Polish "reactionary" to a religious "enthusiast." That he is neither represents the most fundamental spiritual crisis for many Catholics and Christians, for many intellectuals and critics today.

Let me remark on a number of aspects of this document that strike me as weak or ill-argued. I call attention to these things not to seem more "wise" than the Pope, but to engage in that persistent duty we all have to argue clearly and objectively for what is true, all the time acknowledging that other understandings might be better than ours. These concerns are considered here under the understanding in the Encyclical of the notions of work, of rights, and of ecology.

The first issue has to do with the emphasis the Holy Father gives to "work." My problem with what John Paul II says about work, already present in the Pope's Encyclical *Laborem Exercens*, goes back to Josef Pieper who was at pains to reflect on the meaning of work and contemplation. Pieper insisted that there was something Marxist in the notion of "intellectual work."[10] This issue itself goes back to the Greeks and the problem of slavery, to the relation of art or craft to human society. The Pope is most

---

[10] Josef Pieper, *Leisure: The Basis of Culture* (New York: Mentor, 1963).

concerned to dignify the worker. Again and again, he insists that in every industry or business, the most important thing is the worker and his family. The worker is more important than profit or material goods. Moreover, the Pope realizes that there is a kind of proportional dignity among all men no matter what kind of work they do.

In this Encyclical, John Paul II has begun to recognize what people like George Gilder and Peter Bauer have long emphasized, that the real wealth in the world today is not goods but knowledge. This very convergence necessarily takes us back to the Greek discussion of practical and theoretical knowledge and their relationship. Likewise, it forces us to realize again that one of the major reasons for the disappearance of slavery was the Industrial Revolution and all that went with it in terms of machinery and organization. Aristotle had already implied that much work was drudgery, and if it could be replaced by the moving Statues of Daedalus, say to weave cloth, it would be a boon for mankind (*Politics*, 1253b 35). It is not without interest that the weaving of cloth was the first large scale industry of the Industrial Revolution, and it still remains one of the most important industries for human well being.

With the invention of the computer and electronics, the possibility of placing into each man's hands powerful tools of inventiveness has been increased a thousand-fold, something someone like G.K. Chesterton had long wanted to see happen. The point I am trying to make here is that the emphasis on "work" that the Pope insists on seems too much to separate the work and the worker from what in fact the worker does or produces. By emphasizing rather knowledge and enterprise, something the Pope begins to do in the Encyclical, I think it will be possible to restore the distinction between work and contemplation that Pieper sees at the heart of civilization.

The problem is not solved, it seems to me, by calling what the highest activities consist in as "work." What the Pope wants to do is, no doubt, most laudable. He wants to show how each man leads a worthy life by his work. The question still must be asked, "is this work worth it?" By failing to ask this question, we can in principle justify governments that simply "make work" by legislation, or by bureaucracy, or by whatever classical means.

The Pope speaks of the worker so much and so earnestly because he wants a system whereby one's work is really contributing to man's well-being and at the same time offers a means to support a family. This sort of economy, of course, is what the Holy Father is seeking to get at in this Encyclical. What is noticeable is that, while he insists on the need for voluntary societies, he never addresses himself to the more recent questions of the widespread phenomenon of labor union corruption or of the real economic and social necessity of unions themselves. In other places in Catholic social thought, the problem of union corruption, political and criminal, has been reservedly acknowledged. But the widespread decline of unions, their often counter-productivity regarding questions of just prices and contribution of other producers, are not mentioned.

A second major problem that seems to continue in this document, as it has in the major papal documents, is that of the meaning of the word "right." Nowhere in *Centesimus Annus* does there appear to be any reservation about the origins or use of this concept. It is assumed that everyone knows what a "right" is. It is universally acknowledged to be a good thing to promote. "Rights," however, are a product of modernity. If we want to make them concepts from say Aristotle or St. Thomas, we have to undertake the most careful of analysis about their meaning. "Rights" are philosophical words, words that are rooted in a system of thought very alien to the sort of concerns the Pope has in mind in using them.

Clearly "rights" are, at first sight, familiar concepts, used in public documents from the beginning of the modern era. They are found in the American and French documents, in the League of Nations, in the United Nations, in almost every civil constitution. Yet, they are rooted in a system of pure will, presupposed to no natural order. Again and again in recent times, we begin to find that there are "rights" to all sorts of things that are quite incompatible with Christian and natural law teachings.

Conflicts of "rights" now have been transformed into the "duty" of the state to protect the exercise of sundry human disorders. A glowing praise of man's "rights" ends up in wondering how we can oppose a "right" to an abortion, or a "right" to a deviant life style. Moreover, "rights" to work or to housing, economic rights, in other words, have tended to embody the very socialist ideology that has failed. In any case, the point I want to make here is that it is not sufficient to use the doctrine of "rights" without in every case clearly identifying what is meant by them and how they are justified. As they are used in Catholic social thought, I am afraid, they often tend to imply notions quite at variance with what is in fact desired.

A further worry in this Encyclical is the discussion on ecology, itself another potential ideology of the modern era. The Holy Father seems to give little warning about the intellectual background of much of the environmental and ecological movement that is so opposed to many of the very ends that he is proposing. It is not sufficient to say that ecology simply represents a delayed awareness of the limits of the earth and man's greed or lack of control.

Ecology is if anything closer to a new religion that has premises and ends that subsume the individual person back into nature. The anti-growth element of the environmental movement is also an anti-human aspect. Thus far, I see no indication that this side of ecology is understood in its relation to the Church's own teachings and interests, nor do I see the sort of questioning of the validity of the thesis of the movement itself.[11]

---

[11] See Julian Simon, *The Ultimate Resource* (Princeton: Princeton University Press, 1981); Max Singer, *Passage to a Human World* (Indianapolis: Hudson Institute, 1987); James V. Schall, *Human Dignity and Human Numbers* (Staten Island: Alba House, 1971).

VI

If these are some concerns that I have with this document, they are nothing compared with the enthusiasm I have for the extraordinary insights and acknowledgments that have appeared in Catholic social thought as a result of John Paul II's Encyclical. Suffice it to say that it has appeared to many that Christianity would eventually identify itself with socialism. The so-called moral "force" of socialism is apparently very attractive to many religious people who see in the ordinary workings of economy or politics a kind of escapism or self-interest.

Likewise, socialism has appeared to be an ideal way to unify religious and political energies to improve the world. In retrospect, we must be most respectful to the good sense of the Church, beginning with Leo XIII, as John Paul II duly noted, to see in this system ideas and tendencies most at odds with Christian and human understandings of man.

We cannot exactly say that Catholicism has rejected socialism with this Encyclical. Rather we must say that, granting the failures of socialism itself, the Church has finally been able to set aside the century-old obligation of weighing socialist-capitalist claims in tandem to arrive at some sort of middle ground. Without denying its critique of the performance of capitalism, and not forgetting the liberal theory in which it was based, a theory so much criticized by the Church in the last century, we find here a frank acknowledgment that socialism has failed on its own terms as witnessed by events in Eastern Europe.

As a result there is a new look at the theory and practice of those free market economies that have proved their ability to know about the production of an abundance of goods and services, in fact relatively well-distributed within their confines. Since the Church wants poverty confronted, since it wants this confrontation to be done justly and with the interest and cooperation of the workers and the poor, it has had to acknowledge, as did the socialist systems themselves, that there are certain ways that must be employed if mankind is to meet its economic problems.

These ways can be known and imitated, but they must include a juridical system, profit, enterprise, knowledge, exchange, a market, voluntary organizations, a relatively independent economy, private property, and respect for work and excellence.

The Pope proudly notices that the beginning of this crisis of the Marxist states began in Poland with the workers movement. But behind this he sees deeper forces. He takes time to recognize that there was a relationship between modern totalitarian ideology that embraced socialism and carried it to its extremes and its corresponding attack on certain theological and religious notions, beginning with the belief in God. The Pope's analysis of totalitarianism is remarkable in this document. He does not hesitate to maintain that atheism does have political overtones and can result in the most extreme forms of political rule. He does not limit this effect only to admittedly totalitarian regimes of our era. He knows that certain democratic theories of relativism have the same premises as the more extreme theories.

The Pope argues as a result that the basic liberty is that of religion. To acknowledge the reality and force of the transcendent God is the beginning of specifically human freedom. He sees in this direct relationship of man and God the only real power that limits the state from claiming with modernity complete autonomy or power over each man. One of the most striking aspects of *Centesimus Annus*, then, is not its calling religious people to do their duty to the world, though it does this also, but its calling the world to recognize and allow certain relationships to God. The Pope even remarks, rather severely, on those states with established religions — he is thinking of Islamic states, no doubt — that in practice allow no freedom of religion to their citizens either in theory or practice.

VII

If the first unique aspect of this Encyclical is its analysis of the real problem with totalitarianism, the second unique aspect is its willingness to accept the general principles of a market economy.

The Pope insists that there are always many dangers of greed, selfishness, and materialism in this market system. No one needs to deny his point to recognize that he also calls attention to what have become commonplaces among those who have sought to understand how modern societies develop their material bases.

Ever since the Tawney and Weber studies of the relationship of Protestantism and Capitalism, it has been a suspicion that Catholicism was somehow unable to understand the principles that caused the modern scientific, economic, and technological revolutions to take place. Catholic countries were said to be poor because they paid too much emphasis on morality and to the next world. As a result the people wasted time in religion better spent in working. It would be too much to say that this Encyclical is a belated recognition of certain elements in the Reformation, those having to do with a vocation in this world, of hard work, of savings, of sobriety. None the less, all of these things are now present in this document.

The third and final thing that seems to be unique in this Encyclical is the Pope's blunt and frank statement that man cannot achieve his inner-worldly goods or goals without Christianity. One has to know a good deal about the tendencies in modern academia and modern philosophy to realize the importance and radicalness of this aspect of *Centesimus Annus*. We Americans, perhaps, are so used to the exaggerations of our rhetoric on the separation of church and state that we are not prepared to recognize that this separation has something very unnatural about it. But the Pope is not talking about the legal or constitutional principle of how to deal with religion in a civil society. Rather he is dealing with the unity of man in all his aspects, faith and reason, this world and the next, morals and economics.

The Pope takes great care to stress that man's eternal destiny is at stake in any civil society, even in a totalitarian one. Indeed, he suggests that this over-riding concern with ultimate things is just what has happened in Eastern Europe and Russia. On the other hand, the Kingdom of God is not identified with any earthly society. Nevertheless, and this is the point, it does make a difference what we believe and do. Faith is one of the main sources of our doing and making rightly. What exists among us is not just our polities or our philosophies, but grace and faith. Whatever we might say about tolerance and understanding others, it is not fanaticism to say that Catholicism is different and needed to understand what we ought to do.

Perhaps nothing in the modern world drives more people to extremes than the simple and classic religious claim that God did become Man and that this has changed the meaning and history of the world in all its aspects. The emphasis of the Holy Father in this Encyclical is simply factual or historical, however we might designate it. Let me, in conclusion, cite three remarks of John Paul II in this regard. They are cited in the context of the remarkable efforts he has made to know what is going on in the world and to acknowledge the truths of many social, economic, and political facts that have recently come to the fore, facts that have been rooted in experience and practical intelligence.

1) To teach and to spread her social doctrine pertains to the Church's evangelizing mission and is an essential part of the Christian message, since this doctrine points out the direct consequences of that message in the life of society and situates daily work and struggles for justice in the context of bearing witness of Christ the Savior. This doctrine is likewise a source of unity and peace in dealing with the conflicts which inevitably arise in social and economic life. Thus it is possible to meet these new situations without degrading the human person's transcendent dignity, either in oneself or in one's adversaries, and to direct those situations towards just solutions (#5).

2) We need to repeat that *there can be no genuine solution of the 'social question' apart from the Gospel*, and that the 'new things' can find in the Gospel the context for their correct understanding and the proper moral perspective for judgment on them (#5).

3) In order that the demands of justice may be met, and attempts to achieve this goal may succeed, what is needed is *the gift of grace*, a gift which comes from God. Grace, in cooperation with human freedom, constitutes that mysterious presence of God in history which is Providence. The newness which is experienced in following Christ demands to be communicated to other people in their concrete difficulties, struggles, problems and challenges, so that these can then be illuminated and made more human in the light of faith. Faith not only helps people to find solutions; it makes even situations of suffering humanly bearable, so that in these situations people will not become lost or forget their dignity and vocation (#59).

These statements, if I read them correctly, maintain that human social and ethical problems can be understood and resolved in peace, that grace and faith are also necessary to incite men to act properly and to understand fully what their nature and situation demand, and that when all else fails that faith remains attentive to the final reality and destiny of each human person even in suffering and loss.

The tradition of Catholic Social Doctrine, which John Paul II has reflected on and advanced is not merely a philosophical analysis of moral principles, though it is at least that. Nor is it a claim to have something merely beyond the world, though it also claims that. Rather it is a description of the presence of God in the world, in the world of principles as well as in the world of suffering, in the world of production as well as in the world of distribution. The capacity to see the needs of mankind over time, to refine, revise, clarify a full human understanding is the remarkable and unique fruit of *Centesimus Annus*. Does Catholicism still exist? The explication of its doctrines includes an explanation of the world. The person from within, the person who understands that he must be first related to God, is the same person who dwells and acts in existing cities.

CHAPTER XI

American Spirituality

I

C atholicism by its own understanding of itself has a claim, a spiritual claim, to be present in each culture and civilization not merely for the transcendent purposes for which it exists but also, in the light of this purpose, to address the culture in truth about itself. St. Augustine had stated well this priority and relationship:

> Wherefore Thou sayest not, 'Let man be made,' but Let us make man. Nor saidst Thou, 'according to his kind'; but, after our image and likeness. For man being renewed in his mind, and beholding and understanding Thy truth, needs not man as his director, so as to follow after his kind; but by Thy direction proveth what is that good, that acceptable, and perfect will of Thine . . . (*Confessions*, XIII).

I have suggested throughout these reflections that a growing divergence between modern culture and Catholicism exists, particularly in American culture as it separates itself from the classical and Christian principles of its founding. But it remains worthy still to ask whether the peculiar nature of American spirituality and Catholicism are compatible such that the growing alienation of Catholicism and American culture is also a departure of the culture itself from its own origins.

Catholicism, while it recognizes that certain similar elements found in itself also exist in other philosophies, religions, or sects, has maintained that there is only one faith, one Church. A wholeness or completeness surrounds belief and practice. To be itself, Catholicism must maintain itself, must recognize with a certain calm objectivity that certain beliefs, practices, and systems do not correspond to its own self-understanding, to what has constituted its own uniqueness.

Within the Church itself, no doubt, we find differing religious or spiritual traditions. A wide variety of ways to practice the counsels, many differing methods of prayer, many varying sorts of charity directed to the good of others exist within Catholicism. We have active and contemplative orders; we find congregations of men and women devoted to almost every aspect of the human enterprise from education to hospitals to aiding the poor, from visiting prisoners to comforting the lonely.

Still but one true belief or doctrine is recognized, one Mass, one worship of the One Triune God. In the end, the great philosopher Thomas Aquinas and the humblest peasant believe the same thing. It is, to be sure, correct to speak of French or Brazilian "spirituality," or "Jesuit" or "Benedictine" piety but only to the extent that this spirituality or piety maintains contact with the faith itself through the Church with its unity in Peter. Unity in the Church cannot be manifest except through variety, yet the unity remains central.

We are, in fact, without being accused of current relativistic "multi-culturalism," prepared to find lines of a valid spiritual life in Calvinism, in Buddhism, in Muslim books, or in Hindu poetry. These sorts of prayer or devotion or works must still be "discerned" and evaluated. Catholic spirituality has always recognized the abiding possibility of a move of the inner soul away from God toward the self, a move that must be sorted out, defined, acknowledged, and counteracted. Spirituality, consequently, could never be entirely devoid of an intelligible content that reflected Catholicism's precise understanding of what was handed down to it from the beginning.

In recent years, we have heard some talk of an "American Church." But this expression, though it can have a correct connotation, as I shall indicate, usually has the hint of a schismatic or heretical Church. The "American" Church is conceived in opposition to the Roman Church somehow. It rejects or wants to reject one or the other of the basic tenets or practices of the faith as it is given to us. It wants a Catholicism plus contraception, or plus abortion, or minus the authority of the Papacy, or minus the Creed.

Here, however, I wish to use the term "American spirituality" rather in the orthodox sense, analogous to the way we might speak of "Spanish spirituality" or "Byzantine spirituality." I want to inquire what if anything might be an American contribution to spirituality? But I understand that this contribution, whatever it is, is something that is potentially open to and possible for all believers, not just Americans, and this even though they not be obliged to and need not choose to practice its particular approach. That is, without there being any essential difference of doctrine or sacrament or Scripture, are there any signs that American spirituality is identifiable?

Strictly speaking, this spirituality would mean that just as everyone does not have to be a Dominican or a Franciscan, so neither does everybody have to be an American or a German. Indeed, we can say without fear of contradiction that in the history of the Church, only a small minority of its members were either Americans or Germans, Franciscans or Dominicans. Still the spiritual tradition of each Order or country brings out, emphasizes, or deepens some neglected aspect of the wholeness of the faith. It almost seems to imply that the whole of mankind is necessary to bring forth the riches of the entire faith to itself. Indeed, this universality may be the reason we are told as something essential to the missionary nature of the Church to "go forth and teach all nations" (Mark 16:15).

In the Gospel of Luke (2:1), we are told that Christ came into the world during the reign of Augustus Caesar, "when the whole world was at peace." There seems to be something about the relation of God and man that takes into account the conditions in which men find themselves in their own regimes. We do not have to develop a thesis on how good the Roman Empire was on the basis of the fact that Christ was born within its confines, nor even from the fact that Christ at His trial acknowledged Pilate's, that is, Roman authority (John 19:11). In the context of American spirituality, we can at least be aware that differing national customs and attitudes are themselves capable of being used by God and that God's activity is not found totally apart from the ways of men in the world.

II

In a remarkable testimony, Mikhail S. Gorbachev wrote of his correspondence and contact with John Paul II. He acknowledged that no one has played a more crucial role in the transformation of Marxism than this Slavic Pope. The former Russian leader was sensitive to the Pope's political and intellectual influence, but "what I have always held in high esteem about the Pope's thinking and ideas is their spiritual content, their striving to foster the development of a new world civilization."[1] By any standard, of course, this is a remarkable statement.

Considering its source, such remarks from the Russian leader seem, in retrospect, almost miraculous. I cite this passage here both in the context of the difficulties many Americans have had

---

[1] Mikhail S. Gorbachev, "My Partner, the Pope," *The New York Times*, March 9, 1992.

grasping this spirituality of the Holy Father, a difficulty evidently not shared by Mr. Gorbachev. I cite it also by contrast to stress the Holy Father's extraordinary appreciation of what the unique American contributions to and difficulties about such spirituality are.

Though, wherever he is, he almost always speaks over the heads of his critics to go directly to the people, the fact is that the intelligentsia, along with many segments of the clergy and media, have frequently been hostile to John Paul II. No one in modern history, however, has talked to more ordinary people or cultural leaders throughout the world than this Pope. We have not seen anyone like him in centuries, if ever. Something providential seems to hover about John Paul II, almost as if we do not deserve him. The world is being treated especially kindly, it sometimes seems, because of this good and intelligent man on the Throne of Peter. It has been widely surmised that the Bulgarian Secret Police were behind the failed attempt to kill him. His only response was to recover quietly, to thank Our Lady of Fatima at his next opportunity to visit there, and finally to forgive the man who tried to kill him.

In his weekly speeches, in his Encyclicals and letters, John Paul II has literally re-explained brilliantly and clearly the whole of Christian doctrine from the Trinity to Redemption to the Church, to social doctrine, to the sacraments, to the missions, to moral theology, to the importance of the family. On looking at any curriculum in most Catholic high schools or universities, or at the sermons in most parishes, however, it would almost appear that this material does not exist. It is seldom read, touched on, understood, or preached. It is almost as if we have closed souls, afraid of the fact that we may just have the most remarkable man in centuries in the Papal Office, a man who is talking to everyone but ourselves.

Gorbachev remarked that he and the Pope could understand each other much better because both were Slavs. Yet, if John Paul II is not well understood and appreciated, it is not, I suspect, because so few of us are Slavs. To misunderstand or misinterpret John Paul II, I think, we mostly have to will to do so. We have to want not to hear what he says and stands for. We have to understand that to recognize anything truly good, we have to will to understand and love it. There is no other way. The good, particularly incarnate good, is always somehow also itself a sign of contradiction (Luke 2:35).

III

Many have called John Paul II's latest social Encyclical, *Centesimus Annus*, a kind of "American" Encyclical.[2] To be sure, John Paul II does not hesitate to point out things still wrong with attitudes or systems that might prevent human beings from living a fuller life. He is always warning against something called "consumerism." When I hear this rather unfortunate word, it always makes me think of going into any supermarket and buying one of each of everything I see there.

Yet, if we ultimately want to help the poor, to produce and to distribute what we need and want throughout the world, we want an economy in which such efficient and remarkable institutions as supermarkets can exist. We want "consumers" who create a demand that needs to be met by work, production, and distribution at a reasonable cost and profit. Jobs, work, production, distribution, well-being depend on a market open to consumers who can freely decide what is needed and at what price they are willing to pay for it. This understanding is the opposite of an idea, too often espoused even by religious thinkers, that insists that central planning is the only way to accomplish this noble end, a planning that in practice never somehow works.

For the most part, however, this Encyclical described a

---

[2] See *A New Worldly Order: John Paul II and Human Freedom*, edited by George Weigel (Washington: Ethics and Public Policy Center, 1991).

system of democracy and economy that pretty much conforms to the American experience of limited government and vast productivity, of voluntary agencies, private property, profit, initiative. The American founding has been considered unique in that it was the first political system that was intended for the real interest and prosperity of everyone yet with a respect for higher religious and cultural values that each one was free to pursue in truth.

The spirit of the "Declaration on Religious Liberty" in Vatican II was also said to have been inspired by the American experience. Americans in some sense felt that within their system they could say "in God we trust." They even put this phrase on their money, the most worldly of all worldly instruments, almost as if they wanted to affirm that money and God were not necessarily in total opposition to each other as they are often made out to be. We cannot "serve both God and mammon," but we can use the good things of nature and what we do with it for the well-being of everyone. Indeed, the only way to free the material goods of this world to be what they are is for ourselves first to serve God. If man "does not live by bread alone," still he lives by bread. The baker of bread, even of croissants, is doing a work worthy of human enterprise.

The recently concluded Synod of European Bishops, that John Paul II called in order that all of Europe could consult on the peculiar problems of a civilization formed in Christianity, a civilization to which we Americans belong, showed great concern about the condition of faith within its borders, within that culture itself formed by Christianity. "Conditions differ in different regions," the European Bishops stated in their Final Report:

> In various parts of the Continent, particularly among the young, the Christian faith is almost unknown because of the constant spread of atheism, or wherever the process of secularization has gone so far that evangelization has to begin again almost from the start. But even where the presence of the Church has previously been strong, only a

small number take a full part in the life of the Church; in general, there is a notable discrepancy between faith and culture, faith and life.[3]

By comparison with this description, American society seems in many ways like a land of strong belief, granted the vast variety of religious sects and practices in this country.

On the other hand, we have had people like Solzhenitsyn, with whom also the Holy Father has much in common, maintaining in his Harvard Address of 1978, that the spiritual life under Marxism produced deeper and more religious souls than in the West which had not suffered as those believers in the East. Radim Palous, the Rector of Charles University in Prague has remarked:

> You can also think that we have had important moral experience that other societies have not. We have something spiritually valuable to offer the Western world. We lived under a watchdog regime with Western understanding: We know totalitarianism, and we know democracy. We mix these experiences and offer much to the humanities, that is, a history, a philosophy, that has been deepened by what we have been through. So despite these sufferings, we still have much to be thankful for.[4]

Many, including the Holy Father himself, have worried that with the demise of Marxism, what would influence Eastern Europe would not be simply the message about limited democracy and productivity. Rather the materialist culture itself that was said to exist in Western Europe and America, a culture more and more secularized and alienated from its religious roots, would be said to be the cause of Marxism's fall.

---

[3] "Final Declaration: Special Assembly for Europe of the Synod of Bishops," *L'Osservatore Romano*, (December 30, 1991), p. 3.

[4] Interview of Radim Palous with Lynne Chaney, *Humanitas*, 13 (March/April, 1992), 9.

What caused the downfall of Marxism, it is further said, is not spiritual repression but its economic failure. In fact, one of the chief concerns about the new era, typified by Armenia or Yugoslavia, is a renewal of social, ethnic, or religious strife and warfare. Europe's problem was and is, in this view, potential spiritual turmoil caused by religion. Indeed, religion is often identified with fanaticism. Certain theories of modernity would trace the real threat to Europe and to modern governments to any religion, including Christianity, that takes itself seriously. Thus, in *Centesimus Annus*, John Paul II was careful to emphasize that Catholicism was not a "fanaticism" and that relativism could not found democracy.

IV

In recent years, Roman documents have often referred to something called "inculturation." The idea behind this word seems to be that a whole civilization or nation is a peculiar complexus of habits and institutions of a spiritual and moral nature. In a broad sense, the culture informs and explains most actions of a people. No one lives by himself so that habits, manners, and ways of looking at things will reflect philosophical or religious beliefs or attitudes. No doubt, the way a people understand God or reject Him reveals itself most clearly in its habitual ways of doing things, of being born, married, working, dying.

These customs and practices, of course, need to be influenced and, if needs be, transformed by revelation if most people are to live their lives freely and with support of others. The Holy Father in his recent Encyclical, *Redemptoris Missio*, has noticed that Catholics have of late become so interested in adapting themselves to differing cultures and values that they have forgotten to teach and explain what is also unique and proper to Catholicism itself. At the heart of this process still remains the way each person stands to God.

The demise of Marxism has presented a further and most peculiar spiritual problem. The issue was stated in its starkest form by Francis Fukuyama who argued that we are witnessing the end of modernity.[5] The great ideological struggles are over. What has clearly won throughout the world is the western liberal idea of democracy and capitalism. We now know how governments are to be run, how economies to be organized and stimulated. However, this very success of capitalism was itself the origin of a serious problem. Capitalism and liberalism presumably in such a view have no real soul.

As long as it was necessary to oppose Marxism or some other ideology, there was a kind of mission or objective about in free societies. Against this common enemy, everyone could unite and under its threat, everyone could formulate common purposes. But now that capitalism is successful, mankind again realizes the insufficiency of material possessions by themselves. Nothing higher is around to live for or even to die for, so that mankind will become bored. This boredom can easily lead to a kind of decline and fall mentality, a lapse into moral and cultural decadence. Drugs and dissipation are seen as directly related to this malaise.

Addressing himself to this problem, Thomas Pangle has reintroduced the thesis of Alexis de Tocqueville about Christianity and in particular Catholicism in its relation to the American democracy and more basically to all democratic government. "Reminding his readers that he speaks 'as a practicing Catholic,' Tocqueville concedes that what he describes as the felicitous situation of religion in modern democracy is contrary to the historical practice and, what is more, the traditional spirit of Roman Catholicism," Pangle remarked.

---

[5] Francis Fukuyama, *The End of History and the Last Man* (New York: The Free Press, 1992).

> But "I think," he (Tocqueville) avers with uncustomary
> hesitation, that the experience of American Catholicism
> shows that "one is mistaken in regarding the Catholic
> religion as a natural enemy of democracy." In fact,
> Tocqueville goes on to argue, a wise Catholicism would
> see in liberal democracy its greatest political friend. . . .[6]

What is significant is the suggestion that the compatibility of
American and Roman spirituality may perhaps be necessary for
both and have something basic to contribute to the world.

Tocqueville had argued that in certain surprising ways,
Catholicism could counterbalance what were in fact the weaknesses of democracies. In particular, all religions that taught the
immortality of the soul emphasized the seriousness of the moral
life on which democracy depended even against its own instincts.
The freedom of democracy implied that little inner discipline
would come from its own principles. If there were to be limits or
orders within which even democracies must operate, they must
arise from sources outside of the democracy itself but to which it
was open. Thus democracy to flourish needed itself to live within
a religious tradition that provided counterbalances to democracy's
own tendencies to absolute freedom.

V

Christianity has often been accused of teaching men to
follow the after-life and to neglect this one. In a sense, modern
Catholicism has been so much infected with this critique that its
spirituality often appears merely as "faith and justice" or "liberation." Many critics have observed that in the Americas today, both
in North and South America, the Catholic Church in particular
looks more like a political party than like a religion, which

---

[6] Thomas Pangle, "The Spirit of Postmodern Politics," Lecture, American
Enterprise Institute, Washington, D.C., February 22, 1992, p. 21.

appearance is said to be the cause of the attraction of fundamentalist religions to specifically Catholic populations.

The substance of sermons, teachings, and practice, on examination, appears to be concerned mainly with this world. And this interest in politics looks to many to follow a form very much like certain political or ideological movements, not just Marxism, but now rather including ecology, feminism, anti-war, redistributionism, or some other popular ideas. Indeed, the teachings of the Church seem more often to follow rather than to form social movements.

In his book on America, *The Contrast*, Belloc remarked that he did not think the United States was a country of materialism, at least not like the materialism he noticed in France or Europe. The Americans, Belloc thought, do not "love" money for its own sake, but use it for a thousand other purposes. They may use their money badly, but they do not simply hoard or keep it. I recall this remark because I think it fits in with what is most unique about American spirituality.

George Gilder has remarked on the relation of the newer technologies and systems, such as the computer, to human problems and Christian attitudes.[7] In a sense, it is true, as the Holy Father acknowledged in *Centesimus Annus*, that wealth does not consist in things or property as such. Rather wealth consists mainly in knowledge and brains. Indeed, it becomes more and more clear that those nations are poor that do not have freedom or intelligence, not those that have few so-called material resources.

Wealth is created by creating wealth. That is to say, we have to have the spiritual and intellectual resources and will to create wealth and a system whereby it reaches everyone if we are to use modern science and technology for what it is. What is of particular interest to Catholic spirituality, particularly in light of its emphasis on culture, is that certain beliefs, ideas, and virtues are evi-

---

[7] George Gilder, *Wealth and Poverty* (New York: Basic Books, 1981).

dently necessary for both science and economic progress. Put negatively, there are certain beliefs, practices, and habits that will prevent any economic development or prosperity. This fact means that very often religious teachings or virtues, those of justice, or honesty or responsibility for others will be necessary if economic or political institutions are to work.

American political tradition, even beginning with the *Federalist* itself, has held that human vices and self-interest will be operative in every part and subdivision of its own society. This incidence is a fact conformable with the Scriptural tradition of original sin, a doctrine John Paul II in *Centesimus Annus* specifically reemphasized. What this recurrent evidence of human personal and structural disorder means, in terms of American spirituality, is that an effort to understand and counter-balance these tendencies to selfishness, evil, and disorder, whether it be by separation of powers, federalism, the right to bear arms or a local militia, is itself a reflection on the human condition that itself will not change. What this tradition implies is that the existence of human selfishness and tendencies to evil is a fact, a spiritual fact that must be accounted for within a society's understanding of itself. In this sense, there is an Augustinian element in American spirituality that has been present from its beginning.

VI

If we can summarize the nature and tendencies of American spirituality, it is that efforts to create a better this-worldly society are not anti-Catholic or anti-spiritual, provided they do not pretend to be identified with any transcendent or ideological purpose, provided they do not deny implicitly the dire and more dangerous sides of human reality. In the modern world, the effort to substitute politics for religion in an effort to create a Kingdom of God in this world has been very tempting and very dangerous. It is one effort that the central American tradition has instinctively rejected so long as it retained its classical and revelational roots. The spiritual rejection of this aspect of Catholic understanding has been and is one of the many causes of ideology in more recent American politics.

The American political tradition in itself has been careful to limit the state by providing that religion is to be distinguished from the state's immediate interests or purposes. This distinction goes back to the things of Caesar and the things of God. It allows an arena in which the affairs of this world have their importance without making them all-important. Moreover, it allows that there be mutual influence of religion and politics on each other. This relationship accepts the wholeness of the person and does not imply there is any radical distinction between soul and body or matter and spirit that would prevent their acting on each other.

It can be said that there is an American tendency to a kind of incarnational spirituality that would emphasize things like aiding the poor, stress on the independence of each member of society, of allowing each to seek his own proper good, of owning his own property. America has been called an "individualist" society but at the same time it has been characterized by an enormous energy for private or liberal distribution of goods not by command of the state but by leaving much of the effort for enterprises of beauty, knowledge, and goodness in the hands of the private citizens and their organizations. America is thus the home of the world's most varied private charitable and religious voluntary organizations.

The state, of course, in its being properly limited, does not conceive that all these efforts for promoting good works and spiritual goods must be in its own hands. Catholic social thought has long called this approach "subsidiarity," the notion that as many things as possible should be left to individuals and voluntary organizations. Behind this concept of subsidiarity is the more basic notion that individuals have internal resources and are themselves the origins and purposes of all action, even of the action attributed to the state.

In this context of American spirituality and the notion that there are other sources for understanding man besides the state, sources that the state in its own interests should accept and promote, John Paul II in his first visit to Mexico (January 28, 1979) to the Latin American Bishops gathered in Mexico, affirmed: "The Church . . . does not need to have recourse to ideological systems in order to love, defend and collaborate in the liberation of man . . ." (III,2). This position is not intended to deny that certain valuable things about man have been learned in the Latin or North American experiences. The Church does maintain, however, that many fundamental lessons are also derived from faith and that these understandings, that cannot be fashioned by politics or philosophy alone, are themselves contributory to any civil good, including the American one.

VII

The classical objection to democracy, which has paradoxically become itself the modern word for the "best regime," has been that it had no common definition of virtue. That is, democracy was defined in terms of "liberty." But this liberty had no theoretic content other than what the individual citizens wanted or held. This notion of a liberty presupposed to no end or truth has become characteristic of modernity. This freedom has come to mean that man creates his own ends or purposes. No norms or standards are to be found in any other source but in the autonomous will of each. Freedom or liberty becomes self-realization based on nothing but one's own will.

It is this sort of understanding of democracy that seems to be the great threat to any continuing relationship between Catholicism and American spirituality. It is worthwhile spelling this problem out in more detail, as its presence has changed in a fundamental sense the possibility of a compatibility between Roman Catholicism and American spirituality. John Paul II showed his awareness of the seriousness of the problem in *Centesimus Annus*:

Nowadays there is a tendency to claim that agnosticism and skeptical relativism are the philosophy and the basic attitude which correspond to democratic forms of political life. Those who are convinced that they know the truth and firmly adhere to it are considered unreliable from a democratic point of view, since they do not accept that truth is determined by the majority, or that it is subject to variation according to different political trends (#45).

This passage, of course, describes the "politically correct thinking" and relativism that have become commonplace in universities and in many understandings of American democracy. It is a theory that in principle makes Catholicism impossible and legislates it outside the civil society. Such understanding of liberty to mean that no truth is either possible or advisable changes in a radical sense the older problematic of Roman Catholicism and American spirituality that had been based on principles that limited the state and promoted a religious understanding of truth and actions of grace and generosity based on it.

Josef Ratzinger, in a most perceptive manner, has described the sort of thinking within Catholicism that would try to conform itself to this newer sort of relativist liberty and reject the classic notion of doctrine and practice which had in some sense flourished in the American system:

No longer is conscience understood as that knowledge which derives from a higher form of knowing. It is instead the individual's self-determination which may not be directed by someone else, a determination by which each person decides for himself what is moral in a given situation.[8]

The relativist, self-actualizing notion of religious liberty immediately assumes an understanding of conscience that separates itself from any norms in nature or grace. This separation leaves the conscience as not a judge of what is moral on the basis of the order of things but as itself creator of what is right. Democracy in this sense is an internal principle that recognizes no rule but its own.

Ratzinger noted the practical disappearance of three basic elements from Catholic teaching, the absence of which would enable this notion of democratic freedom to transform Catholicism and Christianity itself. These elements are the doctrine of creation, the decline of metaphysics, and the practical elimination of eternal life. The doctrine of creation is what founds the notion that there is something in creation and in man to which the mind must respond to find out what nature and human nature are.

An understanding of nature minus any notion of an order of creation means that the human will can look on nature as merely something open to the human mind. In this sense, the distinction of man and woman, of man and animal, disappears or even is looked upon as an alienation and imposition on human freedom. "Spirituality" then becomes an attempt to remove these natural or created distinctions from nature by the power of the human will of the individual or the state. The glorious diversities from nature become subject to the commonness of will and independent human power.

If creation has no order, then, the very idea of Christ, as the Word made flesh, also disappears. If Christ is not something of being, of reality, of *what is*, then He becomes merely historical and exemplary. If Christ is not the Son of God in some metaphysical sense, He merely represents someone, either a revolutionary or a good liberal, who is trying to will his version of reality into existence and to impose it on the world. And if Christ is only a representative, obviously He did not die or rise again in any meaningful sense. A proper liberal society, in fact, would supposedly have made Christ's death impossible so the Cross as the key to the reparation of human disorder disappears. As Ratzinger put

---

[8] Josef Ratzinger, Address to European Doctrinal Commission, at Laxemburg (Vienna), May, 1989, *Christian Order*, 31 (February, 1990), 108.

it, we must "be saved not through the cross, but from the cross. Atonement and forgiveness are misunderstandings from which Christianity has to be freed."[9]

And if we have no proper purpose for Christ, no resurrection, the doctrine of eternal life must be made to conform to what is possible to autonomous man. "Here we find the deception inherent in the idea of the 'better world,' which nonetheless, appears today even among Christians as the true goal for our hope and the genuine standard of morality," Ratzinger observed.

> The "Kingdom of God" has been almost completely substituted in the general awareness, as far as I can see, by the utopia of a better future world for which we labor and which becomes the true reference point of morality. . . . Where the Kingdom of God is reduced to the better world of tomorrow, the present will ultimately assert its right against some imaginary future. The escape into the world of drugs is the logical consequence of the idolizing of utopia.[10]

These reflections of Josef Ratzinger indicate that spirituality needs to keep close contact with doctrine, with the understanding of faith and its relation to philosophy, including the philosophy that justifies a civil society such as that of the United States or France or any other that describes itself as "democratic."

St. Augustine, to conclude, remarked that we are each made not after the manner of our kind but in the image and likeness of God. Needless to say, this teaching not only grounds the freedom we have from the will of the state that claims no limit but recalls the insistence of the Holy Father that we are each chosen "from conception" to be what we are created to be. No doubt the primary civil instance of a pure will theory, one established and promoted

---

[9] *Ibid.*, p. 113.
[10] *Ibid.*

by a theory of democratic will subject to nothing but itself, is that of abortion. St. Augustine remarked that because we are created in the image and likeness of God, we do not have "man as our director" but we need to be directed to God's "truth" to prove what is "good." In some very real fashion, the question of American spirituality and what has happened to it is bound up in these questions about will without limit and will that is guided by God's truth.

American spirituality in its classical form, one that directs itself in a pragmatic, empirical way to causes of human work, dignity, enterprise, productivity, and freedom is itself very much reflected in Roman Catholicism. The demise of liberation theology, with its attempt to join Marxism with its determinism and collectivity to Catholicism, has failed and been specifically rejected in *Centesimus Annus*. On the other hand, serious issues of understanding, doctrine, and spiritual life remain because of ideas that justify a notion of democracy that would wish to deny any limits to human freedom conceived as a self-actualizing power designed to create its own norms and values.

Over against this latter understanding of the human enterprise, reflection and meditation on Creation, Christology, and eternal life seem to be the central responses of the Christian soul. The American spirit was established on the idea that all men were created equal, that we are a Christian people who do not confuse Christ with a political leader, and that we have here no lasting city, however much we are responsible for the one we do have. The understanding of the compatibility of Roman Catholicism and the American faith of which Tocqueville spoke is very much alive. Its dimensions are today at this most profound level of struggle over whether we are simply founded on the premise of our own will or whether our mind is "renewed" by beholding and understanding God's truth.

CHAPTER XII

Ultimate Questions:
On Joy, Evil, and Sadness

I

If the truth of Catholicism impinges on economic and political questions in its own indirect way, its primary purpose is, within these very contexts, to enable human beings to think about and understand the ultimate questions, those that are common to all men in all polities and in all times. A right understanding of polity or technology and a wrong understanding about what is important for each human being as such is itself a discontentment. To have all things right except the most important things is something that leaves the human heart most exposed and most uneasy. Catholicism, whatever else it is, purports to be an understanding about those things that are most important to our kind.

Johann Sebastian Bach wrote his "Magnificat" in D Major for the Christmas Service at the Thomasschule in Leipzig in 1723. "My soul magnifies the Lord, and my spirit exalts in God my savior." This song is, of course, the great prayer of the Virgin about the dignity of our souls, that we can indeed magnify the Lord, that fundamentally we are to react to God by rejoicing in Him. Nothing else. The version of the "Magnificat" which I came across was recorded at the Third International Bach Festival at Schaffhausen, in Switzerland, as performed by the Wintertur Symphony and Chorus on the Musical Masterpiece Label.

The Introduction to the "Magnificat" on the cover began, "Johann Sebastian Bach's art of religious narration through music stemmed partly from his devotion to the Lutheran religion, the core of which is the inner struggle of the individual." The essence of man, however, is not exactly his "inner struggle," though that indeed often exists, but it is rather a search for wholeness, a belief that all does, in the end, fit together, even evil and suffering. We search for understanding even in our faith.

The properly ordered soul is replete not only with virtues in the ethical sense but also with an adequate understanding about the right order of things. Indeed, Aristotle himself will say that there are certain illnesses of the soul that can only be cured by philosophy, that is, by the right understanding and love of being. Perhaps more than we realize, our difficulties arise in part because certain basic questions remain perplexing to us.

While it is quite true, then, that we can be good without being particularly bright, the fact is that a disordered understanding of certain fundamental issues in human existence will serve to confuse us or even lead us into error if we do not attend to their implications. More often than we care to admit, innocence and naïveté can cause more damage than evil itself because they leave the mind open to erroneous explanations without the effort or intelligence to see things rightly.

On May 30, 1962, Flannery O'Connor had occasion to write to a young college student, Albert Korn, who inquired of her about the difficulties of faith in a modern university. "As a freshman in college," she wrote, "you are bombarded with new ideas, or rather pieces of ideas, new frames of reference, an activation of the intellectual life which is only beginning, but which is already running ahead of your lived experience."[1] She warned the young man that it is dangerous to get so involved in trying to reconcile

---

[1] Flannery O'Connor, *The Habit of Being*, edited by Sally Fitzgerald (New York: Vintage, 1979), p. 476.

intellectually the different faiths such as "Buddhism or Mohammedanism" or modern science that he neglects other means, such as charity and prayer. Finally, she added,

> Don't think that you have to abandon reason to be a Christian. A book that might help you is *The Unity of Philosophical Experience* by Gilson. Another is Newman's *The Grammar of Assent*. To find out about faith, you have to go to the people who have it and you have to go to the most intelligent ones if you are going to stand up intellectually to agnostics and the general run of pagans that you are going to find in the majority of people around you.[2]

This wise advise, no doubt, is hard to come by, but it does not neglect the seriousness of the intellectual side of the faith especially for those whose environment places them in situations where it is not reinforced naturally by adequate exposure to the broader context of Christian thinking.

No doubt, joy, evil, and sadness are the three core issues in human life about which some meditative and intelligent understanding is most necessary. Everyone instinctively understands this. Yet, perhaps as we might expect, here we are most often left in confusion by our civilization, if not by our own choices, sometimes even by our own religious environment.

For right understanding is not exclusively a function of intellectual comprehension but it is also an object of our wills, something we must finally choose, if we are to have it. This is why Flannery O'Connor in her answer to the young student recalled to him the advice of Gerard Manley Hopkins when asked a similar question. Hopkins told the student merely "to give alms." That is, God was to be experienced in Charity, in the divine image in every human being as well as in intelligence.[3]

---

[2] *Ibid.*, p. 477.

[3] *Ibid.*, p. 476.

II

When he was on the Isle of Inch Kenneth with Boswell, on October 18, 1774, Samuel Johnson recounted his stay with Sir Allan MacLean and his two lovely daughters at such a tiny, yet civilized outpost. Before setting off to Icolmkill to view the monastic ruins, Sir Allan, in the afternoon, recounted some of the affairs going on in the American colonies. The same evening, one of the ladies played the harpsichord while the other danced a reel with Boswell. Johnson reflected, poignantly, on their cordial, dignified reception, "We could have been easily persuaded to a longer stay upon Inch Kenneth, but life will not be all passed in delight."[4]

Something about the tone and content of this passage causes us to wonder about the human condition — in particular, our human condition. We are aware of delight, vividly so at times; yet, we are conscious that our present lives will not be all passed in delight, even when we suspect they should be. Why not? Is there a cause of discontents that corrupts even the delight we do encounter? Or are both discontent and delight in the same existence, subsumed into a larger whole?

Ultimately, the world was created in and for joy. We know, however, that it is a sad world in many ways, that even beyond sadness, there is a range of evil that cannot be ignored. In what sense, then, is it possible to speak of the world as created in and existing for joy? Clearly, in no sense, can this affirmation of joy at the heart of reality be at the expense of the sadness and the existence of the evil.

No doubt, these are classic considerations. In part, our willingness to go on living is our tacit assumption that through the disorder and evil we encounter and ourselves do, which we deny at the expense of our integrity, there remains some understanding, some suspicion that any rebellion against the world on the

---

[4] *Johnson's Journey to the Western Islands,* Edited by Allan Wendt (Boston: Houghton-Mifflin, 1965), p. 108.

grounds of the existence of sadness and evil is itself dangerous. In other words, we implicitly believe and acknowledge that joy is that in the light of which all sadness and evil stands.

In a way, this reflection is another side of the classic treatment of tragedy and comedy. Which is the more fundamental, comedy or tragedy, and why? In that odd sort of novel, *The Name of the Rose*, the Christian monks were accused of suppressing Aristotle's treatise on comedy because they thought that joy would be dangerous and would undermine their authority.[5] And it is often thought that a thing is good in proportion to its difficulty or suffering, which is rather not the Christian position at all.[6] Suffering and difficulty, while they may be in some sense natural, only exist in order to lead to what is not suffering or difficult.

And evil, what is it? Ever since at least St. Augustine, of course, evil has not been seen as something positive. It was not a being, or an aspect of being. Evil was not "created" as but one more object of God's powers. Yet, it was not exactly nothing either. The existence of evil is surely the major argument against the existence of God; yet, evil does not exactly "exist." What exists, in all cases, is good. So in a manner, evil is dependent on good. It is not an original creation.

The classical doctrine from Aristotle was that men could commit errors and evils because they could first do good, but that there were many goods that they could fashion into existence in their particular acts. The "practical syllogism" in Aristotle's *Ethics* (Book 7) was designed to explain how it was both that we always chose the good in all our actions, even in our evil ones, and how there could be some disorder in even good actions because we did not put into existence the good we should have placed there. The fault existed in the fact that we knew that it was possible to attend

---

[5] Umberto Eco, *The Name of the Rose*, translated by William Weaver (New York: Harcourt, 1983), p. 112.

[6] See Josef Pieper, *Leisure: The Basis of Culture* (New York: Mentor, 1963), pp. 19-24.

to some other reasoning than the one we in fact put into existence by our choices. This capacity to do good or evil is the legitimate origin of the praise and blame that is due to all our acts.

Thus, it is always possible to give a good reason for any evil in our deeds. We in fact do this. We "explain" vigorously why we did what we did, especially if it is wrong somehow. Furthermore, the good that was in our deeds will continue, in spite of our own disorder. Indeed, this good will provide the possibility for the evil as such to be overcome. In this sense, good is never defeated; it remains itself, even in evil actions. Good does not "come out" of evil, as if evil were its cause.

Rather the already existing good in all of our unordered acts continues to be good — challenging our intellects to explain why. God does not and cannot "bring good" out of evil if we take that to mean that somehow evil "becomes" good or that evil is the proper cause of good. All the evil in our actions can do is to call forth a response based on being, based on good which transcends the evil. This ultimately is the meaning of forgiveness and sacrifice and even suffering.

III

The laughter of human beings is not only a fact, but a bothersome one. Aristotle felt that laughter arose out of our intelligence, out of our capacity to see relationships. Laughter at its best was, moreover, harmless, but it did arise out of our understanding of the incongruity of something. It was precisely that unexpected seeing that causes us to laugh. This capacity was the measure of our wit. Yet, we are familiar with the record of the New Testament which does not tell us that Christ laughed. This same Christ is understood to be the Word made flesh, almost as if to say, He is joy incarnate. "Christianity cannot be reduced to sheer submissiveness stripped of joy nor to a kerygma devoid of culture," Yves Congar wrote.

> There is something about the life of the Church which
> insures that even in the frailty of our human existence here
> on earth it catches something of the radiant joy of those
> who already see God face to face in heaven.[7]

Was Christ's laugher merely hidden then, or did it not exist at all?
We can hardly imagine a human being who does not laugh.
Indeed, it would be a trait that revealed something that distanced
us from the person characterized by no laughter. Yet, if Christ is
like us in all things but sin, then surely He was abnormal if He did
not laugh.

On the other hand, perhaps this "all things but sin" might
explain Christ's lack of evident laughter during his earthly so-
journ. This approach would suggest that sin or evil is so disorient-
ing, if we really saw it for what it was, that it would repress
laughter in any being such as Christ who knew what it was. But
this, of course, would make Christ rather unlike us than like us.
Yet, the connection of sin and laughter seems intellectually a
fruitful one. If we recall the notion that evil can only exist in the
good, then it might follow that the account of evil, its memory,
how it came to exist, may well contain within it elements of humor
that may serve to reorder or refashion the good we do even in our
evil acts. No act is so evil that it contains no good.

One ought not, surely, to romanticize evil or sin, yet all
serious literature and philosophy in some sense must deal with
them. Indeed, their existence seems to define our importance as
beings in the universe. This is what makes any plot, any story,
including the story of our own lives, absolutely stand out of
nothingness in its own integrity and drama. There is an ultimate
risk even in the ordinary thoughts and deeds of our daily lives.
Not only are human beings the mortals, the beings who die and
know that they die, but this death is said to be a result of sin, so that
we are not originally born to die. "Death was not God's doing," we

---

[7] Yves Congar, *Called to Life* (New York: Crossroads, 1987), p. 29.

read in the Book of Wisdom, "He takes no pleasure in the extinc-
tion of the living" (1:12). If this be so, then it is worth thinking out
its implications.

IV

Mother Teresa says that the suffering that is given to us, in
whatever form, is in itself not an evil, but a blessing, that we can
make up by this suffering the disorder in the world, including that
of our own.[8] It is true that the innocent suffer. Even the guilty
suffer too little, but perhaps more than they deserve. But does
anyone "deserve" to suffer? Suffering is, in one sense, a necessary
result of the desire to have finite beings in the first place. It goes
with the territory, so to speak. Suffering is the natural sign that
something is wrong, so that all correction of our ills depends on its
prior existence.

Yet, it seems unjust somehow, even before we figure out that
injustice is itself something rather spiritual. The very notion of
injustice, for example, requires our intellectual comprehension.
We begin to suspect that our greatest sufferings are not physical
pains at all. Indeed, Aristotle remarked that "the greatest evils,
injustice and folly, are the least felt, since their presence causes no
pain" (*Rhetoric*, 1382a 20-21). We have seen people suffer who
have lived perfectly innocent lives. And we have seen perfectly
healthy people suffer immensely because of a disorder of their
own souls or in the souls of others.

Love is shown in deeds and words. No doubt we are accus-
tomed to the notion, valid in its own way, that love shows itself in
deeds and not words. Yet, it also shows itself in words. We hunger
not merely that someone love us enough to do good for us, but that
someone also tell us of their love and esteem. No doubt, words can

---

[8] *The Daily Meditations of Mother Teresa*, edited by Dorothy S. Hunt (San Francisco:
Ignatius Press, 1987), pp. 93-95.

be dangerous or insincere. They can be abused to substitute for deeds. We can lie, in other words. But deeds by themselves are never enough.

We are given speech to articulate what it is we think and feel and desire. Our speech is indeed usually in advance of our deeds in moral sensitivity.[9] Love and words, like anything else, can thus be abused. But they belong together ultimately. The notion in the Gospel of John that the "Word" was made flesh is enough to make us realize that there is some articulation in each thing that exists, some drive for it to be formed in words and for words to be rooted in their turn in being.

And laughter is grounded in our ability to see and to say what it is that is humorous in our relationships with others. We must, probably, distinguish joy and laughter. There is a kind of laughter that kills. But this is an abuse. The delight that makes us what we are includes those things that make us laugh. Belloc in a famous passage in *The Path to Rome* wrote, as a friend recently reminded me,

> Then let us love one another and laugh. Time passes, and we shall soon laugh no longer — and meanwhile common living is a burden, and earnest men are at siege upon us all around. Let us suffer absurdities, for that is only to suffer one another.[10]

There is something enormously poignant in this passage from Belloc, that we are to love one another and to laugh, that there will arrive a time when we can laugh no longer, that we should suffer the absurdities that we are.

---

[9] "Most men come closer to the truth in their public praise than in their private desires because as a community they must restrain the ignoble desires by which they are moved as private men." Larry Arnhart, *Aristotle on Political Reasoning* (DeKalb: Northern Illinois University Press, 1981), p. 152.

[10] Hilaire Belloc, *The Path to Rome* (Garden City, N Y: Doubleday Image, 1956), p. 11.

James Thurber seems to have had something of a similar sentiment in the touching Introduction to his *My Life and Hard Times*. The great humorist finds life essentially sad and ambiguous. He finds himself concerned not so much by the great issues of the world but by those that happen to a very few people in his own life and in the few places in which he lives.

> (The writer) knows vaguely that the nation is not much good any more; he has read that the crust of the earth is shrinking alarmingly and that the universe is growing steadily colder, but he does not believe that any of the three is in half as bad shape as he is....
>
> The "time" of such a writer, then is hardly worth reading about if the reader wishes to find out what was going on in the world while the writer in question was alive and at what might be laughingly called "his best." All that the reader is going to find out is what happened to the writer. The consolation, I suppose, must lie in the comforting feeling that one had had, after all, a pretty sensible and peaceful life, by comparison. It is unfortunate, however, that even a well-ordered life can not lead anybody safely around the inevitable doom that waits in the skies.[11]

The humorist is melancholy. He too awaits his doom, even if his life is well-ordered.

Where is the wholeness of this doom and the laughter? We are all taught to be more concerned about the world than about ourselves. Yet, we know that we are in bad shape, as Thurber said, that our best deeds and words seem to go for naught, that the right order of the world can only begin with the right order in ourselves. And the reason for this is that each of us transcends the world

---

[11] James Thurber, "Preface to a Life," *My Life and Hard Times* (New York: Bantam, 1963), pp. 12-13. See James V. Schall, "On Sadness and Laughter," *The Praise of 'Sons of Bitches': On the Worship of God by Fallen Men* (Slough, England: St. Paul Publications, 1978), pp. 113-24.

directly so that without a proper understanding of our final end, of its completion in joy, we cannot order our lives to attain it, even when we do not create it for ourselves.

V

Is it possible to order joy, evil, and suffering into one articulate whole? Clearly, they must be so ordered in the eyes of God. But we are asking about our eyes. We must at some time seek to resolve what is indeed perplexing. In Aristotle's *Poetics*, we find his famous doctrine of "catharsis," that is, of the feeling of order and peace that comes to us after having witnessed the downfall of essentially a good man who had a fault which brought about his destruction.

What was disordered then was eventually subsumed into a higher order. If, as Aeschylus said, man learns by suffering, then there must be a sense in which the learning redeems the suffering as in tragedy. But that is the word, "redeems." However we think of suffering or evil, in the context of joy, neither can ever be denied its own realities, however it is understood. To pretend that there is no suffering or evil does not in any way really confront the problems that exist for us in their realities.

We ought not, furthermore, think that we can perfectly resolve the perplexities of laughter and evil in one simple formula. Yet, following St. Thomas, we must at least see why it is not contradictory or impossible for them to both exist in our world. Certain Hindu philosophies seem to reduce suffering and evil literally to nothing by undermining the reality of being itself. They both become illusions, and therefore, presumably, bearable. Catholicism is never free to take this route, for the Crucifixion was an historical event. It took place on a certain day, on a certain hill, to a certain man, witnessed and decreed by certain people with names. Whenever we encounter real suffering, it always exists in such minute particularity, particularity that we could not engineer solely from our own minds.

Suffering and evil, no doubt, can be occasions for the increase of suffering and evil. This possibility always remains within the range of free will and finite being. Suffering is ultimately redeemed when it is seen as lying within the spiritual dimension of why the world exists in the first place. The suffering of Christ was not intended to be a kind of endurance test. Nor was it understood to be a sort of qualitative sum larger than the total of all other suffering in the universe.

Rather the suffering of Christ was undergone, with all the realization of Aristotle's observation that the deepest suffering or pain is spiritual, for the purposes of those existences which were not divine. Had there been no world, no human race, there would have been no need for a suffering God. The suffering of Christ is directed exclusively to the final end of each human being, an end that transcends the world, even though men exist in and pass through this very world. The suffering of Christ, in other words, is directed to ultimate joy, as is especially the suffering of the innocent.

A question I have often asked myself is — "Would you abolish sadness if you could?" If this question be taken merely to mean that we should alleviate whatever suffering we can, then it is innocent enough. But if it means that we would reconstruct the world on our own terms, if we would imply that we could make a better world in which suffering had no place, then it is a most dangerous sentiment. Suffering and evil are consequences of our very possibility. Are we willing to have precisely our kind of human being exist, one that does fail, one that is not perfect, one that is responsible for his own deeds?

Boswell recorded a letter Johnson received on March 15, 1782, from a Mr. E. Malone, concerning Johnson's *Life of Addison*. The question came up about whether Addison's faults should have been suppressed in the biography. Johnson wrote as follows on this topic:

> If nothing but the bright side of characters should be shewn, we should sit down in despondency, and think it utterly impossible to imitate them in any thing. The sacred writers related the vicious as well as the virtuous actions of men; which had this moral effect, that it kept mankind from despair, into which otherwise they would naturally fall, were they not supported by the recollection that others had offended like themselves, and by penitence and amendment of life had been restored to the favour of Heaven.[12]

Thus, the darker side of our character exists so that, were we to be shown only the virtuous side, it would undermine the confidence of most of mankind. The proper solution to personal disorder is penitence and amendment of life. Without this, indeed, the despair that there is no hope in our condition as men seems altogether logical. The humorist would become a figure of contradiction, not a sign of hope.

VI

The relation of joy, evil, and sadness, in conclusion, can only be resolved when we can see the results of evil and suffering in gladness, when we can see the whole story of each person resolved so that we can laugh at them in the confidence that they are forgiven in their evils, but that their good continues on into the very infinity that good implies of its very nature. We will be finally free to laugh even at evil when we realize, as a friend of mine wrote, that "the resolution of the evil is complete." This resolution is possible because evil can exist only in the good, or better, can only exist in a good in which something is lacking that ought to be there.

---

[12] *Boswell's Life of Johnson* (London: Oxford, 1931), II, p. 371.

Suffering is itself part of this ultimate resolution in which, what is lacking in the Passion of Christ is made up in the suffering of the innocent and the guilty. This apparent incompleteness does not mean that something was also lacking in Christ, but rather that we are real agents in the drama that is the story of our lives in which we are actually reaching the end for which we were created. But this is to be reached by God's means. We do not and cannot save ourselves from our own evil or make meaningful our own suffering apart from our relation to God.

Some of us, most of us, may indeed fail, for this is the possibility of the rational creature, to prefer himself to what he is given as the joy of his being. The doctrine of hell is thus not a sign of God's vengeance but of our real dignity and freedom. The only alternative God had in making this very world, evidently, was the alternative of allowing the evil and the suffering, or not creating at all.

These disturbing issues of evil and sadness are ultimately resolved, put to rest, when we can see the fullness of the story in which they appeared. When we see them as complete, when we see them as resolved by penitence and amendment, then they become the source of the amusement of those who can now recount their sins in the confidence of their final forgiveness, when it becomes clear that joy is indeed the origin of creation, of the creation of every human being. The origin and the end, the alpha and the omega are the same.

Evil and suffering, no doubt, remain mysteries. We will not abolish sadness in this life. Yet, it is not contradictory that such things exist in our world. Evil and sadness do not defeat the joy of God, but contribute to it. Every tear will be wiped away. The ultimate questions must be asked at the risk of denying what we are. But they must not be given up until they are resolved in laughter and joy, in their completion.

The melancholy and the sadness we often find associated with the humorist are signs not so much of contradiction but of ultimate wholeness, the awareness, the suspicion that even in our most delightful moments as well as in our saddest, something more, something more joyous is to be promised to us, or else delight and laughter could not exist at all.

In the end, don't think you have to abandon reason to be a Christian. The greatest evils cause no pain. The sacred writers related the vicious as well as the virtuous acts of men. Not even a well-ordered life can lead anybody safely amid the inevitable doom. The "inner struggle" is resolved when the story of our lives is complete, when it is told in laughter. Comedy is indeed more profound than tragedy. The frailty of our existence catches the radiant joy of those who already see the face of God. Let us suffer absurdities, for that is only to suffer one another. My soul magnifies the Lord, and my spirit exalts in God my savior. It is in this sense that Catholicism still exists.

Chapter XIII

Life Everlasting

I

In recent years, Catholic teaching and preaching have been filled with what can only be called "causes," almost exclusively social and political causes. We don't hear a lot of praying for rain in congregations these days except for some old fashioned farm parishes. We hardly ever get straightforward instruction in doctrine or what is usually called "spiritual life." We do not think doctrine is important, while spiritual life is understood in terms of politics, of being on the right side.

A few can remember when we used to pray for the "conversion" of Russia. Some even wonder about those prayers, in retrospect, whether perhaps they might well have worked. No one "predicted" the fall of communism. Yet there it was. Curious. It makes us wonder whether the social scientists whose methodology excludes such things as prayer are not missing something.

We are warned, however, about war and nuclear weapons, though all the hype about pacifism and the bishops' pastoral on war seems strangely irrelevant. Catholics in Muslim countries like Sudan or in Catholic countries like Croatia continue to wonder about the non-involvement of other Catholics in their plight.

Thus, we were solemnly warned about the kind of war and weapons that never came about. We were left rather disarmed spiritually when it came to the actual wars like Iraq and Yugoslavia that did happen. Deterrence worked, and we insist on disarming. Eternal vigilance is not our strong suit.

We are constantly warned about poverty, about exploitation, about discrimination, about fascism, warnings with ominous ideological overtones. More recently, and more trendily, we are unsettled about greenhouse effects and ozone depletion. I confess that I cannot imagine praying, "Oh Lord, please keep the ozone within our planetary gravitational pull," or "Prevent, O Lord, both the coming Ice Age and the Warming of the Planet." Over-population rhetoric has reappeared to tell us that there are too many people and too few resources, even though neither of these positions is at all true. Anti-growth and anti-life always seem to be silent partners.

But this sort of secular apocalyptic thing goes on. Our schools take it for their mission. Genesis seems to be reversed. Environment has dominion over us. We worry, with reason, about inflation, about the causes of cancer, about the spread of AIDS, and about the murder rate in the District of Columbia. We read of moral and political corruption, about bank scandals and about slick scams of various sorts. Pornography and abortion are big industries, while other scientists begin to demonstrate that divorce is a great moral scourge. And this list does not even touch drugs, harassment, unemployment, or the condition of a Congress that has successfully isolated its members from the financial problems most people have to face.

Preaching about immediate and politically correct problems seems to be the common thing. Many critics claim they cannot tell the difference between Sunday sermons and political platforms. Marx said that religion was the opium of the people, so many clergy began to preach about something else besides religion. Few know where to go to find religious topics actually presented. Tell me what you preach against and I will tell you what you are.

Nevertheless, it is at least questionable whether our most immediate concerns are issues of this public order sort, however pressing they might be. We are, for the most part, "not perfect," as St. Thomas told us. The Holy Father in *Centesimus Annus* reminded us that "original sin" is still a basic Christian dogma, when it is not merely an observed fact that something seems wrong with our kind. Does religion have anything to tell us about life and salvation other than politics and identifiable economic theories?

Since we are loathe to hear our faults, we are leery of such "outmoded" concepts as original sin, which implies that there is something rather disordered about us, even if we are against the right categories of social preference. And if our private life conflicts with some public cause, nothing is secret. Our sins are shouted from the housetops and from legislative fora. "Private confession" seems to have been replaced by "public confession," with the listeners not priests but politicians and journalists.

The fact is that we want to treat religion as a problem, as something that can solve our social disorders. We even have professionals like A.N. Wilson writing a book *Against Religion* to charge that religious folks have not sufficiently reformed themselves or the world. So religion, in Wilson's analysis, is something of a fraud. Yet, since the doctrine of original sin implies that we will never solve our problems by ourselves, we are damned if we claim the orthodox position that much sin will remain under any system and damned again if we question social utopias, the presumed result of the removal of disorders by political formulas.

We think that correction of evil is something of a technical issue. We just have to define the problem and fix it. It is a question of analysis, energy, and resolution. What is at fault is our "system," not ourselves, not even the stars. If we rearrange certain things — family, property, education, the ecosystem, or the forms of government — we will solve what is wrong. Sin is social. It does not really affect us personally because spiritual disorder is a question of class or gender or rank or dogmatism.

We do not, therefore, need Sacraments but "revolution" and "restructuring." We live in a world full of "victims" but no perpetrators. We do not love the sinner but hate the sin. Rather, we define our categories of political acceptability and unacceptability. We hate those who fall outside of what we choose politically to accept, because we have no theory of personal responsibility or initiative. The guilty and the innocent are defined by the groups or quotas or classes under which they fall, not on the basis of anything that each personally did.

Yet, both the ones who think they can readjust things so that no evil will remain and those who figure that evil will be about no matter what we do speak as if we are in this world only for and by ourselves. Seldom do we hear sermons on what were once called "the four last things." Hell is a sort of weak cuss-word and purgatory something of a theological joke. We do not need such hypotheses, especially if the only wrong we can do is to find ourselves on the losing side of correct political thinking now properly baptized.

Well, we do hear a fair amount about death, as in "death and dying." But we notice that funeral Masses are presented mostly as "celebrations." No more "remember man that thou art dust." We even begin to see the body at the funeral disappear, if that is not too paradoxical a way to put it. We have memorial services, not funerals. We cremate rather than bury. "From ashes to ashes" is now an instantaneous proposition in our funeral homes.

We tell stories about the life of the dead person. We do not think to "pray for his soul and the souls of all the faithful departed." Why should we? Why do the dead need anything? We are pretty sure everyone gets to heaven anyhow. We do Pascal's famous wager one better. We do not bet that God exists against the suspicion that He might not. We rather bet, to steal a theological phrase from Clark Gable, that He does not really "give a damn" what we do, so why all the big fuss about our deeds? God knows we are weak, after all, so He cannot be too hard on us. We cannot do anything that is really very serious. Punishment, especially eternal punishment, is illiberal.

II

The trouble with such reflections is that they make any effort to think carefully about life everlasting superfluous. Peter Kreeft, in his own insightful book *Heaven*, remarked that very few writers have written on this topic.[1] It is one thing to try to say something intelligent about life everlasting, however, and another to inquire how we might obtain it. In terms of popular religious practice, symbolized in our attitude to death ceremonies and to forgiveness, we seem to get everlasting life whether we want it or not.

About the only way to miss everlasting life, it seems, would be to be on the wrong side of certain political questions or movements. Everlasting life is not the reward of a life well spent, so to speak, something that would imply that we had to earn it even when it was given to us, but it is something that an all-good God would not deny to anyone at the risk of His definition. Everybody, it seems, is saved, give or take a few political categories.

Aristotle and St. Thomas discussed the question of human happiness as the first and most essential consideration for understanding human action. They maintained that everyone sought happiness in everything he did. They acknowledged, however, that it made a difference in what we thought this happiness might consist. Thus, we could be wrong. We were usually wrong because we chose to be wrong. And the consequences of mis-understanding what sort of happiness might be ours implied a life of choices and deeds that led to goals and institutions that failed to give us what we seemed most to want.

The most subtle argument against Catholicism is precisely its maintaining that we can get what we most want if we want rightly. Or to use Tolkien's phrase, we should pray that "what should be, will be." This is no doubt among the shortest and most

---

[1] Peter Kreeft, *Heaven: The Heart's Deepest Longing* (San Francisco: Ignatius Press, 1989).

profound of prayers. We are to have the audacity to pray for what we really want as if we could have it.

Thomas Aquinas wrote a brief commentary on the Creed. We are to think about this Creed — how often it is neglected to be recited at Sunday Mass, contrary to what the Church explicitly wants! The Creed's importance is often underestimated by those who do not realize the significance of intelligence to Catholicism. It is even more underestimated by those who do not think that ordinary people need to have their faith accurately stated. The mind is to strive to state the truth even about God. The Church is more democratic than its critics. It is more philosophical than its adversaries.

On Saturday of the Thirty-Third Week of the year, the Second Reading of the Office is taken from Aquinas' commentary on the Creed, specifically from the last two words, "life everlasting." As the readings for the last two Sundays of the year deal with the end of all things, this particular reading on "life everlasting" is especially appropriate.[2]

Aquinas begins by noting how fitting it is that the last words of the Creed correspond with "the end of all our desires." That is to say, what it is we desire most is "life everlasting," our particular life that does not cease. Perhaps it is rash to desire such a thing about whose particulars we know so little. Nevertheless, if we could have it, this is what we want. And by "life" we do not mean a kind of shadowy existence, but "life," life at its fullest. It is "our desires" about which we speak. We are to think about ourselves in a very careful way.

Aquinas proceeds to enumerate what this life might consist in. The very first thing life everlasting implies — the objective existence and nature of which he has established and discussed in his other works — is that we be "united to God." God "is the end

---

[2] See Saint Thomas Aquinas, *The Three Greatest Prayers* (Manchester, NH: Sophia Institute Press, 1990). These prayers are the Lord's Prayer, the Hail Mary, and the Apostles' Creed. The *General Catechism* treats eternal life in #1020-50.

of all our labors." After each substantial statement of what life everlasting will mean, Aquinas will give a citation from Scripture to illustrate and confirm his own conclusion. Scripture seems to flesh out what we want. It seems almost uncanny that there should be such a correspondence between what philosophy wonders about and what Scripture teaches us.

If God is the "end and reward," what does this mean? Aquinas, citing a passage from St. Paul, explains that this union of man with God "consists in seeing perfectly." This is not intended merely as a metaphor. Needless to say, the word "seeing" includes seeing with the eyes and with the mind and heart. St. Thomas had shown that God is not a body, so when we "see" God it is not to be supposed that we suddenly concretize God. Yet, we are Catholics — the Incarnation is a reality. So the Creed speaks literally. We "see" God perfectly. We encounter the exact reason why we are brought out of nothing. Our "seeing" God includes our seeing why we exist in the first place.

III

Yet, if we ask why God bothered to create anything at all so that something other than Himself stands outside of nothingness, we can come up with no good answer unless we meditate on the notion of good. Obviously, if God "needed" to create, He is not the God of Catholicism. That would mean He was lonely or incomplete. The very Creed, before ending with "life everlasting," tells us of the inner life of God, Father, Son, and Spirit. St. Thomas had already said in the *Summa* that we do not call God "Father" on analogy from human fatherhood, but that human fatherhood is itself related to the life of the Trinity.

But calling the world out of nothingness is the proper work of God, if He chooses to create in the first place. The only motive for God's creating thus is generosity or love. Yet, God includes the free rational being in the cosmos. Indeed, the cosmos seems to exist not for itself but for the rational creature's purpose, which is God Himself. What is not God exists then that God might be chosen, not by God but by a creature capable of appreciating Him. So what is it that a rational creature can "do" for God? In one sense, he can do nothing. Yet, St. Thomas says that life everlasting consists in "perfect praise." The rational creature can praise *what is.*

We should not, I think, underestimate the insight in this brief remark about perfect praise. The question being asked is "in what does life everlasting consist?" The answer is that it consists in "seeing" God Himself. But seeing God — and even seeing what is not God — is not complete if we just take or receive it. Each thing has its own reality, its own being. Each thing is marvelous in the way it crowds nothing out of existence, so to speak. The seeing consists, in its completion, in realizing that God cannot command or elicit praise of Himself or of *anything that is* except indirectly. The wonder of His own divine Being, as it were, remains incomplete in the creature until it realizes and responds to its glory.

Praise thus is needed for the completion of the universe. God cannot force it. This means, in a real sense, that the universe is "independent" of God, that God knows that creation is lovely but must await the free creature's own soul to see this loveliness both in creation and eventually in God. Praise is the radical freedom in which we were created by a God who left Himself vulnerable both symbolically and actually before the free creature.

Aquinas then turns to what we "get" in life everlasting. Praise, in a way, is what God gets, though it is also the sign that we have understood and rejoiced in what is first given to us. God does not "need" this praise, of course; yet creation does, we do. We need to state that what is good is good, that we are glad there is something rather than nothing, that we are rather than are not. That is, we need to see that what is not ourselves in its reality is lovely. Our nature is to respond to and to acknowledge our own dependence and our own wonder. But life everlasting is "the complete satisfaction of desire." Then St. Thomas adds, in a most incredible statement, that in life everlasting "the blessed will be given more than they wanted or hoped for."

This notion of being given more than we wanted or hoped for lies at the depths of human experience itself, though this too is directly related to a God who creates what is not necessary, but only what is lovely and good. St. Thomas says that God creates the world and all in it out of mercy, not justice. He means that God does not "owe" the world and ourselves existence. Existence is a gift, something that need not exist, but does out of a kind of abundance in being.

St. Thomas warns us that though our own human desires are vast and great, they are not in reality broad or great enough. We forget that all the serious objections to or systems opposed to the orthodox Creed in which we believe are rooted in their promising us *less* than the Creed does. We are accused of being wrong because we claim too much, not too little. We are asked by philosophy, by politics, by other religions, by our own passions and ideas, to settle for less than God plans for us. We think we are wise intellectuals for so doing. Indeed, for Catholicism it is one of the major functions of philosophy to show this discrepancy between the teachings of the Creed and the meaning of the alternatives to it.

Since we will receive more than we expect, Aquinas continues, this fact explains our very being, our restlessness. It explains us to ourselves. Literally in this life, we will find nothing that can finally satisfy us, even though we do encounter lovely things. "In this life, no one can fulfill his longing, nor can any creature satisfy man's desire," St. Thomas affirms in a statement of great simplicity, accuracy, and honesty. Aristotle and Plato in their own way sought to show this truth also. This position is what the First Book of the *Ethics* is about. It is also the essence of the Sixth Book of the *Republic* and the *Symposium*. "Only God" can satisfy us, Aquinas explains. And his reason for saying this? Because God "infinitely exceeds all other pleasures."

What an extraordinary reason to give! God exceeds all our

other pleasures not by denying our other pleasures exist, but by maintaining that God is more delightful than even these. Aquinas, to repeat, does not at all deny that there are other pleasures. Indeed, the very fact that there are other pleasures and that they are real pleasures is what is to give us pause. Yet, in them, in their very perfections, we still experience an incompletion and longing that the pleasures seem to be designed to bring to our attention.

Naturally, Aquinas here cites Augustine about our restless hearts only resting in God. How marvelous it is that Aquinas is not "jealous" of Aristotle's or Augustine's wisdom but that he is able to praise them by showing us that they too in their own ways understood what the Creed was ultimately getting at. Aquinas expects us to take the trouble to know our own souls and those who have wrestled with its meaning.

IV

Next Aquinas speaks of the life of the saints in their heavenly home with God. Since their longing will be in fact satisfied, "their glory will be even greater." Notice what is said here. Sometimes, we think that the only nobility is in the getting there, in the going. Actually, it is in the possessing. We are less "gloried" persons in our present status because we are not yet what we can and shall be. It is natural to our human status to pass from imperfection to perfection, from beginning to end. To arrive at what we should be means that we have a way along which we first must travel. We are finite beings not complete ones. But we should not ever think that we are now as we shall be, though what we shall be remains exactly us. We pray that "what should be, will be."

Aquinas has spoken much in his works of the notion of "superabundance."[3] Still asking in what life everlasting consists,

---

[3] See James V. Schall, "The Law of Superabundance," *Gregorianum*, 72 (#3, 1991), 515-42.

having explained that God is seen, that our desires are completed, that we are given more than we anticipated, Aquinas adds that "whatever is delightful is there in superabundance." We are to be pleased by what is in fact pleasing. We are to rejoice in what is in fact beautiful. And so here we hear Aquinas telling us, "if delights are sought, there (in life everlasting) is supreme and most perfect delight."

What about everyone else? Did not Aristotle talk about man being a social animal? Did he not tell us about friendship and the difficulty of being friends with God? Did he not hint at our desire to be friends with the whole of another's being, not just his soul? "Again, eternal life consists of the joyous community of all the blessed, a community of supreme delight." The City of God is described in terms of delight — the delight of knowing God and praising Him together with and before the reality of one another, of creation itself.

The noblest act of friendship is to communicate in the highest goods and the truest of things. What keeps us from friendship is both time, the shortness of our mortal lives, and the circumstances of our choices, that we do not really appreciate the same good. Friendship inescapably includes truth. We must not only live in the only world *that is*, but we must understand that we do.

In everlasting life, Aquinas writes, "everyone will share all that is good with all the blessed." Aquinas does not think we will be equal in love or being, simply because he recognizes that our loves are expressions of the different being that God gives to each of us in causing us to be in the first place. Equality and envy theory are not in eternal life. We can rejoice that others are greater than we, that not all gifts and sacrifices are ours. "Everyone will love everyone else as himself." We should love ourselves, however, only insofar as we are, insofar as God created us. If we love others as God created them, we will love properly; we will rejoice in *what is*.

And what will follow? This is the sequence of things: being

- truth - love - joy - praise. Aquinas concludes, "everyone will rejoice in another's good as in his own." And the result of this rejoicing is that "the happiness and joy of each grows in proportion to the joy of all." This is really our experience. Joy is receiving what we love because we are chosen for ourselves, because we too are chosen to be loved in our being. The truth of the being in which we are made, the image of God that each of us is has a joy that results in festivity and celebration.

This celebration is a kind of praise that is greater and more lovely because we all are within it, yet none of us are its cause. This is the great dance, as C.S. Lewis called it. This is "life everlasting" as it is found in the Creed of our faith, in the purpose for which we are called out of nothingness to be what we are so that we might rejoice in and praise what we really want if we could have it. This is our faith, that we can really have it. This is why we pray that *what should be, shall be.*

CHAPTER XIV

The Revolution That is Catholicism

I

T he word revolution means many things. It means something
radically different. It also means the turning of the planets
around a star. It has the sense of always changing but still always
returning to the same point to begin again. In that sense, the
Christendom that grew out of Catholicism is not a revolution, but
a newness that shall not "return" again and again. It bears the
marks of a history with a beginning, a middle, and an end, the end
we call life everlasting.

This "revolutionary" newness, moreover, is conceived as
something given, something entrusted to us to be explained and
passed on. "It was God who reconciled us to Himself through
Christ and gave us the work of handing on this reconciliation," St.
Paul wrote to the Corinthians. "God in Christ was reconciling the
world to Himself, not holding men's faults against them, and He
has entrusted to us the news that they are reconciled" (2 Corinthians
5:18-19).

June 3, 1781, was a Sunday, the first Sunday of the month
when the "Holy Sacrament" was customarily distributed. James
Boswell recounted his going with Samuel Johnson to Southill
Church near Mr. Dilly's. When Boswell noticed that Johnson did
not receive Communion, he inquired why. "I had not thought of

it," was Johnson's curt reply. But Boswell felt that there were other and more spiritual reasons, that Johnson "did not choose to approach the altar without a previous preparation. . . ."[1] Boswell next discussed the three views about the types of preparation for the Sacrament that were then controverted within the Church.

Boswell went on to record the further conversations of this day. The opinion of a learned bishop whom both Boswell and Johnson knew — his view about there being "merit in religious faith" — was brought up. Johnson averred that there was indeed some merit in the good bishop's position: "Why, yes, Sir," Johnson went on, "the most licentious man, were hell open before him, would not take the most beautiful strumpet in his arms. We must, as the Apostle says, live by faith, not by sight." St. Paul, no doubt, has never been quoted in a more quaint context.

The vivid conversation led Boswell and Johnson to the topic of "original sin" and "the atonement made by our Saviour." Further conversation ensued, which Johnson wanted Boswell to record. "With respect to original sin, the inquiry is not necessary," Johnson held, "for whatever is the cause of human corruption, men are evidently and confessedly so corrupt, that all the laws of heaven and earth are insufficient to restrain them from crimes."

Johnson's final comment on such theological topics was succinct: "The peculiar doctrine of Christianity is, that of an universal sacrifice, and perpetual propitiation. Other prophets only proclaimed the will and the threatenings of God. Christ satisfied justice."

On the occasion of the Jefferson Lecture, which he gave in 1989, the novelist, the late Walker Percy, was asked about using in public words such as God, religion, sin, soul, and Jesus Christ. He remarked that the novelist has to learn to speak of such subjects most circumspectly before an educated audience since today's intelligentsia can no longer even hear such words with

---

[1] *Boswell's Life of Samuel Johnson* (London: Oxford, 1931), II, pp. 422-25.

comprehension or sympathy. "The Catholic novelist has to be very careful," Percy cautiously maintained. "He has to be underhanded, deceitful, and damn careful how he uses the words of religion, which have fallen into disuse and almost become obscenities."[2] Similar to Plato or to Leo Strauss, one must use "myth" or "secret writing" even to hint at the truth.

At the end of the eighteenth century two learned men could talk knowingly and believingly of original sin, atonement, and communion without the slightest hesitation. By the end of the twentieth and the beginning of the twenty-first century, however, such topics must be spoken of guardedly. It almost makes one doubt any theory of progress. Obscenities are blared almost everywhere in the modern world with the protection of the law and the promotion of the culture, while faith must be obscured.

In the eighteenth century, a strumpet could bring up questions of eternal punishment in the mind of a licentious man, whereas in the twentieth century she is hardly recognizable as anything other than a bearer of human rights in an ancient and honorable profession. The licentious man, on the other hand, supports some of the most widely read and powerful publications in our society. It might be concluded from this record of two hundred years that Christianity itself, Catholic and Protestant, is in the process of disappearing, at least in the souls of the more literate (and licentious) members of our society. Whether this phenomenon is more of a problem for society's literate members or for Christians remains to be seen.

II

Catholicism does not claim to be either a parochial or a time-bound faith, even though it began at an identifiable time and in a specific place, in the reign of Augustus Caesar, when the whole world was at peace. Indeed, Catholicism does not hold that it

---

[2] Scott Walter, Interview with Walker Percy, *Crisis* 7 (July, 1989).

ultimately began in "time" at all but that it came to be in time through the birth of a child, an event prepared by other events described in the Old Testament. In Catholicism's understanding of itself, the elements of time and eternity are essential, as well as proper and necessary.

Catholicism began as an event, not as an idea or as a doctrine. And when one event happens, others follow from it to the end, even to the end of the world. Catholicism necessarily involves ideas and doctrines because men must explain what the events are about and what they mean. An event without a human word will never appear within the human horizon. The results of events are words. Words in turn lead to events: "In the Beginning was the Word...."

Moreover, this Incarnational religion is intended to be, as Samuel Johnson recognized, a universal faith. This faith is expected to reach, through the human and divine agency of its members, each human being at the core reality in his soul, the reality of the choice where each person makes himself to be what he chooses to be within the initial givenness of his being. Catholicism is designed precisely for one in whatever kingdom or regime someone may be found in, in the best and in the worst, and in those in between wherein most men have lived their days whether happily or sadly.

If we estimate that some ninety billion people have already existed on this planet, and that only some five billion of those are still alive, the fact remains that existing man on earth, in the Christian view, is to explain and direct himself to the transcendent being, to God, from whom each person came and to whom he is to return. This drama of choice is what we observe in the lives of each of the members of the human race. Nothing else really matters, everything else is the background and worldly content of this choiceful *commedia*, as Dante significantly called it. The this-worldly mission of Catholicism is wholly secondary to this essential task that, on its doctrinal and ritual side, is nothing less than its seeking to explain to each man his purpose and his destiny.

There are not, then, two classes of human beings, one intended to reach God and one not. All are indeed made for the same purpose and destiny. But because of human freedom, some may in fact choose not to reach God. This central fact of choice was described already in the fifth century by St. Augustine in the *City of God.* Two cities in fact existed, not one, because the power of choice so radically defines what human beings ultimately are. Whether any individual human beings do not reach God, we do not know. The veil of death ever leaves mankind in doubt, and in hope, and, in some theologies, even in despair.

To believe that some, if not many, are eternally lost, however, is not required by the orthodox tradition. It is only necessary to believe that if any are lost, it is by their own choice. Essentially we must believe that the possibility of man's radical separation from the reality intended for him by God does exist. In a negative sense, here lies the ultimate foundation of human dignity, the guarantee that man's own actions are not finally meaningless.

Classic optimism maintains on its own premises — they are not Christian premises — that a God may not even threaten the most dire of consequences to free man because of his own actions in the world. But this "optimistic" view is precisely the most anti-human of philosophies for it removes any seriousness from the human experience. Doctrinally speaking, the denial of the teaching on hell is the other side of the elimination of any real significance for human action, or its ultimate seriousness before being itself.

III

The first, second, and now the impending third millennium of Christianity underscore in retrospect the improbable fact not of Catholicism's demise but of its strength, its curious lastingness in this world. Whatever else might be said about Catholicism, what is most obvious is that it should not still be here at all. Catholicism is too old still to exist. By any secular norm — scientific, historical, or sociological — this organized faith needs something other than itself to remain what it is. The Catholic faith itself recognizes in the symbolic keys of Peter a guarantee that the gates of hell shall not prevail against it.

The immediate thing to be explained about Catholicism is not whether it will continue to survive, but why it has lasted so long, longer than any other organized institution in human history. There may be scattered tribes and faiths perhaps older than Catholicism, to be sure, though their organization is mostly blood and family, not the product of a rational and willed system. But all the institutionalized nations themselves have come and most have gone or have been so radically transformed that they really are not continuous with what went before them. Scientifically, Catholicism should not still exist.

The interesting thing about Catholicism is not how much it has changed, but how much it has not changed (see Chapter IX). Indeed, this is the most interesting and important thing about it. For if Catholicism actually "changed," as not a few would have it, it would cease to be what it is, which is what makes it worth knowing about in the first place. And whatever we might think of doctrinal development, doctrine does not, strictly speaking, "change."

Unless Catholicism is in some fundamental sense the same as it was from the beginning, then its universal claim is simply non-existing. The claim of Catholicism is also a claim of truth, of a truth that is the same yesterday and the same forever, as St. Paul would have it. If Catholicism does not make this claim to truth, then it simply has no real reason to exist.

In one sense we can consider Catholicism's longevity to be caused by its adaptability. Continuation of principle and rite do not militate necessarily against variety of symbol or wording. But the more profound problem has to do rather with Catholicism's constancy within time. The Nicene Creed is still recited. Communion is still distributed as in the time of St. Bernard of Clairvaux, or of Samuel Johnson, or of Walker Percy. The Gospel of John is still read. Sins are still confessed. The Ten Commandments and the two Great Commandments are still there to be observed or broken by those who affirm their validity. All of these are found in the *General Catechism* as they have been found throughout the two millennia to our time.

Of itself, Catholicism says that when these rites and doctrines cease, it will cease. Catholicism assumes that all other institutions will pass away. The most dangerous threat to universal culture is that Catholicism *will* adapt itself to its surrounding norms rather than remaining itself. The ultimate worth of Catholicism is that it maintains a newness and a freshness able to transcend each nation or people without denying its respective worth.

Catholicism does not consider that this capacity that it has demonstrated about itself in history as an existential fact arises from the strength or genius of individual Catholics themselves. Catholicism's persistence is not considered to be the product of the genius and tenacity of individual believers using their own unaided powers. Thus, in the seventeenth century, Blaise Pascal could write in his *Pensées*, "the Church is in an excellent state, when it is sustained by God only" (#860).

John Paul II has constantly in recent years spoken of the coming "third millennium" of Christianity. Are we to look on it as apocalypse or hope, or both? If we ask whether Catholicism is a "success," again we have to ask whether it is a success in whose terms? Those of that modernity that has defined itself in opposition to Catholicism? Those of Catholicism itself? What would a "successful" Catholicism look like?

St. Augustine seems to have suggested that as the world gets older, fewer and fewer believers will be found. And Augustine did not necessarily think that this meant that Catholicism was thereby "unsuccessful." Catholicism was to be what it was, and only then could it be called successful in its own terms. But even if more and more Catholics were to be found, would that mean necessarily that the ultimate purpose of Catholicism was being achieved? Faith and works —the Reformation struggle was no slight matter.

IV

What is the relation between the nations, cultures, and religions of the world and Catholicism? Again, is this the proper question to ask of Catholicism? Catholicism is not, in its own view, hostile to philosophy, except to a philosophy that presents itself as a humanly closed system, which is in fact the case with not a few. Indeed, Catholicism argues that it alone is compatible with a true philosophy of *what is.* In the thirteenth century, Aquinas also remarked that it is impossible to err without embracing some truth in the process. This truth is why all religions and philosophies have something in common, something universal, to talk about, if they will.

Does Catholicism have an inner-worldly mission? That is to say, is there a right order of the world and is it the purpose of Catholicism to establish it? Are the philosophers not necessary and are the politicians and craftsmen without their own insight? So strongly has modern culture based itself on the condition of man in the world, however, that it often can see no other criterion but its own, presupposed to nothing but itself, by which to judge anything, including religion.

Is there a "Kingdom of God" on earth? And if so, is that what Catholicism is primarily about, as so many, even Catholics, seem to want to believe? Is Catholicism intended to "improve the world"? Or, perhaps better, will it improve the world? And what might the criterion of this "improvement" be? Does faith judge culture or does culture judge faith? Could the immortal souls all be gained and the world lost? And if so, would Catholicism then have proved itself to be a failure or a success?

Do Catholics consequently still repeat the disturbing words, "What doth it profit a man to gain the whole world and lose the life of his immortal soul?" This was the question that St. Ignatius in the sixteenth century used to repeat to the young Parisian college student Francis Xavier, who, when he decided he did not want the profit of the world, proceeded to the Orient because he wanted to see that this religion was known not merely in Europe but all over the world. Is it legitimate to challenge the distant nations with a belief that is not theirs, not their own construction?

Or do the nations, like the Athenians at the trial of Socrates, have the raw power to decide what adherence to their own gods might mean? Was this Xavier a fool? Or was what he brought needed by those to whom he came even if they did not know it? Do the nations ever really know the destiny of the citizens who make up their structures? On the surface, does not the rise and decline of nations and civilizations seem discontinuous and without particular significance?

If the purpose of man's existence on earth is that he live in some perfect, complete, self-sufficient regime, must we not conclude that the question of happiness and meaning for the vast majority of mankind who have ever lived has simply been in vain? Most people most of the time have lived in terrible regimes or terrible conditions, and even the best regimes are few and their days are also distressed.

But it was probably not until the nineteenth century, with its vast missionary works, that Christianity reached the far corners of the earth. Did it come there as an alien power, as so many think, particularly in the light of the Fifth Centenary of Columbus' Discovery of America? Or did it come as it thinks of itself, to dwell within every culture because there are universal questions that all people ask that are not at all culture-bound? Can nations be "saved"? Has the Enlightenment so influenced us that we can no longer ask any questions but inner-worldly ones? Near the end of the Gospel of Mark, the disciples are told to go forth and preach to all creation what they had seen and heard.

Catholic areas are themselves invaded by the other religions — by Islam, by Buddhism, by Hinduism. Science and democracy, what are these? What are their origins? If Catholicism is not universal, surely these latter are? Can science and democracy exist outside of Christendom? Are certain fundamental doctrines and practices implicitly or explicitly necessary in every civilization?

Did science and democracy arise in the west by accident, as a kind of historical chance? Or did they arise there because of the peculiar nature of revealed religion itself? Is faith necessary for science? And is there a natural law that even Catholicism did not invent?

V

The most radical thing that one can say today — radical in the sense of opposed in principle to the commonly accepted norms of contemporary discourse — is that, in the end, it does not make any ultimate difference where one lives, in what regime or society. True, some polities are better than others, that is, if there are right and wrong ways of being human.

If there is no right way to be a human being, then the principal question of political philosophy, of the way men organize themselves, namely, what is the best regime, will not be asked, because all regimes will be equal in principle. In such a case, we could not compare or judge regimes, only describe them, celebrate their structures, whatever it is they do. We could not go to all the nations with anything; the worst regime is as legitimate as the best because there is no way to tell them apart.

Yet, it is true. The connection between souls and regimes is not such that regimes, though they too are of the soul, answer the deepest questions of souls. The Kingdom of God will also be populated by men from the worst existing regimes. Grace abounds. And we must likewise assume that the realm of hell will find within its unhappy confines many of those from the best earthly regimes.

What does this mean with regard to Catholicism in the third millennium? It means that Catholicism must continue to speak to souls over the heads of (or with the cooperation of) existing regimes. Would it not be best, then, as so many later twentieth-century Catholics seem to maintain in their easy accommodation with the after-effects of the Enlightenment, to work to establish the best regimes? Religion, in this view, ought to be politics.

The effort to establish the best regime in this world has invariably been the locus of the most dangerous opponents to what is human in the modern era. Catholicism maintains that it has at its disposal tools that are not available to or for the polity, even though, since creation and redemption are a single whole, right order with the divinity will entail right order within the polity. Faith and reason do not contradict each other.

The fact is that good citizenship does not necessarily entail good belief, and without good belief one will not be saved. Catholicism takes the human intellect seriously, and the function of the intellect is to know the truth. One can have good belief and bad practice. In other words, everyone has both intellect and will and these faculties constitute our unique selves and relationships, the ones that are really ours.

VI

Josef Pieper has made the following remark about Christianity, about its complexity and its simplicity, about what it essentially is, if it be itself:

> According to the theologians, the essence of the Christian faith can be summed up in two words. Those two words are Trinity and Incarnation. The "universal teacher" (St. Thomas) of Christendom has said that the whole content of the truth of Christianity can be reduced to the dogma of the Trinitarian God and the dogma that man participates in the life of God through Christ.[3]

There is a modern reluctance to admit that the purpose of man is, in part, to clarify what it is that he is, what God is, so that his intellect becomes more itself by seeking to know, even to know the divinity.

---

[3] Josef Pieper, "Communication of Reality," *Josef Pieper — an Anthology* (San Francisco: Ignatius Press, 1989), p. 18.

Behind the reluctance to acknowledge the purpose of the human intellect one finds both a skepticism and a kind of purity that would have us give up the effort. However, it is true that we will not be able ever to define what God is in exhaustive human terms. Spiritual beings have this in common, that their capacity to know is that faculty that they share in some fashion with each other, so that not to seek to know and not to define the doctrines would be to fail to exercise one of the given faculties. And since it would be precisely the highest faculty that is doubted, it would mean that man fails in a dignity that most constitutes his being. The failure of intellect thus is also a failure to follow man's natural way to God.

God transcends our formulas. We want not just a definition of God, but God Himself. An existentialist theory of knowledge is not one that ignores this need. In fact, it is one that rests on it in its very operation. The same reality may indeed be explained in different languages and from different aspects rooted in the reality of its being. But contradictory explanations, with both sides true, are not possible. The human mind is not the infinite mind, but it is a mind, and in this sense it must confront what it knows of the Godhead.

The argument among religions and philosophies about what is true even in logic must recognize that not all positions are equally true. A small error in the beginning leads to a large error in the end, as Aristotle had already observed (*On the Heavens*, 271b 9-10). It makes a difference both to civilization and to each person which understanding of God is true. This means that the Hobbesian effort in modernity to remove from the public order a discussion of the highest things in the name of civil peace is itself a betrayal of human dignity, though the effort to insist that this discussion take place in peace is a laudable one.

The city is not the location of the discussion of the highest things that we know about the divinity. But the city can make such discussions impossible or difficult. This possibility is why the problem of the relation of poetry to philosophy and also to politics is and remains the theoretical beginning of all human effort to relate divinity to man. Since man does transcend the city, then the city cannot and must not substitute itself for what transcends it.

Indeed, the main alternative to God in the modern world is the state itself, particularly the state that identifies itself as the instrument or the completion of what is known by man and of what is good for man. It is true that the wars of religion have not resolved the problems that exist between religions, each of which claim the truth. This is why we have and ought to have differing regimes in which at least some possibility of genuine philosophical or religious truth is possible. The way of persuasion, as both Plato and John Paul II argued, remains for all polities as the proper mode of procedure to the highest things.

VII

In the twenty-first century, the third millennium, no doubt, the question of the relation of man to the cosmos and to the other beings of this earth will arise in an acute form because of the problem of the transplanting of at least some human and animal life outside of this planet for a more or less permanent residence. The problem of the twenty-first century, moreover, will not be one in which the main condition of making will be scarcity but abundance.

Computers, fusion, further advances of knowledge and technique will free more and more men and women for the leisure life to which Aristotle referred as the true end of human earthly existence. Whether man is more dangerous to himself in scarcity or abundance remains to be seen, though Aristotle himself had already warned that the most probable answer would be in abundance — would be, in fact, in philosophy.

The question then remains: What sort of existence is that which mankind has been offered in this world? What is to be done with it? If we distinguish an individual existence that will itself transcend the destiny of any earthly city or culture from the purpose of the world itself, we can see that the two questions are not the same. Man is higher than the state, even though man is by nature a political animal. We must assume in revelational terms that the Incarnation will remain a permanent reality of the Godhead.

Hence, as St. Paul remarked in Romans, that creation itself is groaning for redemption suggests that the destiny of the world is related to the destiny of man. Man is not an afterthought of the world, but the world, in spite of its immensity, is an afterthought to the existence of the rational being, the image of God. The ultimate configurations of the world will depend on man, on his choice and technique. But the world does not constitute man's principal choice, which is that of which city he chooses ultimately to join, the City of God or the City of Man.

Each human being has a soul that transcends the world. The nature and the condition of this soul are such that mankind will always be disturbed by man's being insofar as he is not devoted to the openness to which this soul is directed. The twentieth century has seen the alternatives to God elaborated in their most perfect forms. Eric Voegelin has put it well:

> At the extreme of the revolt in consciousness, "reality" and the "Beyond" become two separate entities, two "things," to be magically manipulated by suffering man for the purpose of either abolishing "reality" altogether and escaping into the "Beyond," or of forcing the order of the "Beyond" into "reality." The first of the magic alternatives is preferred by the Gnostics of antiquity, the second one by the modern Gnostics.[4]

Catholicism is not Gnostic in either sense. It does not want the reality of what is less than God to disappear into God or into nothingness.

This position is why Catholicism can assimilate the classic

---

[4] Eric Voegelin, *In Search of Order* (Baton Rouge: Louisiana State University Press, 1987), p. 37. (See above, p. 22.)

doctrine of the immortality of the soul into its own doctrine of resurrection. On the other hand, Catholicism cannot accept the view that the purpose of human and cosmic existence is merely itself or its own making. The spiritual core of man, that includes his connection to all of the cosmos through his own body, longs for that which will fulfill it. The civilizational purpose of Christianity in the twenty-first century is that this longing should not be forgotten or unattended to, even though what man is transcends the world.

VIII

Jean-Marie Lustiger, the Polish-born Cardinal of Paris, has written:

> All the world's problems are basically spiritual problems and they stem from the temptations of Christianity. From this comes the inevitable conclusion that if the world's problems are spiritual problems, then there are Christian answers to the world crisis. I do not derive a sort of spiritual imperialism from this but I point to the evidence for a paradox: the main problems which constitute our world crisis (starvation, underdevelopment, wars, etc.) are capable of a technical solution. We could, *if we really wanted*, feed the whole world of humanity, develop all the Third World countries, and stop the arms race. But in fact, if we do not have the technical means for this at hand, it is because we do not really want these ultimately desirable objectives. So what is making them impossible to reach now is something in our own hearts and wills.[5]

However correct in its essential point, this position is perhaps too one-sided. The problem is not just in the hearts of Catholics and Christians. It is also in the hearts of those who resist — individually,

---

[5] Jean-Marie Cardinal Lustiger, "The World's Problems Are Spiritual Problems," *Dare to Live*, translated by M.N.L. Couvre de Murville (New York: Crossroad, 1988), p. 30.

politically, or academically — listening to its reality or living the spiritual means that faith proposes.

Ultimately the real issue is found in the reluctance to admit that the way to accomplish the technical means for achieving these laudable ends requires a denial, in whole or in part, of the validity and worth of certain historic ideologies, religions, and philosophies. This later spiritual confrontation is the real nature of the struggle of Catholicism in the twenty-first century. Ironically, this struggle over the inner-worldly purpose of Catholicism is found also within the heart of Catholicism about its own essence, about the Transcendent to which it first must be committed.[6] "Seek ye first the Kingdom of God." The third millennium of Christianity will, as in the first and second, have this purpose as the main criterion of what it is about.

Nietzsche wrote in *The Twilight of the Idols*:

> The Christian and the anarchist are both decadent. When the Christian condemns, slanders, and besmirches "the world," his instinct is the same as that which prompts the socialist worker to condemn, slander, and besmirch society. The "last judgment" is the sweet comfort of revenge — the revelation, which the socialist-worker also wants, but conceived as a little farther off. The "beyond" — why a beyond, if not as a means of besmirching *this* world? (#34)

Catholicism in the twenty-first century, as in the first and in the thirteenth, ought not "besmirch" this world — but it should recall that "this world" is not our destiny, nor our final purpose. "The peculiar doctrine of Christianity," to repeat the words of Samuel Johnson, "is that of an universal sacrifice, and perpetual propitiation." This truth, this "dogma," is Catholicism's purpose in any century, in any century of this very real world. As Chesterton said, "Christianity has died many times and risen again; for it had a God who knew the way out of the grave."

---

[6] See James V. Schall, "Transcendence and Political Philosophy," *The Review of Politics*, 55 (Spring, 1993), 247-65.

"The Human Machinery of
a Perfect and Supernatural Revelation"

I n the very first year of the twentieth century, Hilaire Belloc
took a famous walk, on a "path," as he called it, to Rome. He
began from his old French army station at Toul, vowed to walk all
the way South through the Alps and Italy and to be at St. Peter's
in Rome for the Feast of Saints Peter and Paul. During his walk, he
passed "through the high limestone gates of the gorge, and was in
the fourth valley of the Jura." He lit a cigar and asked a local
woman if she could give him something to eat. She said in about
an hour.

He admired the local church and the churchyard. The church
tower was actually built in a stream that flowed about its base. He
thought the faith to be real had to be "something fighting odds."
But here, "to see all the men, women, and children of a place taking
Catholicism for granted was a new sight." He carefully put "his
cigar under a stone" and went into the church where they were at
vespers.

Belloc began to reflect on the meaning of belief. It "breeds a
reaction and an indifference," he thought. It struggles within us,
and in our youth we usually reject it because we are "content with
natural things." Yet, after the walk that is our life, as we have lived
it, we realize the "problem of living; for every day, every experience

of evil, demands a solution." It is at this point that we "look back and see our home."

And we remember that "great scheme" that is our born Catholicism. It is difficult to explain, Belloc thought, and the return is not so easy.

> For there grows a gulf between us and many companions. We are perpetually thrust into minorities, and the world almost begins to talk a strange language; we are troubled by *the human machinery of a perfect and superhuman revelation*; we are over-anxious for its safety, alarmed, and in danger of violent decisions.[1]

In the light of the reflections we have pursued in these pages, these are profound and sobering words. The great scheme remains and it is easy to worry about it, especially the fragile human beings who are here to explain it, live it. They fail often. We are troubled.

And yet, what is it Belloc said? The gulf grows when we remember our faith, that it is coherent. Our wanderings from it, in retrospect, were wrong. The natural things we were content with do not hold. Evil does demand an explanation, especially that evil we cause ourselves. Old Cephalus worried about the same thing at the beginning of the *Republic*. There remains only one coherent explanation, however, that of the "great scheme," of Catholicism itself. We become over-anxious for the safety of revelation. We think we can come to the aid of God as if His grace were not sufficient for us.

And we are in danger of "violent decisions." How remarkable is that phrase! I have often recalled Eric Voegelin's passage in which he says that modern ideology is caused by Christians who have doubted their own faith, doubted its true radicalness. Their doubt flows into the practical attempt to put into the world the

---

[1] Hilaire Belloc, *The Path to Rome* (Garden City, NY: Doubleday Image, 1956), p. 102. Italics added.

promises that were in fact made for eternal life.[2] The philosophers construct a new world, a scheme of their own that is not the "great scheme," as Belloc recalled it. The "violent decisions" we ourselves are tempted to make were in fact made by the philosophers and the politicians who sought to put into the world their own schemes. These are they who cannot tolerate that there is a right order of things that judges their own regimes and their own ideas, their own lives.

Does Catholicism still exist? Belloc put the problem well: "It is hard to accept mysteries and be humble."[3] It is hard because over against the world, over against the alternatives, nothing is more coherent, more satisfying than the mysteries, than the great scheme that man did not give to himself. Walker Percy's question, to recall it again, remains, "What else is there?" And yet, it is precisely this humility that is considered to be the greatest of the weaknesses of Catholicism, the claim that it must be faithful to what is handed down, and not to what man makes for himself.

Ernest Cassirer, in his famous essay "The Crisis in Man's Knowledge of Himself," in comparing Stoicism to Christianity, perceived what is the central issue in its intellectual roots:

> There has always been one point on which the antagonism between the Christian and the Stoic ideals proves irreconcilable. The asserted absolute independence of man, which in the Stoic theory was regarded as man's fundamental virtue, is turned in the Christian theory into his fundamental vice and error. As long as man perseveres in this error there is no possible road to salvation. The struggle between these two conflicting views has lasted for many centuries, and at the beginning of the modern era

---

[2] Eric Voegelin, *Science, Politics, and Gnosticism* (Chicago: Regnery/Gateway, 1968), p. 109.

[3] Belloc, *op. cit.*, p. 103.

— at the time of the Renaissance and in the seventeenth
century — we still feel its strength.[4]

At the end of the twentieth century, indeed, we feel its strength
even more forcefully.

The "asserted absolute independence of man" is in Christian
theory man's "fundamental vice and error." Cassirer was right.
Catholicism is not opposed to this sort of absolute humanism
because it is not a noble enterprise. The opposition comes rather
from Belloc's "looking back and seeing our home." That is, it
comes from the fact that Catholicism not only recognizes the fact
of man's finiteness, that he is not absolutely independent, but that
what he is intended to be and do is something more glorious and
exalted than the philosophers have realized. It is in this sense that
St. Augustine's concept of the will remains at the heart of our
reality. We can indeed choose to reject what we are and what we
are offered. The fabric of this rejection is the history of our times.

Bernard Williams, in his *Shame and Necessity*, toys with the
idea of a world history in which Christianity did not exist as the
interpreter through which we understand the metaphysics and
morals of the classical Greeks.[5] What is true about such a reflection
is, of course, that the Nietzschean alternative to the weakness of
Christianity is possible. Likewise, in basic theology, revelation
need not have happened. Other forms of human history or other
forms of God's intervention in history can be imagined. What
Catholicism stands for is the uncanny suspicion, spelled out in the
accurate accounting of what revelation is, that it bears within its
logic what is best for man because it understands what it is the
human intellect knows and can know. Faith is rooted in existence,
not in itself.

---

[4] Ernest Cassirer, "The Crisis of Man's Knowledge of Himself," *An Essay on Man*
(Garden City, NY: Doubleday Anchor, 1944), p. 24.

[5] Bernard Williams, *Shame and Necessity* (Berkeley: University of California Press,
1993), p. 12.

Does Catholicism still exist? It is not enough to denounce evils, though we should denounce them beginning with our knowing what they are, something, as St. Thomas said, that often requires the help of revelation (*Summa Theologiae*, I-II, 91, 4). We should be sympathetic to the poor, but largely by knowing how to help them not to be poor. In his biography, Ian Ker cites a remark of John Henry Newman to the effect that Catholicism would "look pretty silly without the laity."[6] Newman, furthermore, could not find anything in principle wrong with the notion that if one observed the commandments, practiced charity, honor, thriftiness, and justice, the people would prosper.[7]

The reality of what we see in the world includes the disorder. Newman continued:

> "Intellect, and even moral virtues, will frequently be found dissociated from the Church" because she "calls especially the poor, the sinful, and the ignorant; not that she calls them *peculiarly*, but because her *including them* repels the rich, the self-righteous, and the intellectual."[8]

This remark of Newman brings me back to where I began, with the particular problems in the modern world rising from intellectuals, the problem of Stoic and modern pride that would place all under our autonomous reason and the humility that would recognize that the alternatives to Catholicism, the ones that exist and the ones that are thinkable, are themselves not worthy of what it is that human beings are called to know and enjoy.

To return to the initial question, does Catholicism "still believe in something" or is it "beginning to doubt everything"? The shortest answer is, "yes, there are those who doubt everything;

---

[6] Ian Ker, *John Henry Newman* (Oxford: Oxford University Press, 1988), p. 479.

[7] *Ibid.*, p. 485.

[8] *Ibid.*

yes, Catholicism still believes in something." We do worry about "the human machinery of a perfect and supernatural revelation." But when we finally examine the content of this perfect and supernatural revelation, even when we do so with Belloc walking in the Jura, we find ourselves in agreement with Walker Percy, who when asked near the end of his life why he believed in Catholicism, responded, with some exasperation, "What else is there?"

Index

• p 30 - Ogden Nash on sins - ORTANT and SHUDDA

• p 32 - Adam † Eve : Thought that the distinction between good and evil would be <u>theirs</u> to make.

p54— Compassion misplaced if located in the intellect.